A PRACTICAL GUIDE TO PLANT ENVIRONMENTAL AUDITS

A PRACTICAL GUIDE TO PLANT ENVIRONMENTAL AUDITS

H. William Blakeslee
Manager, Environmental and Energy Conservation
CertainTeed Corporation

and

Theodore M. Grabowski
Sun Refining and Marketing Company
Senior Environmental Engineer

VNR VAN NOSTRAND REINHOLD COMPANY
New York

Library of Congress Catalog Card Number: 84-13051
ISBN: 0-442-21421-9

Manufactured in the United States of America

Published by Van Nostrand Reinhold Company Inc.
135 West 50th Street
New York, New York 10020

Van Nostrand Reinhold Company Limited
Molly Millars Lane
Wokingham, Berkshire RG11 2PY, England

Van Nostrand Reinhold
480 Latrobe Street
Melbourne, Victoria 3000, Australia

Macmillan of Canada
Division of Gage Publishing Limited
164 Commander Boulevard
Agincourt, Ontario MIS 3C7, Canada

15 14 13 12 11 10 9 8 7 6 5 4 3 2 1

Library of Congress Cataloging in Publication Data

Blakeslee, H. William.
A practical guide to plant environmental audits.

Bibliography: p.
Includes index.
1. Environmental impact analysis—United States—Handbooks, manuals, etc. 2. Factory and trade waste—Environmental aspects—United States—Handbooks, manuals, etc. I. Grabowski, Theodore M. II. Title.
TD194.6.B55 1985 658.2 84-13051
ISBN 0-442-21421-9

Preface

Over the last ten years, the United States has witnessed an enormous growth in both the number and the complexity of environmental constraints placed on industrial operations. This growth is vividly illustrated by the increase in the number of pages devoted to environmental rules in the Code of Federal Regulations, which rose during the last decade from approximately 450 to over 5900—a 1300% increase. Although it is unlikely this growth rate will be sustained, it is clear that new regulatory programs and modifications to existing rules will be necessary.

Recently, environmental audits have been proposed as a cost-effective means to help manage the environmental aspect of plant operations. Although the total literature base on the subject of environment audits is not large, there have been discussions on topics ranging from their benefits to legal ramifications. Studies have been conducted that contrast alternative audit approaches as well as detail audit report formats. Throughout this exchange of information, there has clearly been a lack of specific direction on the "how-to" aspects of plant audits. This book attempts to give that practical, down-to-earth advice. The procedures and observations contained herein are a result of actual experience with auditing industrial plants. The subjects have ranged from small fabrication shops and warehouses to large, integrated manufacturing plants. Altogether, the authors have conducted more than fifty audits. Although the procedures and recommendations outlined here are both realistic and effective, it is also clear that alternative approaches exist, and the authors welcome the opportunity to be made aware of them.

This book is organized into seven logically arranged chapters. Chapter 1 defines an environmental audit and contains a list of answers to the question, "Why conduct an audit?" Our intention is to include enough material for anyone to "sell" the concept of an environmental audit to a supervisor or customer. The meat of the book is contained in Chapter 2, "How to Conduct the Audit." It outlines the steps followed in preparing for and conducting an audit, and addresses many details that may appear small but are nonetheless significant. By including them, it is hoped the reader can avoid some small pitfalls that easily waste valuable time and resources. This chapter also discusses the final audit report, its preparation and organization. Chapters 3 through 7 provide information necessary to audit plants in individual environmental situations. Regulatory discussions are included for the major areas, such as air and water pollution as well as waste management. In addition, data sheets are included to help organize the information collected during the audit. The inclusion of data sheets should not imply that an environmental audit is an exercise in paperwork. Data sheets, checklists, or audit manuals simply serve as a guide for the auditor to pace his efforts and ensure that important areas are not omitted. Although they serve meaningful purposes, data sheets cannot replace a concerted personal effort directed at plant operations.

Less universal environmental programs are listed in the appendix. This section consists of short descriptions of federal laws so the auditor can quickly determine their applicability. The intent is to provide an overview rather than exhaustive coverage.

The major chapters of this book are as self-contained as possible, so that readers can quickly review areas of specific interest without risk of losing continuity. We recommend however, that Chapter 2 be reviewed in all cases because it complements each regulatory chapter. With self-contained chapters, interested readers can perform "staged" audits of their own facilities as time and resources permit. In this fashion, they can address one or two areas at a time, instead of reviewing every area at once. Similarly, the first audit can be focused on a few areas, recognizing that future audits will eventually cover all. We do not recommend that "staged" audits be conducted as a matter of policy; it is far too easy to miss major problems with limited audits. However, it may be necessary to "sell" a limited audit to management as a test of its effectiveness prior to instituting a formal program. The issue of an audit's scope is discussed further in Chapter 1.

The potential users of environmental auditing information can come from many different areas. The practical aspects of this book may appeal to plant engineers, who are typically responsible for much more than environmental regulations. Consultants and agency personnel may be interested in alternative ways to organize their audit and inspection efforts, whereas corporate personnel may be interested in audit implementation. With this broad range of potential interests, it is necessary to make several assumptions about environmental audits:

1. The plant to be audited has never received a formal audit before. Although the audit described here can certainly be applied to previously audited plants, it may be easier to continue using the prior format, and merely to use the information contained here as a check for completeness in those cases.
2. The person conducting the audit is not necessarily an expert in all environmental regulations. He should be generally familiar with such rules and should have access to experts, legal counsel, or other information resources. Environmental audits generally identify and list problems for others to solve, such as internal experts or consultants. Where appropriate, the auditor can recommend solutions he knows are effective.
3. A single audit will not address every potential impact the first time around. For most plants, the subject of environmental compliance is certainly too complex for a single three- or four-day review to solve. As plants receive further audits, perhaps on a scheduled basis, the coverage increases until all areas are addressed well.
4. The ideal plant for the audit described here is small to medium in size. It may employ from 100 to 300 people and occupy approximately 50 to 150 acres. This audit can certainly accommodate smaller or larger facilities, but some modification will be necessary. Where possible, these modifications are described in the text. In general, large plants are split into manageable parts for auditing purposes.
5. The auditor has already received proper management approval and support to conduct the audit. Without it, no concerted effort should begin. The purpose of an environmental audit is to identify and list previously unknown problems. This identifi-

cation carries with it a responsibility to authorize actions to address these problems. In addition, the auditor must have authority to review potentially sensitive environmental problems. Management must be willing to give this "front end" commitment before an audit takes place.

6. The personnel used to conduct these audits are not employed at the plant to be reviewed. They may be employees of a retained consultant or may be employed by the company at a different location; the use of group, division, or corporate level personnel is common. While it is possible for plant employees to audit their own facility, this assumption merely recognizes that it may be difficult for them to remain objective and also recognizes the benefit of having "fresh eyes" perform the audit.
7. The environmental audit described here is not used to satisfy specific court or legal requirements. The Securities and Exchange Commission (SEC) for example, has required in at least one case that a company retain an outside consultant to review environmental compliance costs and report the results to the company's board of directors. Although some facets of these audits may be similar, the basic motivations are vastly different. The audit described in this book is basically concerned with the individual facility, its success with environmental compliance, and measures to improve its performance. The audit required by the SEC generally uses the stockholder's or investor's interest as its motivation. Although they may support each other, the basic requirements differ and should be approached in different ways.
8. Any program aimed at conducting plant environmental audits should receive input from legal counsel regarding protection from disclosure. Since audits are designed to uncover previously unknown problems, it may be important to minimize premature disclosure. Although it remains unclear whether all audit results can successfully be protected under attorney–client privilege, it is necessary to address this issue prior to audit implementation.

Although the subject of environmental auditing is relatively new, many companies have recognized that a formalized internal review process can support important company objectives in a cost-effective manner. With continued support from government agencies and industry trade associations, this recognition will grow. Although most people are aware that environmental audits cannot be as "standardized" as financial audits, it is clear that a need exists for a practical approach to environmental audits. The authors hope this book helps to satisfy this need.

Contents

A PRACTICAL GUIDE TO PLANT ENVIRONMENTAL AUDITS

1
Introduction to Environmental Audits

For most plants in the United States, the task of complying with environmental requirements has become increasingly difficult. This situation is due mainly to the unprecedented growth of environmental rules and regulations, which has precipitated a clear need for effective management and monitoring of plant operations. The presence of an environmental coordinator at each plant may no longer assure continued compliance. Many firms have met this environmental challenge by instituting a formal, periodic audit program. This book describes a practical approach to environmental audits and contains information regarding standards of evaluation. To obtain maximum benefit from this book, it is first necessary to define the term "environmental audit," the functions it serves, reasons for its use, and methods to manage its implementation. These topics are discussed here.

DEFINITION OF AN ENVIRONMENTAL AUDIT

An environmental audit is a management tool used to help measure a plant's environmental performance against internal and external standards. It consists of an organized review and reporting process that uses personnel interviews, plant inspections, and records reviews to develop an accurate performance picture of each facility.[1] Because our definition stipulates that the audit is a tool, it does not replace an ongoing environmental awareness, nor can it be implemented in a

1. Depending on management objectives, these steps can be complemented with actual measurements of plant effluents, emissions, and wastes.

negative, "fingerpointing" atmosphere. Its true effectiveness rests with the positive results it achieves by objectively evaluating reality at the plant against known standards and goals.

The audit described here will yield a significant amount of current information regarding a plant's effluents, emissions, wastes, and operations. It can be likened to preparing a plant environmental profile. This profile is complemented, through several steps of the audit, by an examination of past activities and future liabilities. For this reason, it may not be entirely appropriate to call an audit an "environmental snapshot in time." Although a performance "picture" is taken, it is not static or unchanging.

In addition to evaluating obvious points of environmental impact, the audit described in this book will evaluate activities subject to regulation. Examples include operating and maintenance functions as well as storage or treatment activities. Finally, the audit will also focus attention on materials and substances that may be present but do not meet the description of emissions, effluents, or wastes. Examples are found in the proper use of polychlorinated biphenyls (PCBs), the removal of asbestos, and the storage of oil.

FUNCTIONS OF AN ENVIRONMENTAL AUDIT

Although an audit program can contribute to many desirable goals and objectives, its main functions can be loosely grouped into two separate areas: confirmation and identification. All environmental audits should be structured at least to address these important objectives.

Confirmation. The classic role of an audit program is to verify or confirm a plant's compliance with various environmental rules such as emission limits, effluent standards, and waste management practices. Independent of whether an audit is used or not, this ability to comply is measured in several ways, such as agency inspections or citizen complaints. The real attraction of an audit program is its ability to measure total performance in a systematic fashion using in-house resources. In this way, problems that may interfere with normal business activity are communicated to management.

With proper design and implementation, an environmental audit can also be used to measure the effectiveness of a plant's existing environmental organization. In many companies, the plant environmental organization varies from location to location, and may range from a part-time coordinator to a full-blown department. By examining these organizations and documenting the reasons for their variety, an approximate picture of the optimum structure can be found. Most environmental regulations require periodic or episodic reporting to outside agencies, and management must be sure these responsibilities are not needlessly hampered by organizational structure. The audit can confirm who is responsible and accountable for meeting these requirements.

Like most other departments at industrial plants, the environmental function must respond to and manage daily emergencies. This ability to "fight fires" is an obvious standard for performance measurement. Unlike some departments, however, the environmental department also carries an additional responsibility to anticipate, plan, and adapt to change. Changes may take the form of new agency regulations, manufacturing processes, or chemicals usage. This aspect of a department's performance is sometimes difficult to measure but is important nonetheless. An environmental audit can be structured to gain valuable insight regarding this skill.

Additionally, an audit can be used to measure the effectiveness of prior capital investment in plant pollution control equipment. If persistent noncompliances continue after installation, it strongly suggests the investment has not generated the desired return. On the other hand, oversized equipment may represent a needless expenditure in nonproductive assets. The audit can provide information for determining whether expenditures were productive and, by doing so, can prevent future errors.

Identification. In the process of confirming a plant's compliance status, organizational structure, and capital expenditures, an environmental audit naturally identifies areas of weakness. In fact, the audit should be designed and implemented specifically to achieve this objective. Thus management will adopt a proactive approach to agency enforcement by consciously identifying problems before they become hurdles. This identification role assures that problems are solved internally without external interference, an approach that usually results in the most cost-effective solutions.

In the widest sense, the identification function of an audit can protect company assets by averting environmental catastrophies. Many examples exist of illegal actions at a single plant that severely impacted major corporations because they persisted so long. If such practices are identified soon enough, the risk of enormous impact is dramatically reduced. In this regard, an environmental audit can be used as a risk management tool that complements a firm's existing risk reduction program.

Environmental audits should be structured to identify strengths in plant environmental programs as well as their weaknesses. In this way, positive reinforcement is built into the system which serves to encourage effective environmental management. This approach also recognizes that, for most plants, compliance with environmental regulations is difficult, and examples of success deserve recognition. Positive reinforcement encourages continued compliance and guards against a "return to normal" after the auditors leave. Such a positive approach can result in fewer and less severe enforcement penalties and, more important, less chance for litigation or other court actions.

The final identification function of an environmental audit is directed at recognizing potential areas of opportunity. For example, plants with several air pollution sources, each controlled separately, may be able to combine them and control all the emissions simultaneously. Similarly, companies may want to evaluate the opportunity to "bubble" all emissions and increase their operating flexibility. For emissions such as sulfur or hydrocarbons, "bubbles" can result in real savings as fuel-consuming control equipment is replaced with cheaper controls at other sources.

An environmental audit frequently identifies pieces of pollution control equipment that have been idled because of process changes or shutdowns. This equipment may now be available for use at other company locations or even for sale to third parties. As the cost of new pollution control equipment continues to rise, the sale of unused pieces becomes more likely.

The ultimate environmental opportunity may be the chance to commercialize internal treatment processes or capacity. In some cases, pollution control equipment was designed to handle future projected loadings as well as those presently experienced. If company plans for further expansions or new processes have changed, this capacity is now available for marketing. A reasonably common example is an "oversized" wastewater treatment plant. If the plant is located in an industrial park, nearby plants may be potential customers.

REASONS TO CONDUCT AN AUDIT

The previous section listed the two major functions of an environmental audit as confirmation of a plant's compliance status and identification of a plant's strengths and weaknesses. Given the large potential penalties associated with noncompliance, it is clear that these functions may be the main reasons to conduct the review. However, a company may enjoy many other important benefits from conducting an audit, in many areas. Some examples are discussed below.

Credibility with Others. The fact that a company periodically reviews the environmental status of its plants can and does affect the image it projects to others, such as government agencies, employees, and the general public. Although few agencies are in a position "officially" to sanction or reward internal auditing efforts, they can afford some latitude to responsible firms. An audit can also be used to establish an effective communication channel with company departments such as public relations, external affairs, or employee relations. The audit can give them examples of when the company can be justifiably proud of significant progress made in environmental control.

Securities and Exchange Commission (SEC) Rules. Regulations promulgated by the SEC require all publicly held companies periodically to report current and future expenditures for environmental compliance, as well as present and anticipated enforcement activities that may have a "material" effect on the firm. While some ambiguity still surrounds these reporting requirements, it is clear from cases brought before the commission that these rules are taken seriously. Properly designed, an environmental audit can serve as the tool senior management uses to comply with these reporting requirements.

Insurance Companies. Specific sudden and nonsudden insurance requirements have recently been imposed on facilities that treat, store, or dispose of hazardous wastes. As these requirements passed from proposed to final standards, it became increasingly obvious to the insurance industry that insufficient risk information is available to set rates, deductibles, and policy limits. Without such information, insurance companies are more or less forced to review each facility—or group of facilities—on a case-by-case basis. These reviews typically focus on potential losses from present, future, and past practices. In these cases, it is common for the insurer and the client jointly to retain and pay for an acceptable consultant to perform an audit of the client's facilities. With an internal auditing function already in place, it would be possible to negotiate a less exhaustive, hence less expensive, insurance audit for determining insurance parameters.

Resource Planning. In addition to merely identifying and listing environmental problems at an individual plant, an environmental audit can also attempt to prioritize these concerns. A prioritized list can be used to plan the deployment of company resources to address each area. In this way, the available supply of manpower, equipment, and money can be logically committed to the most compelling problems first. The audit may also identify areas where small expenditures made today can prevent the need for large commitments in the future. Even in cases where expenditures cannot be avoided, their commitment may be timed to coincide more closely with projected cash flows and hence reduce cost.

Personnel Training. With the complexity of today's environmental standards, it is clear that both plant management and the plant environmental function need some level of training. Some regulations, such as those regarding hazardous waste, oil spills, and hazardous material transportation, specifically require that employees be trained periodically. In many plants, the sheer volume of these requirements is too burdensome for employee training simply to be added to a person's workload. The audit can serve as a valuable training exercise, and the audit report can even be used as a text for employee training purposes.

Another significant area of personnel training is the preparation of the plant environmental coordinator for the inevitable agency inspection by using it as a "mock" government visit. The person responsible for conducting agency personnel throughout the plant can be briefed on the requirements and methods of handling this important facet of plant life. This "training" is especially important at facilities that receive few government visits. Because an environmental audit results in an organized and comprehensive report, these reviews can also be used to help promote continuity in the plant's environmental function. In some facilities, personnel turnover is so high in the environmental area that a collection of audit reports is useful as a continuous thread of information from the past to the present.

Determining Compliance Status with Proposed Standards. In most cases, a significant lag time is not unusual between the first proposal of new regulations and their final promulgation. This time is generally devoted to a public review and comment period when interested parties can offer input to the rule-making process. For proposed rules with a large potential impact, companies may choose to conduct audits at several plants to determine this impact and provide feedback to the rule-making agency. In this way, a proactive approach is adopted that typically results in workable and realistic standards. Even if such input does not materially change the proposed rules, proactive companies have at least succeeded in preparing their plants for future requirements.

Decisions to Buy/Sell Facilities. As industries' past environmental problems become public, it is clear that companies interested in the purchase, sale, or lease of facilities must be aware of any real or potential liabilities associated with the transaction. Although it is tempting to think only of plant sales in this light, the same considerations extend to used equipment purchases. Although the purchaser may initially be most interested in documenting the risks associated with the sale, the seller often derives comfort from an informed transaction. He can now be reasonably sure that undisclosed liabilities will not come back to affect future operations. As the number of corporate acquisitions increases, one can expect interest in such audits likewise to grow.

Expansion Planning. The lead time associated with expansion of existing facilities has continued to grow. Much of this growth can be attributed to the need to obtain environmental permits. In many cases, the negotiations between the company and the agency can consume months of effort, and are further complicated by the need to perform exhaustive and time-consuming environmental monitoring. In some cases, this monitoring alone can take a full calendar year.

Although few environmental audits will discuss expansion planning in detail, the audit report will contain much of the information necessary to evaluate this important business area. In most cases, air pollution concerns will dominate this evaluation. The audit report, in discussing the air pollution situation of the facility, will outline its current emissions and their respective permit limits. The difference between the two figures represents the amount of "new" pollution available. Although this is certainly a simplified approach, it can be used to rank "sister" plants for expansion potential.

In reviewing a facility's expansion potential, it will be important to note whether or not the plant is located in an area that is in attainment with ambient air quality standards. This single determination can affect the amount and type of air pollution control that any new source will be required to utilize. Similarly a review should be conducted to determine if New Source Performance Standards for the appropriate industry have been promulgated by the United States Environmental Protection Agency (EPA). If the facility discharges process water to a local publicly owned treatment works (POTW), this too can become a limit to future expansion.

Information Clearinghouse. In companies with many individual operating locations, it is easy to document cases where complex problems are easily solved at one location, while the same problems continue to confound others. The reality of intra-plant competition sometimes assures that this will remain true. In some organizations, sister facilities very seldom have the chance to meet and compare notes. However, company management has a vested interest in seeing that its environmental problems are addressed in the most cost-effective manner possible. An environmental audit can support this important objective by documenting cases of successful problem solving and distributing them to sister locations. In this way, the company helps minimize the cases in which each operation makes the same mistake at least once. By comparing notes, the number of mistakes, and thus the cost, are reduced.

Increased Management Confidence. In the final analysis, perhaps the main reason to conduct an audit is the increased level of confidence it can bring to management. This results from the informed evaluations that are made and the proactive measures taken to address problems. Plant managers are now free to conduct their daily business activities, while senior management can focus on company direction. The cost–benefit associated with increased management confidence is impossible to calculate but is real nonetheless.

AUDIT IMPLEMENTATION

In the previous sections, the definition and functions of an environmental audit were presented, as well as a list of reasons to conduct audit programs. Because the decision to begin can result in significant cost, it is important to identify some of the flexibility associated with implementation. Generally it is easiest to implement an audit program if the approach is phased in over time. This phased approach is not only attractive from a total cost viewpoint, but also permits the company to gain valuable experience before a large commitment is made. At another level, it allows the auditors to gain familiarity with the plants, personnel, and processes. By phasing-in the program, management has the opportunity to test-run an audit prototype at several representative plants and facilities. Prior to audit implementation, six basic parameters must be reviewed, which can be varied to accommodate budget and resource limitations. Each is discussed below, and they are summarized in Figure 1-1.

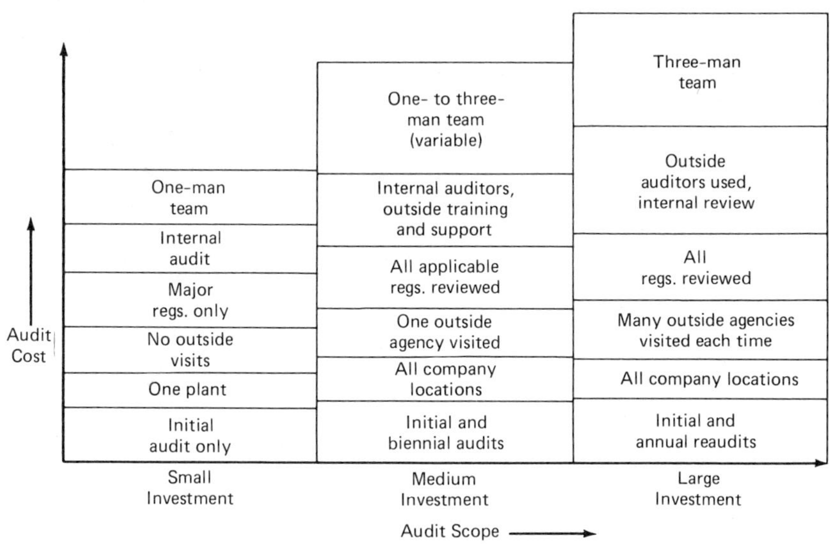

Figure 1-1. Audit implementation: basic audit parameters.

Audit Team Size. An obvious parameter that can be varied to suit budget restrictions is the size of the team used to conduct each audit. The flexibility of this parameter is limited by the complexity of the facilities subject to the audit. For small plants or warehouses, a single auditor can easily suffice. As the size of the facility increases, it becomes more likely that multiple-member teams will be necessary. For exceptionally large complex plants, teams composed by four members are common. An important consideration is the effect an audit has on the plant's environmental coordinator. The coordinator still has his own job to perform and duties to discharge, a fact the auditor should remember in order not to use his time unfairly.

Independent of the team size, one person should always be designated the "team leader." The leader should be responsible for directing the audit's overall progress and assuring that it stays on schedule and focuses on results. A general rule in determining team size is that big is not necessarily better.

Internal vs. External Team. For the most part, environmental audits should be conducted by company employees. Environmental consultants do indeed play a role in proper auditing, but this role should be kept to one of advise and support. The consultant can be used to help prepare the audit checklists or manuals and may even help train the auditors. Certainly, the consultant can be used to help address any environmental problems the audit identifies.

The use of company employees ensures that environmental problems remain within the company's sphere. As all companies have finite resources, it is simply prudent to keep the entire problem-solving process—from identification to solution—internal. By reducing the chance that problems will become public prematurely, one increases the probability that senior management will accept the audit concept.

The selection of the actual audit team is an exercise in balancing several important considerations. On one hand, environmental audits can benefit from using "fresh eyes" to review relatively unknown processes and plants. These eyes are able to look at each facility more objectively than those that spend their daily workday at the plant. Very often problems go unnoticed simply because they've always been there. As we discussed, it is also beneficial to use company personnel as the auditors. Many firms have been able to meet these conflicting requirements by using personnel from division or corporate headquarters. An alternative staffing mechanism consists of using environmental personnel from sister plants within the company.

Besides the actual choice of auditors, it is important to address the flow of information that an audit will generate. If division personnel are used as the audit team, the data generated will be collated at division headquarters, refined, and compiled into a final audit report. At this point the compiled report may be distributed to key plant and division personnel for their comment and action. By soliciting a schedule of corrective action, the audit effort assures that true progress will be made. Because the audit effort will generate a significant amount of background data, it is clearly important to track this information flow—a task that is facilitated by using internal personnel.

Regulatory Scope. The time, effort, and cost associated with performing an audit are direct functions of the number of regulatory programs subject to review. As the number of environmental laws and regulations increases, so does the effort to prepare and implement the audit. In most cases it is unrealistic to use a comprehensive approach initially. Because most environmental problems can be loosely grouped into air, water, and waste, it may be better to focus attention on these major areas first. By restricting the audit's initial scope, its cost is significantly reduced. As the audit effort gains experience and acceptance, its scope can likewise be expanded.

Off-site Visits. A comprehensive environmental audit recognizes that a plant's performance is also a function of the contractors and vendors it chooses to use. This recognition is especially true in the area of solid and hazardous waste. For this reason, a complete audit may include visits to landfills, treatment facilities, and other off-site locations involved with the plant. A review of this aspect of the plant's environmental picture makes those contractors and vendors aware of the importance of compliance on behalf of the plant. Such visits also serve to identify and document the company's good-faith efforts concerning compliance by vendors. As discussed in Chapter 4, local publicly owned treatment plants may also be eligible for visit.

Other off-site locations that may deserve attention during the audit effort are the several government agencies that inspect or maintain records on the plant. Typical agencies include the local, municipal agency (if applicable) and the state office, as well as the appropriate

EPA regional office. During these visits, the agency files on the facility are reviewed for accuracy, completeness, and content. Of particular importance are those documents that the company has rightfully declared confidential. It is reasonably common for information such as process parameters, formulas, and other trade secrets to be found in agency files that are accessible to the general public. By identifying these documents, the audit helps reduce the chance that such information will be wrongly distributed.

Although the importance of such agency visits is easy to recognize, these efforts are time-consuming. For this reason, the initial audit may not include any visits. This audit parameter remains flexible and can accommodate any budget or time restriction. The number of outside visits can be kept to one or two per audit until each agency is eventually reviewed.

Number of Facilities. Many industrial firms have several operating locations throughout the country. Although a comprehensive audit program would review every location, this parameter can also be modified to accommodate the budget. For companies with many locations, the initial effort may involve auditing a representative sample of each type. The results of this review may be used to indicate the magnitude and complexity of environmental problems likely to be encountered through the entire company. Succeeding audit efforts may use different company locations as the sample until every facility is eventually reviewed.

Similarly, initial audits can be restricted to major facilities within the company. By consciously classifying each company location according to potential environmental impact, budget restrictions can be accommodated while auditing efforts can progress. A simple note of caution applies to this parameter. Even though several facilities may be classified as minor, this subjective classification should not be used to rationalize away the need eventually to review their environmental compliance. Very often minor facilities lack the day-to-day attention necessary to assure continued, trouble-free operation. A simple one- or two-day effort may be all that is required to confirm their minor classification.

Reaudit Effort. The function of an environmental audit is to measure a plant's environmental performance against internal and external standards. Because this performance can and does change over time, it is also necessary periodically to review each plant's status. Although typical practice may encourage an annual review of each facility, once again this parameter is flexible.

For major plants that have large potential impact, an annual reinspection may be called for. On the other hand, minor operating locations may only need biennial review. For facilities with truly minimal potential, a single audit may suffice. By consciously tailoring the reaudit effort to real or perceived plant impacts, the cost of these valuable inspections is managed while their effectiveness is enhanced. A simple and logical reaudit scheme dictates that locations with poor performance be reviewed more frequently than those with minimal problems. In this fashion, the audit program serves to help motivate the plant personnel to better performance.

2
How to Conduct the Audit

INTRODUCTION

The job of the environmental auditor is to judge the degree of a plant's conformance at the time of the audit with standards set by federal, state, and local regulations as well as by corporate policy. This requires a working knowledge of applicable regulations and a thorough familiarity with the criteria for conformance. The preparation for the audit must include both these areas. All specific regulations and corporate policies relating to the environment for that plant must be reviewed before the auditor travels to the plant. In addition, the control equipment typical for the industry should be studied, as well as the characteristic water pollutants, waste streams, and toxic materials. At the plant, all the documents, reports, forms, manifests, and other administrative procedures required by the regulations and corporate policies must be inventoried and assessed. These may include inspection reports, maintenance logs, emission test results, and routine effluent analytical results. Many audits end at this point and do not consider the criteria for conformance.

The fundamental purpose behind all environmental regulations is the protection of the environment. Thus, an environmental audit must include an assessment of the impact of the plant on the environment. This means that, as a part of the audit, the auditor must inspect all process and fugitive sources of air pollutants, all points of water pollutant discharge to the surface or ground waters including the sewers, all storage or handling areas of toxic or hazardous materials, and all other aspects of the plant that may have an environmental im-

Figure 2-1. The auditor inspects an impact point in order to evaluate how well it conforms with environmental standards.

pact. Each inspection point must be judged with respect to its conformance with specific criteria that are required by either environmental regulations or corporate policy. These criteria for conformance relate to each type of impact point and often are determined by the size or type of industry being audited. For example, an emission source at a recently constructed plant may have to comply with EPA's new source performance standards as well as any more rigorous regulations imposed by state or local agencies. The control equipment used to achieve compliance with these standards must be inspected so that the auditor can judge how well it is operating or, in other words, how well the impact point is conforming. For this reason, checkpoints such as pressure drop and temperature are among the criteria for conformance that must be included in an environmental audit.

There is no uniform procedure for conducting an environmental audit. Auditing programs are tailored to meet the particular needs of the company being audited. In 1982, the Edison Electric Institute surveyed the auditing practices of over 40 utility companies and found a great variety of audit programs. These diverse programs were designed to meet a wide range of company management goals. Some companies used highly structured audit programs; other companies used more informal programs. Many larger companies used auditing staffs specifically dedicated to environmental compliance; smaller companies assigned the task to one individual, who probably had other responsibilities. Some preferred outside consultants, whereas others used environmental personnel from different plants.

The environmental auditing program presented in this chapter can easily be adapted to meet the management objectives of any company conducting an environmental audit. There are no hard and fast rules, and, unless EPA publishes guidelines (an unlikely occurrence), every company is free to design a specific audit program to accomplish its compliance objectives. The steps in the program discussed in this chapter are: preparation; meeting with the plant manager; collecting plant information; touring the plant; visiting with the appropriate agency; reviewing findings with the plant environmental coordinator; summarizing with the plant manager; and contributing to the audit report. These steps are described in the following sections.

The program described in this chapter is adaptable for use by in-house auditors as well as by outside consultants. It can be used just as effectively by an auditing team as by an individual auditor. Each member of a team, for example, could apply the program steps to the environmental area (air, water, solid waste, etc.) with which he is most familiar.

Background and Training of an Environmental Auditor

A word can be added here about the background and training required of an environmental auditor. An auditor should be well acquainted with the latest environmental regulations. He can familiarize himself with the regulations both by reading the environmental literature and by taking short courses such as those offered by the Air Pollution Control Association. Knowing the regulations, however, does not automatically mean that an auditor will be able correctly to determine whether a plant is complying with the regulations. Such determinations require a technical or engineering background because the control of every area of a plant's environmental impact involves

Figure 2-2. The auditor must be able to determine if spill containment satisfies regulatory requirements in terms of criteria such as volume, impermeability, and precipitation control.

engineering technology to some extent. For example, secondary containment can prevent oil spills. Engineering knowledge is necessary to determine whether a certain method of containment satisfies the regulatory requirements in terms of criteria such as volume, impermeability, and precipitation control.

In addition, a thorough understanding of the science and technology of pollution control is important. An auditor can learn about pollution control by taking several of the many available environmental science courses. A few years of on-the-job experience can also provide the auditor with this knowledge.

No formal academic program in environmental auditing yet exists. In fact, such programs might not be practical because of the wide range of industries, processes, and technologies that an audit might cover. However, specific courses about environmental subjects are available. For example, since the promulgation of the RCRA (Resource Conservation and Recovery Act) regulations, various training organizations have sponsored comprehensive courses in the area of waste handling and shipping. It is important for an auditor to be aware of the legal ramifications of an audit; this area has been the subject of many industry seminars. Up-to-date training in visible emissions reading is useful in auditing plants that have emission sources. Finally, EPA has published training guides for NPDES (National Pollutant Discharge Elimination System) and PCB inspectors. These guides are available through the U.S. Government Printing Office.

PREPARATION

Preparation for an environmental audit comprises three steps: (1) defining the audit parameters, (2) collecting preliminary information, and (3) preparing the equipment and materials needed to perform the audit. Defining the audit parameters requires determining the scope of the audit. The scope of any audit is based on the objectives of management in requesting the audit. For example, management might request a "snapshot" of the plant's compliance status. This type of audit might emphasize certain regulations, such as RCRA and PCB regulations. Or, management might request a study of compliance trends and the plant's potential liabilities in terms of proposed regulations. The amount and type of information requested will determine the length of time that the auditor needs to spend at the plant and also the complexity of the final report.

The second step required in preparing to audit a plant involves collecting preliminary information about the plant. Table 2-1 is a comprehensive list of background information that helps the auditor prepare for a plant audit. The list must be modified according to the scope of the audit. If sufficient lead time is available, the auditor might be able to obtain much of this information by providing the

Table 2-1. Preliminary Audit Information.

- General information about the plant
  - Mailing address
  - Phone number
  - Directions to the plant
  - NONcontiguous locations
  - Hours of operation
  - Plant safety requirements
- Vicinity of plant
  - Nearest municipality
  - Local governing body
  - Access to rail, water, or highway transport
  - Land use of immediate vicinity (e.g., farming)
- History of plant
  - Date constructed
  - Date and nature of major additions or alterations
  - Near-term plans
- Names of key individuals
  - Plant manager
  - Plant engineer
  - Environmental coordinator
  - Purchasing agent
  - Maintenance supervisor
  - Laboratory manager
  - Shipping supervisor
- Products or services of plant
  - SIC Code(s)
  - Type and volume of products
  - By-products
  - Type and number of manufacturing processes
  - Raw materials
  - Power (energy) modes and requirements
- Air pollution
  - Emission sources
  - Nature of emissions
  - Control equipment
  - Permit numbers, limitations, expiration dates
  - Recent NOVs, fines, problems
  - Monitoring equipment, reports
  - Recent source test results
  - Local agency regulating plant
  - Name of agency contact
  - Class and attainment status of region
- Water pollution
  - Outfalls and/or sewer connections
  - Receiving body and/or POTW
  - NPDES and/or POTW discharge permit dates
  - Treatment or pretreatment facilities

(*Continued*)

Table 2-1. (*Cont.*)

Test schedules and results
Recent problems or complaints
Local agency regulating plant
Solid waste
RCRA status
Names and addresses of haulers
Names and addresses of disposal sites
Areas of accumulation
Treatment on site
Oil storage
Locations, volumes, and contents of tankage
Spill protection
Date of SPCC plan
Recent spill history
PCB equipment
List of PCB transformers
Test results
Number of PCB capacitors
Other PCB equipment in use
PCBs in storage
Storage area

plant manager with a questionnaire to be completed and returned before the auditor visits the plant. Examining old corporate or agency files before a plant visit is not advisable because they might contain erroneous information. After the plant visit, however, the information gained might be used to update these files. The preliminary information need not include exact details about the plant such as how air emissions are controlled or what wastewater permits exist. Any information not readily obtainable should not be a concern because its relevance and importance will be more easily judged during the plant visit itself.

A substantive knowledge of the industry will enable the auditor to ask informed questions of plant personnel. If the auditor is unfamiliar with the industry, he should review the general industry information available in a technical or scientific encyclopedia. In addition, the auditor can check with the library of the regional EPA headquarters, which has several sources of industry-specific information such as technology transfer booklets, regulatory background documents, and contractor reports.

The last area of pre-audit preparation concerns the equipment and materials needed to perform the audit at the plant. These are shown in Table 2–2.

Clothes

Traveling clothes are suitable for the first day at the plant when the auditor meets with the plant manager. After that, work clothes are a must; the auditor's clothing should be able to take an occasional splash of oil or mud. In rainy weather, a rain parka will be invaluable. Safety shoes are mandatory; high ones are recommended in case the plant tour includes walking through underbrush. The plant will supply hard hats, hearing protection, and safety glasses if the safety program calls for them. The auditor must use these items if they are required. The auditor should also obey any other plant safety rules such as not smoking in areas designated as "no smoking" areas.

Instant Camera

Other equipment needed includes: an instant camera and film, a clipboard, a pad, ballpoint pens, and a tape measure. The instant camera is the single most important tool for conducting a thorough audit. The one-step, color models are the easiest to use because there is no waste paper produced during the photographing. Many plants already have instant cameras in the quality control lab or the engineering depart-

Table 2–2. Audit Equipment and Materials.

Preliminary plant information
Work clothes
Rain parka
Safety shoes
Safety glasses*
Hard hat*
Hearing protection*
Instant camera and film
Clipboard, pad, ballpoint pens
Tape measure
Source data inventory forms

*Supplied by plant.

ment. If the auditor plans to use the plant's camera, however, he should be sure that it has enough resolution to produce useful photographs. The camera should have adjustable focusing (i.e., it should be a range finder camera). Self-focusing is useful but not necessary. In addition, the camera should have automatic exposure control. Even with this feature and a flash, pictures taken indoors are unlikely to have enough definition to be of much use except as a memory jogger. The auditor should have plenty of film because the initial audit at an unfamiliar plant may require 40 to 50 photographs.

Most plants have strict policies concerning photographs taken by visitors. The auditor should ask the environmental coordinator about the plant's policy before carrying a camera into the manufacturing area. The auditor might need to obtain the permission of the plant manager, or a review of all photographs by the plant engineer might be required. The auditor and the plant manager (or the environmental coordinator) should agree on the disposition of the prints after completion of the final audit report. If an in-house auditor is performing the audit, the photographs might be filed for future use. If an outside consultant is performing the audit, the photos should be either returned to the plant manager or destroyed.

Data Inventory Forms

Data inventory forms provide an efficient means of collecting information and data on all plant environmental systems during a plant audit. In a comprehensive audit, one data inventory form should be prepared to record information about each of the following: (1) air emissions, (2) water effluents, (3) waste handling, (4) oil storage, and (5) PCB equipment. The design of each form depends on the complexity of the environmental system at the plant being audited and the level of detail required by the audit. For example, if the plant has extensive air emissions and major investments in air pollution control equipment, the air pollution inventory forms might be very complicated. In fact, one or more separate forms for each source or piece of control equipment might be required to list information such as: type, manufacturer, rating, and installation date; test data, permit limits, and monitoring records; performance history; major rebuilds; and problems. For a plant with fewer or less complex air emissions, a single form listing, for example, exhaust fans or heater vents might be sufficient.

Taken together, the data inventory forms relating to a specific plant become a manual that provides a guide for conducting the audit. As such, it should be designed during the preparation for the audit using the knowledge gained about the plant and the reasons management had for requesting the audit. When carefully prepared and organized, this manual can help prevent oversights and omissions in the data-gathering stage of the audit. Furthermore, it will aid in the preparation of the audit report. If environmental systems that were not identified and included in the pre-audit preparation are discovered at the plant, the auditor can easily prepare a form on blank paper to log the data. Carefully organizing each data inventory form (either during pre-audit preparation or at the plant) will help the auditor to collect all the information necessary to assess adequately the environmental impact of each system at the plant.

Information will be recorded on the data inventory forms throughout the audit. Much of the background information will be available during the pre-audit preparation stage. A great deal of information, however, will be recorded on the forms during the remaining steps of the audit. In short, the inventory forms are the work sheets of the audit.

If a plant is being audited for the first time, the auditor should keep in mind that the purpose of the first-time audit is to obtain as comprehensive a picture of the environmental impact of the plant as possible. The auditor cannot afford to get caught up in detailed investigations to confirm suspected environmental problems. Concerns about suspected problems and recommendations for correction should be noted on the data forms. Once the plant manager has been notified of a problem area, plant personnel can initiate a more detailed analysis of the situation.

Follow-up-Audits

On follow-up audits or visits, it might be necessary for the auditor to bring along enough portable equipment to check on any problems noted previously. If plant personnel corrected a previously identified problem, a test will confirm the correction. If the problem was not

Table 2-3. Examples of Follow-up Audit Equipment.

Duct air-flow meter
Manometer and Pitot tube
Pyrometer
Pocket thermometer
Sound level meter
Indicating tubes and pump for gas tests
Sample jars
Water quality test kits

corrected, testing can add factual data to support the previous recommendation, which can then be resubmitted. Table 2-3 provides a list of the portable equipment that an auditor might use on a follow-up visit to a plant. Examples of testing that would be within the scope of a follow-up audit are: checking to see if the outlet flow of a duct or vent is within equipment specifications; testing to see if the temperature of a water outfall is within the permit limitation; taking a sound level measurement at a plant boundary if an ambient noise problem is suspected. In addition, samples of effluents, waste oils, insulation, and so on, can be taken for analysis by independent laboratories. The auditor doing the sampling must be aware of proper sampling procedures, which include consideration of: sample uniformity, contamination, nonreactive sample containers, stabilization and preservation, and chain-of-custody documentation.

MEETING WITH THE PLANT MANAGER

In most plants, the plant manager, like the captain of a ship, is ultimately in charge of and accountable for everything that occurs within his jurisdiction. Thus, it is more than just common courtesy that the auditor's first responsibility after arriving at the plant should be to meet with the plant manager or his designee. An appointment should be made as far ahead of time as possible to ensure that the plant manager will be available. At the meeting, the auditor and the plant manager will have the opportunity to discuss the subjects listed in Table 2-4.

The reaction by the plant manager to an environmental audit might easily be negative because the only people usually interested in a

Table 2-4. Subjects to Be Discussed in Introductory Meeting with Plant Manager.

Introduction of auditor(s)
Authority under which audit is being conducted
Purpose of audit (management goals)
Advantages of audit to plant
Confidentiality considerations
Environmental concerns of plant manager
Recent inspections by agencies
What the audit consists of
How the audit will be done
What the audit report will contain
What follow-up will take place
The audit schedule
Request for organization chart
Request for facility and plot plan
Request for work area for auditor
Request for permission to use a camera
Request for permission to enter all plant areas
Introductions to plant staff

plant's environmental status are agency enforcement personnel, whose interest often carries the threat of citations or fines. If the plant manager's attitude is negative, the auditor should stress the positive side by explaining some of the advantages of an audit (discussed in Chapter 1). In particular, the auditor should emphasize the importance of an audit's expert appraisal of the plant's compliance status. With this assurance, the risk of inadvertent violations will be reduced, as will any attendant damage to public relations.

The plant manager's knowledge is required for the success of the audit. The auditor can elicit this knowledge by questioning the plant manager about any environmental concerns he might have. As a resident of the local community, the plant manager will probably be aware of environmental news such as changes in local regulations or nearby Superfund investigations that would impact on the audit. Relative to this, a major concern of the plant manager regarding the audit itself is likely to be confidentiality. Any examination of plant facilities has the potential of bringing to light unforeseen hazards or improper disposal practices. There is no way to ensure that the audit report will not become public once a problem is exposed. Some firms employing outside consultants as auditors attempt to shelter these documents under attorney–client privilege; however, until there is a test case in the courts, this privileged treatment must be considered uncertain. Under these circumstances, some managers are very cautious about engaging in an auditing procedure that could uncover the need for an expensive compliance activity or cleanup. Once a problem is discovered, these expenditures would be mandatory because any resulting agency litigation concerning violations that were discovered and not corrected would be very serious. On the other hand, discovering and correcting plant environmental violations in-house by means of internal audits can save money in the long run. It will be easier and less expensive to correct a violation that is brought to light internally than to correct a violation discovered through a complaint or an agency inspection. Internal audits can also provide sufficient information to assess potential problems that could become violations if not dealt with.

The plant manager's concerns might include actual or impending inspections or surveillance by regulatory agency personnel. The auditor should point out that the audit will help to prepare plant personnel for these agency inspections because the audit is itself a non-threatening inspection that provides direct feedback to plant personnel concerning such things as levels of cooperation, volunteered information, and reporting responsibilities. If the plant was inspected by a regulatory agency within the previous year, the auditor should request the name of the inspector as well as any correspondence files concerning the inspection. This information will help the auditor understand the plant from the agency's viewpoint, and this understanding will be useful to the auditor who plans an agency visit as part of the audit. (Agency inspectors are usually very willing to explain any criticisms in their inspection reports to a representative of the plant. Too often, plants fail to use this readily available agency assistance.)

The plant manager might express concern about the adequacy of certain pollution control equipment in the plant or the legitimacy of some plant disposal practices. The high cost of operating pollution control equipment, of disposing of regulated wastes, and of renewing permits is another concern likely to be voiced by a plant manager. In addition, there may be uncertainty over plant practices, such as on-site disposal of hazardous plant wastes, that might have occurred in the past.

The plant manager is affected by media reports like everyone else, and he is probably wondering if he is doing everything from an environmental standpoint that he should be doing. Does his plant have the most cost-efficient control equipment? Are any water pollutants sneaking by? Is all hazardous waste going where it is supposed to be going? If a convincing case has been made for the advantages of a plant audit, the plant manager should be anxious to receive assurances on these points by way of the audit.

Special permission from the plant manager might be necessary for the auditor to enter some restricted areas of the plant. If so, arrangements for lighting, security, and safety should be made as well. If the plant has property that is not contiguous with the primary location, or if the plant property is exceptionally large, arrangements for transportation and access to all areas might be necessary. If necessary, the auditor must obtain permission to use a camera on the premises. Any special requirements in this area should be reviewed.

The auditor should have adequate work space in the plant offices to use throughout the plant audit. Ideally, the work space should be equipped with a desk, a telephone, and some table space where documents and pictures can be organized. It should be near both the plant's environmental files and a copy machine. A conference room usually has plenty of table space for spreading things out; however, during the course of the audit, the room will probably be needed for at least one plant meeting which would require the auditor to leave. Because such delays are disruptive to the efficient conduct of an audit, a smaller work space that is exclusively available to the auditor is preferable.

The auditor should explain the auditing procedure to the plant manager. In particular, the auditor should explain the audit schedule and the hours during which he will require access to the plant. It is also important at this introductory meeting for the auditor to schedule a concluding interview with the plant manager to summarize the findings of the audit.

In the introductory meeting, the plant manager might not have time to discuss everything in Table 2–4. Instead, he might have the plant superintendent or the plant environmental coordinator discuss some of the subjects with the auditor. ("Environmental coordinator" might not be an assigned title, but every plant staff has one individual who is responsible for environmental regulatory concerns such as permit renewals. This individual might provide some input regarding plant policy in environmental matters, and, in more progressive organizations, he might also have the authority to shut down any operation he has determined to be out of compliance. In smaller plants, the environmental coordinator is usually the plant engineer.)

Finally, the plant manager will introduce the auditor to key plant personnel including the environmental coordinator, the purchasing agent, the shipping foreman, the plant engineer, the maintenance superintendent, the quality control manager, and the electrician. Probably, the plant manager will assign the task of making introductions to a subordinate; however, the plant manager should at least make certain that (1) all key personnel are aware that the audit is in progress, and (2) all key personnel are directed to provide information or assistance to the auditor when requested.

COLLECTING PLANT INFORMATION

The job of reviewing pertinent information about the plant's environmental control systems begins with a meeting with the environmental coordinator. He will have been instructed by the plant manager to render whatever assistance the auditor needs during the audit. If the audit is intended primarily to aid the plant manager in his environmental compliance program, the environmental coordinator might effectively become an assistant to the auditor for the duration of the plant visit. Other audit purposes might, however, be hindered by this degree of plant personnel participation. In any case, the environmental coordinator will be the primary contact between the auditor and the plant.

Obtaining Plant Diagrams

Diagrams and maps of the plant will help the auditor become familiar with the plant itself. The first diagram the auditor should ask for is the plot plan, which shows the legal property boundaries of the plant. Any noncontiguous properties either owned or leased by the plant (e.g., warehousing, parking lots, or rail sidings) should be included on the plan.

The second diagram required is the plant layout, which indicates the type of manufacturing operations conducted in each building or area of the plant. Third, a U.S. Geological Survey 7.5-minute quadrangle map of the immediate vicinity would also be useful. This map will show the locations of nearby bodies of water and will indicate local land uses. (The map's revision date is important. In some cases, a drive around the vicinity of the plant might provide more current information about the neighborhood than the map will.)

For auditing purposes, the most useful form of plant map or diagram is an 8½ × 11 outline that can be readily copied. In this way, information about each environmental system can be recorded on a separate sheet. If the plant has several manufacturing facilities and other areas such as tank farms, outside chemical process equipment, and storage yards, one diagram for each area might be necessary along with a master diagram showing the relative positions of each plant area. Precise scale or accuracy is not important as long as the relative locations of buildings and facilities are shown. Simple sketches by the environmental coordinator from whatever drawings are available or from his knowledge of the plant are acceptable.

Walking Around the Plant with the Environmental Coordinator

The second thing the auditor should do before he reviews the plant's environmental files is take a walk around the plant with the environmental coordinator. The purpose of the walk is to familiarize the auditor with the layout of the plant. Before beginning the walk, it is important for the auditor to understand the route they will take with respect to the diagrams. This will enable the auditor to use the diagrams later to tour the plant alone without getting lost. The auditor will not need the camera on the walk, which is intended mainly to familiarize him with the plant and its processes.

The walk may take an hour or more, and if the environmental coordinator is very busy, he might delegate the job of accompanying the auditor. This would be less satisfactory than having the environmental coordinator's firsthand comments on each system's operation. In particular, questions about his environmental concerns are likely to produce a great deal of information during the walk, which is a good time to ask questions about what is seen (or not seen). "What is that smoke there?," "Where does that drain go?," and "Should that (control device) be operating?" are all valid questions and should elicit candid answers. If they are not answered, or if the answers are evasive, the environmental coordinator has not understood the purpose of the audit.

Once the walk is finished, the environmental coordinator should understand that the auditor will make a more extensive tour of the plant later. Following that tour, which may take a full day or more, the auditor will have a list of questions to discuss with the environmental coordinator. This discussion will take at least several hours; so at the end of the walk the auditor should schedule this meeting.

Reviewing the Plant's Environmental Files

The largest amount of environmental information at the plant will be in the plant's environmental files. The environmental coordinator should be well acquainted with the information in the files because every letter, questionnaire, or document related in any way to pollution probably arrived at his desk for action. Most of these documents would have eventually been filed, though not necessarily in an orderly way; in many plants, documents not directly related to manufacturing are not filed carefully. Thus, the environmental file might consist of one or more overstuffed file folders or drawers. Most likely, the folders or drawers are not the only place where environmental documents are routinely filed. Some environmental regulations contain specific requirements for records retention and periodic reporting. Most plants affected by these regulations have had to develop orderly record-keeping systems for important documents. Hazardous waste manifests, for example, might be filed in the office of the shipping supervisor, the person responsible for tracking the copies and filing annual reports. Emission monitoring records or effluent tests might be kept in the plant laboratory, and any required reports filed by the laboratory supervisor. These records can be examined during interviews with the individuals respectively responsible for these activities.

Going through the plant's general environmental files means looking at each individual piece of paper and evaluating it. If the files are very unorganized, the first step might be to sort the papers into four separate categories: (1) air pollution; (2) water pollution; (3) solid waste; (4) other material. During the second review of each pile, the auditor can record pertinent information on the proper data inventory form. When reviewing the "air pollution" pile, for example, the auditor should pay particular attention to active permits, agency inspections, compliance test reports, and maintenance records. State air pollution inventories often contain information such as stack heights and diameters, exit temperatures and volumes, and manufacturer data. Invoices for equipment might provide installation dates, performance specifications, and the nature of any major upgrades. Memos and inspection reports provide insight into equipment performance histories. As this material is put in chronological order, the auditor should be able to fill in most of the information required by the data inventory forms and, at the same time, form conclusions about the adequacy of the plant's control equipment. The described procedure is then used to record the information contained in the "water pollution" pile, the "solid waste," pile and the fourth pile of "other material."

Interviewing Plant Staff Members

Once the auditor is satisfied that he has collected and recorded all the pertinent information from the environmental files, he should start interviewing the plant staff members whose jobs are related to the plant's environmental functions; for example, the purchasing agent, the shipping supervisor, the quality control manager, the maintenance foreman, and the electrician. This list will be different for each plant, and the plant's organization chart will help to pinpoint the best individuals to interview. The most important one is the environmental coordinator. He will know what procedure, if any, the plant follows to ensure proper operation of all control equipment. He should also have access to all emergency contingency plans (which may contain spill reports and PCB inventories), and he probably was given the responsibility of assuring that they are workable. He will be aware of the plant's status insofar as RCRA, air, water, and PCBs are concerned.

Solid waste information can be obtained from the purchasing manager and the shipping agent. They will know what enters the plant as raw material and operating supplies and what exits the plant as

Figure 2-3. The plant tour provides verification that the elements of a plant's pollution control system are as described in the permits.

products, by-products, or waste. They should also know how the wastes are disposed of. If any wastes are hazardous, a variety of documentation must be on hand. Wastewater information is usually maintained by the quality control manager because the required testing can be done in the plant's laboratory. He will be able to explain routine laboratory procedures that generate wastes and how these wastes are disposed of. The maintenance foreman may have further knowledge about how the plant manages its wastes. He should know about degreasing solvents, boiler chemicals, cleanup materials, and process wastes created during maintenance or repair procedures, and maintenance schedules for pollution control equipment. Finally, the electrician will be able to point out any electrical equipment that might contain PCBs. It would probably be his job to maintain the log of regular inspections of PCB equipment.

THE PLANT TOUR

In the plant tour, the auditor makes a firsthand assessment of all elements of the plant that have potential of actual environmental impact. Included are pollution control systems, wastewater outfalls, PCB equipment, oil storage tanks, and waste disposal facilities. These elements should all have been listed on the data inventory forms that were filled out as part of the plant information. The plant tour will provide verification that they are as described. In addition, the plant tour will provide data on the condition and adequacy of each element. Another, equally important purpose of the tour is to identify any environmental impacts that have not been listed. For this reason, the tour of the plant must be done in several segments, one of which involves a walk around the property line of the plant. This may seem to be a useless physical exercise, especially if the plant is large. Actually, it is a very valuable way of uncovering environmental oversights such as unpermitted outfalls and improper dumping. The other tour segments include inspections of the various manufacturing processes, chemical units, tank farms, storage areas, shops, and shipping or receiving facilities that make up the plant being audited.

In a large, complex facility, the tour segments should be made individually using the area diagrams obtained from the environmental coordinator. Each of these areas could be considered to be a small plant, in that each might have several different types of systems to be examined. Thus, to prepare for a tour segment, the auditor must first review the data inventory forms relating to systems located in the area of the plant to be visited. A manufacturing area, for example, might have a baghouse controlling dust emissions, a cooling water system with a drain to the sewer, several gas-fired space heaters, and some PCB capacitors in a motor control center. To tour this segment of the plant, the auditor would put the four data inventory forms relating to these systems on a clipboard, along with the area diagram of the manufacturing area. He would then take this clipboard and his camera to the area to examine each system.

The camera should be used primarily as an aid to memory. Photographs of each system, if properly taken, will help establish its location and orientation in addition to possibly showing the operational condition at the time of the audit. An obvious subject for photography is any environmental oversight discovered by the auditor, such as oil spills, improperly discarded wastes, unauthorized discharges, or excessive emissions. These photographs will be invaluable during the review meetings with the environmental coordinator and the plant manager when references are required for specific questions or comments. More importantly, they will provide a means for recalling the details of each system during the writing of the final report. If they are retained by the auditor, they will serve the same purpose each time questions are brought up about plant environmental systems.

For the photographs to be most useful, it is important for the auditor to get enough detail into each one to be able to positively identify it at a later date. Ideally, each photograph should show the item of interest plus enough background to confirm its location. Building walls or major pieces of process equipment are useful for this purpose. Including something for scale comparison, such as a person, automobile, or even a clipboard, is also helpful. The photographer should be aware of lighting angles so that the desired details are not obscured by deep shadows. One advantage of instant photography is that an inadequate photo can be retaken before the auditor leaves the location. Photographs taken inside a manufacturing area will rarely be very informative, even when flash is used, unless the camera is very close to the item of interest.

It is good practice to write enough information on the photograph as soon as it is printed so that it will be easy to relate it to a data inventory form at a later time. Writing on the plastic surface of Polaroid or Kodak instant photographs presents a special problem. Most ballpoint pens are not very satisfactory. Pencils will give a light mark that can be rubbed off. The soft-tip pens are no good at all, even for taking notes, because their marks run together and become unreadable if the paper gets wet. The Polaroid print has a strip of paper on the back that can be written on with a ballpoint pen. One solution that works well is to number and date each photograph on the back as it is taken. Any notes or questions relating to a photograph can then refer to the number. In the office, the photographs can be stapled onto cardboard file folders for reference. Six will fit onto an 8½ × 11 sheet. If it is necessary to title them, a piece of mending tape on the botton of each one will provide a writing surface.

Along with photographing each system, the auditor must carefully evaluate it. Does it conform with the information on the data inventory form? If not, the auditor should take notes concerning the variances. Items requiring particular attention are nameplate infor-

Figure 2-4. The auditor evaluates the operating condition of a control device, noting visible indications of proper function or malfunction.

mation, visible indications of proper function or malfunction, meter or gauge readings, and signs of deterioration or poor maintenance. These comments should be added to the inventory forms. Subsequent chapters of this book review the information that should be checked in each category of environmental equipment.

When all the inventoried items have been found, the auditor should make sure that every room or area in the plant has been inspected, and that every roof surface has been checked for stacks or vents. Some items may be discovered for which there are no inventory forms. These may be unpermitted emission points, or they may simply be the result of misplacing documents in the files. In either case, a blank data inventory form should be filled out for each, and further investigation done in the plant office. On the other hand, some items for which forms were filled out will not be found. Probably the equipment was replaced, but the files were never updated. Again, this should be noted on the form and a recommendation made to delete the file and, if necessary, cancel the operating permit.

Figure 2-5. Every roof surface must be checked and all stacks and vents identified.

Once the examination of a segment of the plant is completed, another segment should be started, until the entire plant has been inspected. The plant tour may take as long as several days in a large plant. If several auditors are working as a team and each has expertise in one environmental area, the tour segments should be scheduled individually by each member for maximum efficiency. The team members should be prepared to compare notes at regular intervals and to lend assistance whenever problems are encountered. Once exception is the tour of the plant's perimeter, which they should conduct as a group.

The plant perimeter tour differs from the other tour segments in that there are no specific items to be sought. The outfalls or other items that are located along the perimeter should have already been addressed in one of the tour segments. The perimeter tour is strictly for the purpose of discovery. The walk is easier if all fence lines have been mowed—an important factor to plant security as well. Items that might be discovered in the perimeter tour include unauthorized outfalls, contaminated runoff, forgotten trash accumulations, abandoned equipment, and evidence of process upsets. All discoveries should be noted and photographed.

Figure 2-6. The walk around the perimeter of the plant is easier and more informative if the fence line has been mowed.

The end of the plant tour does not conclude the information-gathering part of the audit; the accumulated information must be sorted and organized. Most of this should be done at the plant so that any uncertainties can be cleared up. The first priority is to identify all apparent or possible violations for review with the environmental coordinator. The rest of the information should be checked over to be sure that all the questions have been answered. Enough information should be available to enable the auditor to put together a comprehensive audit report.

VISITING THE AGENCY

Agency personnel can provide a unique view of the plant not obtainable elsewhere. Some are almost as familiar with plants in their districts as the plants' personnel. This is because turnover and advancement in governmental positions occur at a slower pace than in private industry, even though agency administration and policy seem to fluctuate almost continually. The career engineers and inspectors try to stay immune from policy matters as much as possible, and while their emphasis must change as new directives come down to them, their basic perception of what is right and wrong remains the same.

The agencies that regulate the various aspects of a plant's environmental impact are different in every region of the country. For air pollution, state or local agencies usually have enforcement authority. The state or local air pollution agency usually knows the most about the plant, particularly if the plant has a number of emission permits. Water discharges to a Publicly Owned Treatment Works (POTW) are regulated by the municipal authority operating the POTW although EPA's pretreatment standards may also apply. NPDES permits may be issued and enforced either by the state or by EPA. Similarly, the disposal of hazardous waste may be controlled by the EPA regional office or by the state, if the state program has been approved by EPA. Consequently, no one office is able to provide a comprehensive picture of the plant.

It is not necessary to visit every agency that has any control over the plant. In fact, it may not be practical or useful to visit any agencies at all on a first audit. The plant's file should have everything in it that the agency's file has, and it is not unusual to find that the agency's file is just as disorganized as the plant's. On the other hand, if the agency office is easy to reach in the course of the audit trip, the aforementioned agency perception of the plant would provide a valuable adjunct to the audit. Particularly valuable would be discussions with inspectors who have dealt with the plant. The names of these individuals may appear in the plant files or the environmental coordinator may know them, if there have been frequent visits or inspections.

If the auditor decides to visit an agency, a good approach is to call the inspector who is most familiar with the plant to request an appointment. The stated purpose of the meeting would be to review the file that the agency has on the plant. It is not a good idea to suggest discussing any specific permit or pollution problems. Rather, the auditor should present himself as corporate representative who is trying to learn as much as possible about the plant from an environmental standpoint.

Before visiting the agency, the auditor should be well informed about any problems that the plant is having with that agency. The subject probably will come up unless legal action is being taken by the agency. The auditor should not attempt to negotiate any issues for the plant during the agency visit, for several reasons. The main one is that this would very likely discourage agency personnel from giving an unbiased viewpoint concerning the plant. They might not accept the auditor as a neutral third party. Another reason is that the tone of the conversation would no longer be about the overall compliance of the plant, and some potentially useful information might be missed. The recommended approach is to learn as much as possible about the agency's view of the problem without offering any rebuttal. In the final audit report, some ideas could be offered as a defensive strategy for use by the plant in negotiating the issue.

The agency should have a file on the plant, which might vary in complexity from a manila folder to a computerized file. Most states have a computer listing of permit fees paid by the plant, and some have emission inventories with details such as source descriptions of every piece of pollution control equipment. These often serve as input for computer models to determine compliance with National Ambient Air Quality Standards. If the plant does not have up-to-date copies of the state's emissions inventory in the environmental file, the auditor should request them. They will be very useful for comparison with the data inventory forms that were filled out throughout the audit. In fact, the auditor should request copies of any agency documentation concerning the plant that is not in the plant files. It might also be useful to request a copy of the latest version of the agency regulations.

A careful review of the state's emissions inventory may reveal errors that have been perpetuated over the years. The auditor is in an excellent position to correct them because he has up-to-date knowledge of the plant's emission control equipment. The state personnel will generally be grateful for this input, and if part of the updating involves getting some minor sources permitted that somehow slipped by in the past, no punitive actions are likely to be taken. More likely, corrections will consist of deleting control equipment that has been replaced, changing firing rates or fuels, or correcting process descriptions to correspond with current conditions.

If there was a recent unfavorable inspection or a notice of violation

(NOV) issued by the agency, the auditor should try to get the inspector's viewpoint on it. It may have resulted from a misunderstanding on the plant's part about a regulation, or something that the plant had simply been ignoring. Again, the auditor must bear in mind that the sole purpose of the agency visit is to collect information, not to negotiate. When the auditor leaves the agency office, agency personnel should have a strengthened impression of the plant's environmental conscientiousness. This attitude will pay inestimable dividends over the years.

REVIEW WITH THE ENVIRONMENTAL COORDINATOR

The steps of organizing all the environmental information concerning the plant onto data inventory forms and then confirming it by inspecting the actual equipment or systems will produce an accurate and up-to-date picture of the plant's compliance status. However, it will most likely be incomplete, and the auditor will have a series of questions about missing data or oversights that came to light during the audit. Many of these situations will have been documented with photographs, which will be among the key findings of the audit. Thus, another essential step of the audit procedure is to meet with the environmental coordinator to fill in the gaps that still exist on the data inventory forms and to resolve any questions concerning permits, oversights, or malfunctions. This should be done at a scheduled meeting that may take several hours to complete.

The auditor should have developed an overall perception concerning the adequacy of the plant's environmental compliance program, and it would be a courtesy to review this perception with the environmental coordinator. Repercussions resulting from criticisms contained in the audit report will most likely be directed to him, so this pre-review may eliminate some misconceptions on the part of the auditor and allow the reporting procedure to focus on verifiable problems. That is not to say that the review should catalog only problems; it is important that the auditor stress his observations concerning the positive aspects of the plant's compliance program. In the environmental coordinator's job, there are very few opportunities for positive feedback.

It is not the intention of the review step in the audit procedure to provide a detailed oral report on the auditor's findings for the benefit of the environmental coordinator, nor would some audit purposes be well served by this. For example, if the audit was intended to evaluate the plant's environmental compliance program, such a review would provide the plant with an opportunity to address each point before the release of the audit report. This could seriously reduce the impact of the report, thereby lessening the ability of the audit to serve its intended purpose. On the other hand, it is the auditor's responsibility to see that corrective actions are taken as soon as possible for spills or other imminent hazards discovered in the course of the audit. There may also be reporting obligations in the case of spills. Thus, it is the responsibility of the auditor to see that the meeting with the environmental coordinator, like all other steps in the audit, achieves the purposes for which the audit was intended.

The most important function of the review with the environmental coordinator is to supply answers to the auditor's questions. Most of these should be accompanied by photographs that not only provide documentation of the current situation but also may eliminate the need to walk out to the site to confirm something. In many cases, the environmental coordinator will want to see the actual locations in question anyway, and it would be most efficient to look at them all in one final walk at the end of the review meeting. Before that, all the questions should be asked and any information gaps on the data inventory forms reviewed. If the forms are not too numerous or extensive, it would be useful for the environmental coordinator to look over all of them. In this way, misconceptions or errors on the part of the auditor could be caught and a more accurate data base produced.

The final subject for discussion is the tentative list of recommendations, if this coincides with the audit's purposes. The auditor should strive to maintain the constructive attitude of the rest of the interview, as there is no fundamental intention to criticize. Rather, the audit is intended to help the plant achieve and maintain compliance with environmental regulations in an organized and cost-effective fashion. The environmental coordinator should realize that an auditor may visit a wide variety of plants and thus be exposed to similar situations under other circumstances. What could seem to be a trivial complaint at this plant may have resulted in fines or excessive costs at another plant. Throughout this discussion, the auditor must keep an open mind with respect to rebuttals from the environmental coordinator. If a piece of control equipment was inoperative, for example, the reason could have been a back-ordered part. The follow-up questions that then should be asked include: Was a variance requested? Is there documentation? Should spares have been available? How long was the interval between the initial failure and the ordering of the part? This discussion will have the effect of converting the list of specific problems into the basis for a program of procedural changes by which these problems can be eliminated in the future. These procedural changes can be added to the list of recommendations to review with the plant manager in the summary meeting.

SUMMARY MEETING WITH THE PLANT MANAGER

Before the auditor completes a plant visit, courtesy again demands a meeting with the plant manager. The plant manager should be very interested in this meeting because it will give him some idea of the direction that his environmental compliance costs will take. He will expect information from the auditor's review of his plant pertaining to the adequacy of current control devices and whether the plant personnel are following the rules. The auditor may not be able to answer all his concerns on the basis of a one-time survey; also, it may not serve the purpose of the audit to do so. On the other hand, some observations resulting from the audit may demand immediate correction.

It is very important to the success of the audit at the plant level that all comments, both written and oral, be expressed in positive terms. Success of an audit depends on the reaction of the recipients of the final document. If they accept the auditor's approach as knowledgeable and unbiased, they will make every attempt to follow the recommendations. On the other hand, if they perceive the auditor to be a hypercritical environmentalist, the audit report may never even be read. To maintain a positive approach with the plant manager, the auditor should first discuss all the positive aspects of the plant's environmental compliance program before reviewing the recommendations that resulted from the audit.

If the audit included visits to any of the agencies, it would be valuable to review what was learned. This will also help in writing the final report because the plant manager most likely has a better perception of the agency's regulatory activities than the auditor would be able to gain in a single visit. If the plant is engaged in a dispute with the agency, the plant manager's point of view must be taken into account to achieve a balanced understanding of the problem. The purpose of the audit may be to assess plant liabilities; therefore, a comprehensive discussion of any agency dispute would be a requirement for the audit report. If the auditor's opinion of the dispute goes against the plant, it would tax his tactfulness to convey this to the plant manager; nevertheless, it would be a service to the plant to do so.

The plant manager should receive a list of recommendations for immediate actions to be taken to correct potential or actual violations. This is a "must do" list that could include nonfunctioning control equipment, spills that have gone unnoticed, or toxic materials that are improperly stored. Second, the plant manager should get a "to do" list to correct environmental problems that do not pose imminent hazards or involve violations. This list should be prioritized to maximize the effectiveness of any expenditures of labor or money. Finally, the auditor may communicate a "wish" list. This list contains actions that might be taken to improve the compliance posture or efficiency of the plant. An example might be the replacement of an afterburner with a condensor, both to eliminate fuel costs and to recover solvents. Disposal of PCB equipment before the mandated times might be another wish. Wishes could also include identifying environmental opportunities such as waste trading with other firms, sales or banking of emission credits, reducing compliance costs by using a "bubble" strategy, or delisting hazardous wastes. There might also be steps that would make anticipated regulation changes easier to comply with.

The plant manager's comments on all recommendations should be noted, particularly if they involve schedules for correcting noncompliance situations. Any agreements on corrective actions resulting from this meeting should be documented in the audit report. The recommendations as well as the corrective actions will provide the starting point for the next audit.

AUDIT REPORT

The "product" of an environmental audit is a written report intended for corporate or plant management and containing all the findings of the audit. Oral comments and criticisms made during the course of the audit including those made to the environmental coordinator and the plant manager have very little lasting impact. In fact, such comments can be counterproductive; oversights may be corrected at the time they are pointed out but allowed to lapse soon after the audit is completed. "Policing" activity is a responsibility of plant supervision. The audit report, on the other hand, should document situations where policing has been inadequate, allowing lapses to occur in the plant's environmental compliance. The report is in effect a tool to upgrade a plant's compliance management so that environmental incidents such as spills or violations are less likely in the future. In achieving this purpose, the audit could be considered a preliminary information-gathering step necessary for the preparation of the report.

The format of the audit report should serve the purpose for which the audit program was intended. There are many specific reasons to conduct an audit, for example, assessing potential liabilities for insurance purposes or evaluating assets for expansions or mergers. A review of typical audit "purposes" is included in Chapter 1. The audit report must answer the questions for which the audit was performed. In general, the audit will fall into one of two categories: (1) audits designed to aid plant management in attaining or maintaining environmental compliance; or (2) audits designed to inform corporate management of the plant's environmental status and liabilities. In the first case, the report should include recommendations to correct any deficiencies that the auditor identified at the plant. The report for corporate management, on the other hand, should be limited to factual descriptions of all findings and exceptions. Most audits in smaller corporations will be used for both purposes. One way to satisfy both is to issue two reports, one to the plant manager with recommendations for achieving compliance and one for corporate management assessing the liabilities of the plant.

In either case, the audit report must start out with a brief statement of the purpose of the audit. Equally important, it must provide the dates of the audit and the names of the participants. These items are often overlooked in the typical memo-reports that are sometimes used to document plant inspections, diminishing any value as a record of the plant's compliance status at the time of the visit. A properly documented audit report can be used as evidence of the plant's compliance status at a specific point in time. Likewise, a group of reports for all plants in a corporation documents the corporation's environmental conscientiousness as well as its compliance status.

An audit report should be organized into at least four sections: introduction; scope of work; review of the findings; conclusions. Audit reports intended for corporate management or ones that are very long and detailed should include an executive summary at the beginning. The type of information that can be included in each section of the report is shown in Table 2-5.

Table 2-5. Information Included in an Audit Report.

INTRODUCTION

1. A brief statement of the purpose of the audit.
2. The audit dates and participant(s).
3. The procedures followed in the audit.
4.* A summary of the mandatory recommendations for plant management.

SCOPE OF WORK

1.** A brief description of the plant, including its history.
2.** The environmental impacts of the plant.
3. All environmental permits and restrictions, including date of issue, expiration date, test requirements, and all limitations.
4.** Review of the federal, state, and local environmental regulations affecting the plant, including all reporting requirements.
5. Review of any corporate environmental policies or procedures affecting the plant.
6. List of citations, fines, inspections, complaints, court actions, notices of violation, etc., that the plant received involving environmental activities since the last audit.

REVIEW OF RESULTS

1. A description of each source of environmental impact including each air pollution source, water effluent outfall, sewer discharge, solid waste depository, hazardous waste facility, oil storage container, PCB item, etc. The original inventory forms could be used in this section.
2.** A specific assessment of each item concerning its compliance with all applicable regulations and policies. This should include acknowledgement of proper operation as well as documentation of deficiencies.

CONCLUSIONS

1.** Summaries of all comments, both positive and negative, concerning plant operation.
2.* Specific recommendations to the plant manager of items needing prompt correction.
3.* General recommendations to the plant manager of policies and procedures that would assure better compliance. Improvements in the plant operation and maintenance program are an example.
4.** A narrative summary for corporate top management of the plant's status, including assessing all liabilities, reviewing the adequacy of all environmental control systems to meet current and anticipated future needs, and discussing any restrictions (such as PSD) to expansion at that location.
5. A comprehensive summary of the plant's reporting requirements to meet environmental regulations and corporate policies.

*Audits for plant management only.
**Audits for corporate management only.

The inventory forms could be included in the report as the "results" section, provided they are sufficiently detailed and understandable. Used this way, they would also supply much of the information called for in other sections of the report, simplifying the overall report writing. For example, the air emission source forms include: the type of source; the type, date of installation, and capacity of the control device; the location, height, width, and emission rate of the emission point; the permit number, date of issue, expiration date, and requirements; test results on record; and comments on the operation and maintenance of the system. The only additional requirement for the report under the subject of air pollution would be a list of recommendations based on the comments on the inventory forms. This approach to the audit report, however, is not recommended for several reasons: the inventory forms are meant to be work sheets and as such are not easy for the reader of the report to interpret; the standard format of the forms would mean that many pages would have to be included in the report to convey a relatively small amount of information; and, in most cases, the forms would have to be copied over lessening their value as a record of the audit.

Audits for Plant Management

The report for an audit that is designed to aid the plant manager should be brief. Though addressed to the plant manager, it will most likely be turned over to the plant engineer or maintenance superintendent, neither of whom has much time for reading. It should contain a minimum of background information and concentrate instead on listing the items needing immediate attention, including specific instructions where necessary. This list of items should be as close to the beginning of the report as possible, perhaps even condensed into a preliminary summary section. The recommendations to the plant manager can be divided into two categories:

1. Those that must be followed up immediately (mandatory).
2. Those to benefit the plant (discretionary).

Included in the first category is the correction of any violation or exception brought to light during the audit. Discoveries such as an active spill, an illegal disposal procedure, or a nonfunctioning control device require an immediate response by the plant, which could be a cleanup, an agency report, or a maintenance work order. The Clean Air Act, the Clean Water Act, the Toxic Substances Control Act, the Resource Conservation and Recovery Act, and the Comprehensive Environmental Response, Compensation, and Liability Act all include obligations to notify appropriate authorities under certain circumstances. The auditor's role as the discoverer of the circumstance is to notify plant management of its obligation. Other situations requiring immediate response include imminent hazards. Inadequate spill protection, unlabeled PCBs, improperly stored toxic materials, and deteriorating asbestos insulation are all examples of imminent hazards that require immediate action.

In a first-time audit report, a discussion section could be used to review the specific regulations or corporate policies with which each correction item is intended to comply. There is little need to review the sources that are in compliance except when the compliance is marginal. These could be put into a subsequent section listing nonmandatory items. The auditor can provide a compliance schedule for the mandatory items if he has that authority. A follow-up visit should be included to review the results of the corrective activities. An alternate approach is to require a response from plant management concerning each mandatory item. This could consist of the plant's own schedule for compliance for each item or a written argument on the validity of an item. In the former case, a follow-up audit would still be beneficial; in the latter, a response is required from the auditor, followed by some sort of resolution of any difference of opinion.

Nonmandatory items that would be of interest to the plant manager are included for the most part in a discussion of the "quality" of the plant's compliance efforts. This discussion should be provided in a section following the mandatory list. Examples of quality considerations include the following:

1. Energy efficiency
2. Cost of maintenance
3. Product recovery
4. Compliance with future regulations

Consideration of these items will aid plant management in making decisions concerning compliance activities. Some will enable the plant's environmental compliance activities to contribute to cost savings, by either reducing energy consumption, reducing labor requirements, or improving product yield; others will put the plant in a better position to comply with anticipated changes in regulations.

Energy efficiency is of primary importance to almost every plant manager; any suggestions should be welcomed on ways to reduce the energy budget for environmental control equipment. For example, the auditor might recommend the installation of a solvent recovery system to eliminate the need for incineration as a method of hydrocarbon emissions control. The combustion of high-BTU wastes as an alternative to disposal can have a major impact on plant energy costs in addition to reducing disposal costs. Recommendations for installing energy-efficient motors or high-efficiency fans, however, are outside the scope of an environmental audit. Inefficient control devices should be pointed out if more efficient technology is available, but sufficient information for accurate assessment of the possible economic return should be included.

Maintenance efficiency often runs hand in hand with energy efficiency in pollution control technology because the older control equipment is usually less efficient than the new. The actual costs are difficult to evaluate, however, unless a large portion of the expenditures go for replacement parts, or unless the maintenance department has a good record of time assignments and hourly costs. High maintenance costs can be the deciding factor for the replacement of aging control equipment when energy efficiency is only marginally improved.

Product, by-product, or raw material recovery is rapidly becoming an important issue in a plant's environmental compliance program. Formerly, the value of recovered material was often minimal in comparison with the additional equipment costs necessary to achieve recovery. Recent substantial increases in disposal costs, however, have altered this economic picture. If the material is listed as hazardous, any possible recovery is almost mandatory. Even ordinary wastes are becoming an increasing financial burden. Moreover, virtually every industrial waste stream has the potential to become a liability because of current trends of public opinion regarding industrial wastes.

The increasing liability of plant wastes may be considered with respect to future regulations. Many wastes currently disposed of by plants as ordinary trash can be expected to be included in future hazardous waste regulations. Lubricating oil is an example. The plant that has a head start in reducing or reclaiming these wastes will have an advantage over its competitors when and if the regulations are promulgated. The auditor, through his routine reading of the environmental literature, should be aware of all legislative trends involving federal environmental regulations. Many states and regions go beyond the EPA regulations because of specific local considerations. Plant management or the local agency may be able to inform the auditor about local regulatory trends so that appropriate recommendations can be made.

Audits for Corporate Management

The reports for audits designed to inform corporate management of a plant's compliance status and liabilities should be comprehensive with respect to each of the audit's intended purposes. In most cases, the readers will not be intimately familiar with the plant and therefore will have to base their judgments on the information provided in each report. The corporate legal counsel, for example, may never have visited a plant. They will need to know the location of the plant (state, city, and county) as well as the vicinity of the plant, population density, nearby bodies of water, and local land use. A description of the plant itself should be provided, including a short history, the makeup of the plant's work force, and some quantitative estimates of its primary product lines. If the plant has had major environmental compliance problems in any specific area, these should be described as part of the plant's history, with the dates and descriptions of any milestones in the problem.

A detailed description of the audit procedures should be provided in addition to the information in the summary. The names and qualifications of each member of the audit team should be included, as well as names of each plant employee interviewed. All questionnaires and data sheets should be included as an appendix, with the information given in the procedures section. An audit schedule listing the date and time of each audit milestone should also be included as a table.

For audits intended to provide management with the status of a plant's environmental compliance program, a detailed review of all environmental regulations and corporate policies affecting the plant should be provided. This can be categorized according to air, water, solid waste, and so on. Under each heading, a description of the plant's compliance status should follow the regulation review. Reference should be made to the data sheets on each individual control system or waste stream if more complete information is included.

If the audit is intended to document present or future liabilities, only the areas of liability should be covered in this section. For example, if the plant emits a hazardous air pollutant that exceeds present limits or that would exceed a proposed limit, the discussion should be as comprehensive as necessary, including evaluations of alternate technologies that would eliminate or mitigate the liabilities. There is no need to review present compliance with other regulations.

A separate section of the report could include specific findings during the audit that do not directly affect overall compliance. This section should parallel the section in the audit report for plant management that covers nonmandatory items, but it should include far less detail. Rather, it should focus on general trends shown by the leaders in the industry in their ongoing compliance programs. Thus, if a plant is becoming obsolete because of its inability to recycle water or waste streams, and regulatory trends are encouraging this obsolescence, the audit report should say so. Individual oversights such as broken bags in a baghouse, unlabeled PCB equipment, or nonregulated discharges should be mentioned only with respect to their "root causes." That is, the plant's organizational failing that enabled the oversight to occur should be discussed. The audit concentrating on liabilities should review the potential liabilities brought on not only by the oversight itself but also by other oversights that could occur.

The last section of the audit report should list the recommendations of the auditor or the audit team. These should be presented as decision guidelines for the intended readership of the report. The recommendations will obviously reflect the author's perspective, derived from his training, experience, and awareness of current trends. Thus, the recommendations can constitute "advice" from the environmental standpoint that the readers will combine with management goals and perspectives or legal opinions to forge corporate environmental policy decisions.

The corporate information audit report should undergo a review step before being published and distributed. This should include a representative of the legal department (unless this department was represented on the audit team). The importance of this review cannot be understated because of the far-reaching legal implications of the audit report. Questions of disclosure, confidentiality, attorney–client privilege, and so on, must be answered before the report is published. This legal review will provide timely expert guidance on the handling of any exceptions, which might require immediate reporting to EPA, the Coast Guard, or even the company stockholders. In such cases, the final report will not only review all deficiencies; it will also describe any required responses and provide assurances that all reporting obligations have been met. In this way, upper management can concentrate on the long-range implications of the report without having to become concerned with immediate responses. Obviously, the manager of the audit function should review the audit report, as should any other members of the corporate staff that the manager deems necessary. It may not be desirable, however, to include plant management in the review step, particularly if the report is critical of plant management. Any review under this circumstance would suggest possible compromise of the intent of the corporate audit program. On the other hand, a thorough review of all facts in the report should be made before report publication. This might entail plant review of all data sheets.

An audit report intended to aid plant management should be reviewed in draft form by the plant manager. This review will serve to initiate the corrective dialog that is the purpose of the audit program, and will provide the plant manager with the opportunity to act before any information is published that might reflect on his management.

FOLLOW-UP

Although publishing the final report is the natural culmination of the audit, it is by no means the end of all activities. In fact, for an initial audit, the final report might be considered to be the point of departure for a comprehensive environmental compliance program. This would involve the correction of any deficiencies brought to light by the audit, and then initiation or upgrading of programs designed to prevent recurrence of the problems. These might be preventive maintenance programs where control device problems were uncovered, or regulatory compliance programs where noncompliance situations were found. Examples of the latter might be the need for a spill prevention program for a plant with large volumes of oil stored in drums, or a PCB compliance program where PCB capacitors were found in motor control panels. Follow-up audits are also necessary to assess the effectiveness of the new programs and to prevent backsliding. Even when adequate compliance is found, follow-up audits are essential because environmental regulations are in a constant state of change. So too are operating industrial plants, not only in production rates and processes but also in personnel and policies.

3
Air Pollution

Every industrial plant regardless of size has sources of air pollution, ranging from gas-fired space heaters or dusty parking lots to blast furnaces or coke ovens. Likewise, problems from air pollution are not the exclusive domain of big industry. Odors emitted from roof vents or wall fans have caused major headaches for small manufacturers, just as sulfur and particulate emissions have for their larger cousins. Usually, these problems are solved by installing control equipment to reduce the emissions to acceptable concentrations. Odors, for example, are often controlled by filtration, adsorption, or incineration. All

Figure 3-1. Every industrial plant regardless of size has sources of air pollution.

the devices using these principles, however, have unavoidable operating expenses and maintenance requirements, none of which adds to the plant's productivity. The same applies to most other air pollution control equipment, including cyclones, baghouses, precipitators, and scrubbers. They must be kept operating efficiently in the same manner as the plant's process equipment, regardless of the cost. The air pollution audit is a way of checking to assure that this is being done.

The air pollution audit must take into account all sources of air pollution at a plant and provide an evaluation of the present effectiveness of any control devices that have been installed to reduce emissions. It should also provide a review of the regulations that govern the plant and the regulatory agency that enforces them. This will tell "how the plant is regulated." The auditor might include a brief history of the plant's battle to control its emissions and determine how it arrived at its present status. From these inputs, the auditor through his report will be able to assist the plant in plotting its course, either to maintain its status of environmental compliance or to correct deficiencies in a cost-effective manner.

AIR POLLUTION REGULATIONS

Air pollution was the dominant environmental concern of the general public in the United States for the first half of the twentieth century. For this reason, the most complex set of federal, state, and local environmental regulations concerns the control of industrial air emissions. These rules have been promulgated at various levels of government since the end of World War II, and in some urban areas, much earlier. The regulation of air pollution on a national scale started in 1963 when Congress passed the Clean Air Act (CAA). The intention was to encourage state regulatory bodies to control and abate air pollution while providing for federal enforcement authority where necessary. The initial preference for the states as the primary regulatory bodies has continued to this day. Consequently, a thorough knowledge of federal air pollution regulations will not provide much assistance in judging an existing plant's compliance; most of the regulations that it must comply with are state or even local regulations. However, knowledge of federal regulations will be useful in utilizing the audit report to determine the plant's status insofar as expansion or modification is concerned.

The Air Quality Act of 1967 reinforced the states' role of having the primary responsibility for controlling air pollution; but, at the same time, it strengthened federal programs where state control was too weak or entirely absent. To do this, all federal programs dealing with pollution were consolidated under a new agency, the Environmental Protection Agency (EPA). In the Clean Air Act of 1970, this agency was charged with the responsibility of defining National Ambient Air Quality Standards (NAAQS) for major air pollutants. As a result, EPA promulgated primary and secondary standards for criteria pollutants, which are particulates, sulfur oxides, nitrogen oxides, carbon monoxide, hydrocarbons, ozone, and lead (Table 3–1). The primary standards are intended to protect the public health with an adequate margin of safety. Secondary standards protect the public welfare against other adverse effects, such as damage to soils, crops, wildlife, weather, visibility, climate, economic values, and personal comfort and well-being. Each state was divided into air quality control regions that are designated attainment or nonattainment for each criteria pollutant, according to whether the air is better or worse than the primary standard for that pollutant. EPA required each state to develop and adopt a state implementation plan (SIP) in order to bring all regions of the country into attainment with the NAAQS. The deadline for the states to complete their SIPs was 1975. EPA reviewed each state's SIP and determined whether it was sufficiently stringent to enable the state to attain the NAAQS in a reasonable period of time. When this was not the case, EPA augmented the SIP with additional requirements.

Other 1970 CAA amendments required EPA to set national emission standards for hazardous air pollutants (NESHAPs) and to promulgate new source performance standards (NSPS) for almost 30 classes of major (emitting over 100 tons per year) industries. Citizen suits were permitted in the defense of clean air, and EPA was given the right of entry to enforce its regulations. While some states already had aggressive pollution control programs, the CAA amendments of 1970 forced the others to action. Many state industrial air pollution control programs in effect today date from the early 1970s, the result of newly formed or invigorated state agencies encouraged by increasing public awareness and pressure.

A new body of amendments to the CAA was enacted by Congress in 1977 that resulted in EPA regulations in 1978 for the prevention of

TABLE 3-1. National Ambient Air Quality Standards

POLLUTANT	PRIMARY	SECONDARY
Sulfur oxides	ppm	ppm
annual average	0.03[a]	
24-hour average	0.14[b]	
3-hour average		0.50[b]
Particulate	$\mu g/m^3$	$\mu g/m^3$
annual geo. mean	75[a]	60[a]
24-hour average	260[b]	150[b]
Carbon monoxide	ppm	
8-hour average	9[b]	same
1-hour average	35[b]	
Ozone	ppm	
1-hour average	0.12[c]	same
Nitrogen oxides	ppm	
annual average	0.05[a]	same
Non-methane HCs	ppm	
3-hour average	0.24[bd]	same
Lead	$\mu g/m^3$	
calendar quarter	1.5[a]	same

[a] Never to be exceeded.
[b] Not to be exceeded more than once a year.
[c] Standard attained when expected number of days per year with maximum hourly average above 0.12 ppm is equal to or less than one.
[d] Applies 6 A.M. to 9 A.M. daily.

significant deterioration (PSD) of the existing air quality in all regions of the country, whether they were in attainment or nonattainment with the NAAQS. This required those desiring to construct a new major source to undergo a new source review (NSR) process to ensure that the source would not reduce the existing air quality in the region. Several classes of pollution control equipment were defined for the purpose of achieving compliance of new sources. Which of these is required depends on whether the location of the source is in attainment with the NAAQS for the pollutants being controlled. In order of increasing stringency, these classes are: Reasonably Available Control Technology (RACT), Best Available Control Technology (BACT), control technology specified in the NSPS (which is usually the same as BACT), and Lowest Achievable Emission Rate (LAER). BACT differs from LAER in that BACT takes economic and energy usage considerations into account, whereas LAER does not do so. In cases where the plant being audited is planning major modifications or expansion, the auditor may need to identify the category of controls on existing sources and the offsets (pollution credits) that would be available if they were upgraded to BACT or LAER.

State and/or regional air pollution regulations that have been enacted or modified to meet the SIP can be moderate or severe, depending on the amount of industrial development in the state or region and the degree to which attainment has been achieved with the NAAQS. These regulations apply to existing sources and new ones for which NSPS do not apply. Many are modeled after the NSPS for some industries, but generally most are not source-specific but are structured around the type and amount of pollutants emitted before controls are applied.

Two important categories of regulation involve opacity and sulfur oxide emissions. Opacity is usually regulated at percentage levels from zero to 20%, with higher percentages allowed for occasional short-term upsets. Twenty percent opacity corresponds to a Ringleman number of one. The auditor should be able to estimate this opacity even without visible emissions training at a "smoke school." More precise readings are outside the scope of an audit, but if the auditor feels that the emissions could exceed 20% from a stack or vent, he should note it on his report. Care must be taken not to be confused by water vapor. This will dissipate rapidly, while particulate emissions will fade only with dilution downstream.

Opacity measurement is an easy means for states to regulate particulate emissions, because no interactive testing is required. Sources can be evaluated quickly from a distance—often outside the plant property line. A plant manager may be required to have particulate tests run on a source that he believes to be in compliance with mass emission standards even though the opacity exceeds the regulations. Particulate testing may also be required routinely for larger sources or upon start-up of new control equipment prior to issuance of an operating permit.

Sulfur oxides are easily regulated in many states by blanket restrictions on the sulfur content of industrial fuels. Some states scale the allowed emissions to source sizes and stack heights. Only the largest sources such as power-generating plants can afford to scrub sulfur oxides from their emissions and thus be able to utilize fuels with high sulfur contents. These sources must prove to the agency through rigorous testing that their emissions meet the regulations. In addition, the agency will usually require continuous monitoring of their emissions.

State or regional regulations may be encountered for volatile hydrocarbons, nitrogen oxides, and odors. Fugitive emissions may also be separately regulated. Volatile hydrocarbon regulations impact upon fuel storage and transport and metal coating and finishing industries. The extent of controls required depends on the regional attainment with the NAAQS for ozone, and the vapor pressure and reactivity of the hydrocarbon species being emitted. Where control is required, the agency may require some proof that it is operated continuously and that it is maintained properly.

Nitrogen oxides, odors, and fugitive emissions are usually not strictly regulated because of the difficulty of measuring and controlling them. This situation may change for nitrogen oxides as EPA applies more pressure on the states to seek attainment with the NAAQS for NO_x. Odors and fugitive emissions are nuisances to surrounding communities and may result in citizen complaints followed by agency investigations.

AIR POLLUTION SOURCES AND CONTROLS

Industrial air pollution sources can be broadly defined as those locations at a plant that have an impact on the atmosphere around the plant. In most cases, the impact has been substantially reduced by control equipment installed between the source and the emission point. Individual sources typically fall into one or more of the following classifications: combustion equipment, process units, dry material storage and transport, and fluids storage and transport. For the most part, these are point sources, in that the emissions to the atmosphere occur as discrete locations such as stacks or vents. A characteristic of point sources is that they are easily evaluated by testing a sample of the flow at the emission point. Fugitive emissions are another category of industrial air pollution. Dust or fumes escaping from doors and windows or blowing off storage piles or dusty lots are examples of fugitive emissions. They are very difficult to evaluate by traditional testing procedures. Nevertheless, any survey of industrial air pollution must take into consideration all the point and fugitive sources at a plant.

Combustion

Combustion sources are found at almost every manufacturing site—if not in the process, then as a part of steam generation or space heating. It is the rare plant that can transfer all of its combustion requirements to the local utility (through electric heating or the purchase of steam). Besides space heating and steam generation, other combustion sources could be dryers, process heaters, calciners, furnaces, smelters, or incinerators. The latter include units for the disposal of solid, liquid, or gaseous wastes. These might be dedicated units or equipment designed for other purposes such as process heating or steam generation. Also included are flares for the disposal of high concentrations of volatile hydrocarbons.

External combustion of fossil fuels produces primarily carbon dioxide and water vapor. Other pollutant species are functions of the fuel being burned, the nature of the combustion chamber, the material being heated, and the efficiency of combustion. Two important pollutant species are nitrogen oxides and sulfur dioxide. The former result from the oxidation of atmospheric nitrogen and are produced in proportion to the combustion temperature and the amount of excess air. (In addition, there is a small amount of dissolved nitrogen in petroleum-based fuels that oxidizes during combustion.) The concentration of sulfur dioxide is a function of the amount of sulfur in the material being combusted, the temperature, and the amount of excess air. Sulfur trioxide or sulfur compounds with lower oxidation states may be formed as well, depending on combustion conditions.

Particles produced during combustion are a result of any of the following: incomplete fuel utilization, a noncombustible fraction in the fuel (ash), fire box erosion, and product ablation or volatilization. The ratio of one to the other of these is determined by the fuel and the process. Natural gas generally burns completely and has no ash content; so any particulate formed is from the equipment used for burning or from the material being heated. Solid fuels such as coal, lignite, or wood, on the other hand, have a relatively high ash content, some of which becomes fly ash during combustion. All the ash becomes fly ash when the fuel is pulverized before burning, and, in addition, some unburned fuel may escape with the emissions because of inadequate residence time in the combustion chamber. Liquid petroleum fuels, such as kerosene, diesel, bunker C, and light and heavy residuals, produce particulates in proportion to their ash contents and the ability of the burner to atomize the liquids.

Particulate may be formed during combustion when a product or raw material is heated by direct flame impingement. Product-generated particulate is a function of the product's friability and volatility, and of the angle and velocity of the flame. The same factors apply to the material lining the combustion chamber. High-temperature furnaces lined with ceramic refractory materials produce measurable quantities of particulate from refractory erosion. Glass furnaces, rotary kilns, and smelters are examples.

Plant vehicles and stationary engines constitute a special combustion case known as internal combustion. Because of its inherent inefficiency and mechanical complexity, internal combustion rarely plays a large enough role in plant operations to contribute substantially to the emissions. In addition, the emissions of most vehicles are regulated as mobile sources and not as part of a plant's total emissions. Stationary engines are generally restricted to uses such as to power fire pumps or auxiliary generators and are excluded from the plant emission inventory.

The emissions from internal combustion sources include a substantial fraction of carbon monoxide in addition to all the other gaseous combustion products. There may also be substantial quantities of particulate, depending on the fuel being burned. Diesel engines, for example, are notorious for their particulate emissions. Unburned and partially burned fuel may also be found in internal combustion emissions. The quantities of these pollutants are very dependent on the quality of carburetion being achieved. Turbine engines, which are often used to power auxiliary (peaking) generators, are more efficient than reciprocating engines and therefore produce less carbon monoxide. On the other hand, they produce more nitrogen oxides including nitrogen dioxide, often resulting in a characteristic brown plume over the source.

Most smaller industrial noncontact combustion sources are not required to have emissions controls by local regulations. An exception might occur in the case of particulate resulting from solid fuel combustion in locales where opacity limits are very stringent. Horizontal plenums or high stacks, however, often remove enough fly ash to achieve compliance. If further control is necessary, one or more cyclones may be used, possibly in combination with a baghouse. Sulfur dioxide is commonly regulated by restricting the percentage of sulfur allowed in fuels. This restriction sometimes varies with the type of fuel in order to encourage certain fuel usages. Control devices (scrubbers) to reduce sulfur emissions are not common or even encouraged for small sources because they are generally unreliable. Only a facility on the scale of a utility can provide the investment necessary to keep sulfur dioxide scrubbers operating dependably.

Combustion sources involving product contact are regulated in accordance with the potential for generating particulates exceeding the limitations imposed by the SIP. When a control device is required, the selection is dependent on the same factors as for process units (discussed next). In some cases, the product being heated effects a reduction in emissions. Such a situation occurs in lime, cement, and magnesite kilns where sulfur dioxide is absorbed into the product as a sulfate. The operators of these units can petition to use lower-cost, higher-sulfur fuels by proving with source testing the reduction being achieved. Some experimental facilities have even been set up to combust hazardous waste in cement kilns. Up to 30% waste has been successfully incorporated into the fuel.

Process Units

The greatest variety of air pollution sources is included under the heading of process units. Examples are mixers, cookers, dryers, grinders, reactors, coaters, extruders, pulpers, and distillers. The description of each is beyond the scope of this book, but it remains the responsibility of the auditor to become familiar with the process units in the plant he is auditing. A good starting point for this information is the Air Pollution Engineering Manual (AP-40), available through the U.S. Government Printing Office. This manual is based on practical knowledge gained by Los Angeles County in its pioneering efforts to control air pollution. The auditor should also review the NSPS for the industry, promulgated by EPA, even if the plant has no new sources.

The NSPS will usually describe all the process units specific to that industry and define the type of controls that meet BACT. State regulations specific to the industry being audited should be reviewed to see what the state agency considers to be BACT and how it regulates emissions in existing facilities. It might also be useful to know the type of controls required by the most stringent state because this defines LAER for the industry. The emission reduction credits that a plant would achieve by substituting BACT or LAER for the present control equipment could be used as offsets for future expansion or modification.

In contrast to the wide variety of air pollution sources, there exist only a limited number of control technologies. These are based on an equally limited number of physical characteristics of the emissions, such as bulk, inertia, resistivity, solubility, combustibility, reactivity, and adsorptivity. In the case of a fine particulate, for example, emissions can be controlled by utilizing its characteristics of bulk with baghouses, inertia with venturi scrubbers, or resistivity with electrostatic precipitators. The newest installations of these devices may contain high-technology improvements, but the basic principles are the same. Also, within each equipment category individual manufacturers have developed unique configurations for the specific needs of certain industries or to provide real or imagined advantages over their competition. Thus, the auditor is often confronted with a seemingly endless variety of control equipment. For the most part, however, it operates according to a few basic principles.

Process emissions consist of gases, solids, and liquids that are expelled into the atmosphere through the operation of an industrial process. To design a control device, the engineer must have as much information about the process as possible. For example, he must know the rate at which the emissions are released; whether they are continuous or intermittent; whether they are constant, increasing, or decreasing; and what their temperature, pressure, and humidity are. The gas phase could contain any inorganic or organic compounds that are gases under the exhaust conditions, although it will be primarily air or combustion products with a percentage of water vapor ranging from zero to saturation. The emissions probably contain particulate, which may be solid or liquid in narrow or broad size distribution. The particles may be hard, soft, low-melting, reactive, or adsorptive. Finally, some of the gaseous or solid components of the emissions may be odorous. All these factors must be taken into consideration in order to ensure that a control device is effective, efficient, and reliable.

The following paragraphs discuss the operating parameters that the auditor should be aware of concerning the more common types of control equipment: cyclones, scrubbers, baghouses, high energy filters, coalescing filters, electrostatic precipitators, absorbers, adsorbers, condensors, and incinerators.

Cyclones. Medium to coarse particles (larger than 10 μ) tend to separate from a gas stream by inertia at any change in direction of the stream. This often occurs at elbows and transitions in duct work, and can lead to plugging if not accounted for in the design. The cyclone takes advantage of particle inertia to achieve air cleaning. It consists of a circular chamber with a tangential inlet. Here the particles concentrate along the wall and migrate toward a restricted outlet at one end while the gas stream spirals through another outlet at the other end. The usual configuration has a horizontal inlet, particulate removal at the bottom, and the outlet directed vertically at the top. The particulate can be liquid or solid, but should not be sticky enough to build up on the cyclone walls or agglomerate to plug the discharge. Another means of achieving inertial separation of liquid particles is to utilize vanes within a duct to spiral the air stream while providing a means for collection and removal around the perimeter of the duct. The efficiency of all inertial separation processes is dependent on particle mass, inlet velocity, and cyclone dimensions.

As the size of individual particles in a gas stream decreases, the efficiency of their cyclonic capture is diminished. It can be improved to some extent by increasing the velocity through the cyclone and reducing its diameter. There is, however, a limiting velocity after which turbulence sets in. Increased velocity also increases the pressure drop in the system, reducing the volumetric throughput. Multiple, high-efficiency cyclones working in parallel can provide good volumetric flow while removing particulate as fine as 5 μ . This is well into the respirable size range where the inertial structures of the human upper respiratory tract also lose their efficiency in particulate removal.

Cyclones are inexpensive to purchase and operate. Also, they are

Figure 3-2. A cyclonic oil mist knock-out. Inlet at the top; outlet at the bottom. Some oil leakage is visible.

unaffected by a wide range of temperatures, pressures, and atmospheres; so they are useful in many industrial situations, either alone or in combination with other control equipment where a portion of the particulate is applicable to cyclonic capture. As preconditioning devices, cyclones often permit smaller and more efficient control equipment to be used, protecting it from damage or overloading from large particles. They also provide a means for product recovery by passing fine particulate and pollutant gases while separating coarser particles than can be returned to the process.

It is difficult for an auditor to determine whether a cyclone is operating correctly. The pressure drop across the unit is not a sufficient indication because the usual source of failure is plugging of the solids discharge, which would not affect the pressure drop. On the other hand, stand-alone cyclone installations are usually used to control highly visible particulate such as sawdust; so a plugged solids discharge would be very noticeable from the emissions or settled deposits around the outlet. If the cyclone feeds into another control device, it should be checked whenever the other device fails because of overloading. The rate of discharge from a cyclone is also a good indication of its operation. Any reduction from normal quantities is an indication of possible plugging.

Scrubbers. Particles that are too fine to be captured by a cyclone can often be removed from a gas stream by wetting them with water to increase the mass and then relying on inertia for removal. Devices to accomplish this are called scrubbers, and because water also dissolves some solids and liquids as well as gases, they are very useful for air cleaning. A wide variety of scrubbers have been marketed over the years, differing mainly in the configuration and/or mechanism used to contact the air stream with water. The efficiencies of these scrubber designs are a direct function of the degree to which they wet the particulate, which is usually proportional to the amount of energy consumed. Thus, high-efficiency scrubbers are usually expensive to operate.

The principal phenomenon by which all scrubbers achieve particle wetting is turbulence. Examples of mechanisms to achieve turbulent contact between a particle-laden air stream and a water stream include packed counterflow towers, high-pressure sprays, whirling plates or vanes, submerged orifices, and venturis. Of these, venturi scrubbers are currently among the most popular for particulate control because they achieve high efficiencies with low maintenance. Other designs may be less costly to operate or may provide cooling as preconditioning for other control equipment; so the auditor must be aware of all types of scrubber technology. This is especially true at older plants where obsolete scrubbers may still be in operation. The venturi scrub-

Figure 3-3. A venturi scrubber and separator chamber.

ber creates a high-velocity mixing area by forcing the air stream through a narrow throat where it comes into contact with water or a scrubbing solution. The low pressure created in the throat can be used to aspirate the liquid through an orifice in the throat. Liquid injection with a pump is more common because the required amount of scrubbing liquid usually exceeds the vacuum available. Part of the scrubbing liquid is often injected in front of the orifice to wet the walls. This prevents a buildup of particulate around the orifice that would result in eventual plugging. Critical to the operation of a scrubber is the throat velocity, which must be kept within narrow limits for maximum efficiency. To maintain constant flow when process emissions are variable, some scrubber designs include a variable cross section in the throat.

Scrubbers require a source of particulate-free water, which most often can be recirculated after the captured particulate has settled out. However, if there is a high proportion of soluble particulate or gas in the exhaust stream, recirculation is not possible unless the water is first processed to remove the solutes. Disposal of the wet sludge is an increasing problem because operators of landfills are becoming more and more reticent about accepting liquid industrial waste. Thus, many scrubber owners are finding it necessary to dewater the sludge before disposal. In effect, scrubbers convert air pollution problems into water pollution or solid waste problems.

Maintenance problems with scrubbers include mechanical failures caused by pump malfunctions, line or orifice clogging, corrosion due to low pH or abrasive particulate, or freezing of the scrubbing liquid. An efficient demister is usually necessary to remove entrained droplets from the exhaust stream, and this equipment also can become plugged or corroded. Visible emissions are a sign of improper operation, but even when the scrubber is operating properly, a scrubber's exhaust may become saturated and condense in a cool or humid atmosphere.

The primary indication to an auditor of the operating status of a scrubber, other than visible emissions, is the pressure drop. This is useful, however, only if the design pressure drop is known. Where that information is not available, the auditor could compare the current reading to the maintenance log, going back several months to see if there is any change from normal operating conditions. If such logs are not being kept, a recommendation to keep them should be made. The auditor should also check to make sure any recirculating pumps are operating properly, that there are no signs of corrosion on the plumbing to the scrubber, and that any settlement equipment is free from excessive solids.

Baghouses. Fabric filtration is a very versatile method of removing dry particulate from a gas stream over a wide range of air flows, temperatures, concentrations, and particle diameters. It is ac-

Figure 3-4. An aging baghouse. Newer equipment has been constructed around it.

complished in a baghouse in which the exhaust stream is forced through a layer of cloth. The fabric captures enough of the particulate in the air stream to form a filter cake on the dirty-air side of the fabric; this then becomes a highly efficient filter. The filter cake removes substantially all the particulate from the exhaust until it becomes too thick to pass enough flow to be useful. Before this point is reached, the filter cake must be broken free of the surface of the fabric and removed. This cleaning cycle can be accomplished by shaking the cloth to flex and break the filter cake or, when felted fabrics are used, by high-pressure reverse jets of air. The filter cake is allowed to fall into a hopper for removal, and the cycle is started again. The placement of the fan to drive the system can be either before or after the baghouse.

The fabric in baghouses is usually formed into long, narrow tubes that are oriented vertically, parallel to each other. Typically, these are 6 or 8 inches in diameter by up to 10 feet long. Larger bags can be 12 inches or more in diameter by up to 30 feet long. Other configurations include flat or envelope-shaped bags. The number of bags required is determined by the desired air-to-cloth ratio. This is the ratio of volumetric exhaust flow to the square footage of fabric. It determines the velocity at which the gas passes through the cloth, which can range from one-half foot to six feet per minute. Generally, the smaller the particle size or the higher the concentration, the slower the recommended velocity. The correct velocity permits the most economical baghouse operation without the risk of packing the filter cake so densely that particles are forced into the weave of the fabric. This would result in "blinding" the fabric and consequent bag failure. High-volume air flows may require hundreds of bags in order to maintain a required air/cloth ratio.

The temperature and chemical properties of the exhaust gas and the physical properties of the particulate must be taken into account in selecting the type and weave of cloth to be used in the bags. Cotton, for example, is used where the temperature is low and the particulate noncorrosive. Glass fabric, on the other hand, works well in high temperatures or corrosive atmospheres. Other fabrics include wool and synthetics. The type of fiber, the characteristics of the yarn, and the weave and finish of the fabric all affect the filtration ability of the bags under various conditions. Other variables in bag selection include: initial cost, power requirements, probable life, and replacement cost.

The bags are mounted in a baghouse according to several configurations. These depend on the mechanism used for cleaning. The most frequently used configuration brings the dirty air into the inside of the bags. The lower ends of the bags are securely fastened to ports on an airtight floor sheet oriented over an enclosed hopper with a mechanism for removing the captured solids. The upper ends of the bags are either closed and suspended from a shaking mechanism or open and fastened to an upper tube sheet. In the former design, the air to be cleaned enters below the floor sheet, rises into the bags, penetrates the fabric, and exits the baghouse. Cleaning is accomplished by periodically stopping the air flow and either shaking the bags or providing a reverse air flow to cause the filter cake to drop into the hopper. The bags that are open at both ends are cleaned by pulses of air directed down each bag. Alternatively, rings with compressed

Figure 3-5. A baghouse with a cyclonic preseparator.

air jets traveling up and down each bag dislodge the filter cake. Air jet cleaning can be carried out without stopping the flow through the baghouse.

The periodic removal of the filter cake from the bags can be controlled by a timer or a pressure sensor. The latter detects a rise in the pressure drop across the fabric from a normal operating range of two to three inches of water to six or more inches. Before shaking can be effective, all flow through the filter must cease, and the cloth must be able to collapse back to its natural shape. For continuous operations,

Figure 3-6. Silo baghouses. Note pneumatic conveying conduits.

this often means that the exhaust flow must be diverted to another identically sized unit. Single-unit baghouses can be timed to shake after manufacturing shutdown each day, provided they have been sized properly. Bin and silo baghouses are usually timed to shake after each filling.

The filter cake that is freed from the bags will fall into the hopper portion of the baghouse, where it must be removed. Removal is usually achieved by means of a screw conveyor and a rotary valve, which may be operated on a batch cycle or continuously. However, there is a risk of compaction or bridging if the hopper becomes too full. The baghouse will eventually become plugged under this condition, requiring a costly maintenance procedure. To ensure proper solids removal, insulation, vibrators, or air jets may be necessary to prevent compaction in the hopper.

The pressure drop across the baghouse is the key to the condition of the bags. If it is too low, it is a good indication of one or more broken bags. Exhaust opacity is also an accurate sign of bag leaks because a baghouse in good operating condition should exceed 99% efficiency. Transmissometers that respond to an increase in opacity are available to detect broken bags. These are particularly useful if the baghouse exhaust is to be recycled for any purpose. Too high a pressure drop indicates plugged bags, which could be the result of a failure in the shaking mechanism, or blinded bags. The latter may be caused by excessive moisture in the exhaust stream or improper bag material. Some baghouse failures may not be indicated by the pressure drop across the bags. A partially plugged hopper that interferes with the inlet air flow, torn bags that have been pulled into the outlet, or leaks in the duct work are examples. The pressure drop across the fan or the entire system flow should be measured for proper evaluation of the baghouse operation. The auditor may not be able to obtain these data, but secondary indications such as poor dust control or reduced solids removal can be relied on to indicate problems.

High Efficiency Air Filtration. Control of organic particulate such as oil mists or resin fumes cannot be achieved in an ordinary baghouse because there is no buildup of filter cake that can be periodically removed. High efficiency air filtration (HEAF) can be used to control these emissions, however, in devices designed so that the filter medium can be discarded after becoming plugged with the catch. To achieve an economical filter life, the filters are fairly thick, dense fiberglass mats into which the organic mist can penetrate before coalescing and becoming trapped by capillary action. A high pressure drop, hence high energy, is necessary to provide enough flow to be useful. In smaller HEAFs of 100 CFM or so, an increase in the pressure drop beyond a prescribed limit indicates the need to change the filter. This is done manually by shutting off the flow and opening the unit. On larger HEAFs, the filter medium is supplied in a roll form. These automatically advance the roll to a clean section every time the pressure drop gets too high. In auditing HEAFs, the auditor should check the pressure drop during the audit with respect to the change cycle. The equipment operators or maintenance mechanics should know the limiting pressure drop. Evidence of incomplete fume clearance in the work area or oil stains around the outlet stack are indications of either malfunctions or inadequate capacity. The auditor should also question the method of disposal used for the exhausted HEAF filters.

Coalescing Filters. A low-energy method of controlling organic mists involves cooling the exhaust stream to condense the vapors and then passing it at a very low velocity through a thick filter bed. The long residency time in the bed allows the mist particles to coalesce by Brownian motion into larger droplets that impact on the fibers and are drawn together by capillary action. As more fumes coalesce, the collected liquid becomes heavy enough to run down through the filter bed into a sump. Thus, the coalescing filter is a continuous control device requiring infrequent filter replacements.

The filters are manufactured in various shapes, including flat beds and round "candles" of several diameters. The design parameters are similar to those for the baghouse, in that enough surface area must be available to reduce the velocity through the filter bed to an acceptable rate. Experience has shown that a velocity of about 5 FPM will provide adequate flow for the control of oil mists. Too high a velocity will reentrain liquid droplets at the exit side of the filter. To treat a 10,000 CFM exhaust stream, for example, without exceeding a velocity of 5 FPM through the bed requires over 50 candles measuring one foot in diameter by 12 feet in length.

The air flow through a coalescing filter using cylindrical candles is from the outside of the candle into the hollow center and then up through the top. The candles are sealed to a tube sheet near the top of the unit and allowed to hang down. Demist pads at the top of each candle eliminate minor amounts of reentrainment that may occur as the candle becomes saturated. The captured liquid runs down the candles and drips off the bottom into a sump. A prefilter may be included to remove particulate that would blind the coalescing filter sur-

Figure 3-7. A single candle coalescing filter. Fuel tank contains solvent for rinsing the candle's surface to remove solids that could reduce the flow.

face and shorten its life. To cool the air stream, cooling coils, water sprays in the inlet duct or scrubber trays may be used. One device with a flat filter bed has a water spray directed at it from the side of the entering air stream. This has the effect of cooling and washing off the collected liquid. Because of the importance of cooling to the efficient operation of these units, the auditor should note whether the filter temperature is in the recommended range. If the temperature is not available and there is any evidence of opacity, a temperature measurement of the exhaust may show if there is sufficient cooling.

The key indicator to proper filter operation other than the inlet temperature is the pressure drop across the filters. As the surfaces inevitably become blinded with fine particulate, the flow through the unit will decrease. This will be obvious from an increase in the pressure drop across the bed and from the inability of the unit to control the design capacity of fumes. In this way, all control devices using filtration are fail-safe; that is, when they are plugged, they stop removing fumes. The uncontrolled fumes then back into the process again or into the work area, forcing the operator to correct the malfunction. By contrast, an electrostatic precipitator or a scrubber passes uncontrolled fumes to the atmosphere whenever it malfunctions.

Electrostatic Precipitators. Electrostatic precipitators (EPs) are among the oldest air pollution control devices, having been developed by Frederic Cottrell at the University of California in 1907. They are

Figure 3-8. A small EP used for oil mist removal.

also among the most versatile because they can be designed to collect a wide variety of liquid and solid particles in sizes ranging from submicron to as large as 100 μ at temperatures from ambient to over 1000°F. Unit capacities range from a few hundred cubic feet per minute for controlling oil mists in machine shops to hundreds of thousands of cubic feet per minute in power plant applications. The low pressure drop and high efficiency make them attractive for large installations.

An EP removes particulate from an air stream by causing an elec-

Figure 3-9. A large EP used to control glass furnace emissions.

trostatic attraction between it and a collection plate. A charge is induced on the particles by passing them through a corona. Positively charged plates then attract the charged particles and pull them out of the air stream. Periodically, these plates must be rapped to dislodge the collected particulate, allowing it to fall into a hopper to be removed in a manner similar to removal in a baghouse. Alternately, in a wet EP, the plates may be washed with water sprays to remove the particulate. Oil mists controlled by an EP coalesce into liquids that are usually fluid enough to run off the plates to a sump.

Cottrell-type EPs pass the air stream between the discharge electrodes and the collector plates. The largest industrial units use this configuration. Smaller precipitators are often two-stage units where the air stream is first passed by the discharge (ionizer) electrodes and then by the collectors. These may have mechanisms to rotate the collectors through a wash bath for particulate removal. Several passes through discharge/collector banks may be necessary to achieve the degree of control desired.

Proper EP (Cottrell) operation requires the voltage differential between the electrodes and the plates to be high enough to allow occasional arcing. This "sparking," usually between 50 and 100 per minute, may be audible from outside the unit. If so, the rate can be counted and compared with manufacturer specifications as an indicator of EP operation. Likewise, the frequency of rapping can be noted. These are only indications, however, and a program of regular internal inspections is necessary to assure reliable operation.

EP malfunctions can be caused by flow obstructions due either to plugging of the prefilter or inadequate cleaning of the plates. Electrical failure can be a result of insufficient or excessive voltage differential, loss of discharge wires, warpage of plates, or shorting due to particulate buildup on the plates or in the hopper. Malfunctions due to the original design include undersizing, excessive particulate resistivity, inadequate prefiltration, or poorly distributed flow. None of these problems can be detected by the auditor except by secondary evidence such as unacceptable opacity or insufficient flow capacity. In these cases, the maintenance records should be checked to see when the last inspection took place. If there has not been a recent inspection, a recommendation may be necessary to do one as soon as possible and to beef up the inspection schedule.

Absorbers, Adsorbers, and Condensors. Sources of volatile hydrocarbons such as surface coating or bulk liquid transfer and storage can be controlled in a variety of ways. One of the oldest is absorption in a countercurrent tower using a packed bed. The gas to be controlled must be soluble in the scrubbing liquid, and some means of disposal or reuse of the spent liquid must be provided. An example of an absorption system would be bulk solvent transfer in a refinery using oil with a lower volatility than the solvent's as a scrubbing fluid. The captured solvent can then be reclaimed in a routine stripping process. In addition to volatile hydrocarbon vapors, countercurrent absorption is also useful for scrubbing acid gases using water as a scrubbing liquid.

Adsorption is useful for controlling lighter hydrocarbons or odors. It uses activated charcoal or other granular solid with adsorbent characteristics. This is packed in canisters or beds over which the exhaust stream is passed. The active sites on the particles capture and hold the pollutant molecules until all the sites are filled and the bed is saturated. A purge cycle must then be initiated by taking the bed out of service and subjecting it to vacuum, heat, or both to drive the trapped molecules off the solid for disposal by absorption, condensation, or incineration. Portable adsorption devices are sold primarily for odor control, and are usually discarded after saturation or returned to the manufacturer for recharging.

Condensation is used to control light hydrocarbons such as gasoline when recovery of the vapor is desired. It involves passing the exhaust stream across chilled plates onto which the vapor condenses. A highly efficient refrigeration machine is required to provide sufficient cooling for adequate control efficiency. An occasional warming cycle is necessary to drain the condensed liquid off the plates. This must be done after process shutdown unless short periods without control can be tolerated.

Without inlet and outlet source testing, it is generally not possible for the auditor to tell if any of these control devices is operating properly. The vapors are not visible, and even if the source were generating odors, the auditor might not be able to position himself so that he could tell if the odor were being reduced. Instead, he must rely on plant maintenance records and agency complaint files for indications of problems with the units. If problems are indicated, then control efficiency tests should be recommended. These tests are relatively easy to perform because particulate and flow measurements are not required. An estimate of efficiency can sometimes be obtained through the use of indicator tubes.

Incinerators (Oxidizers, Afterburners). Incineration is an effective means of disposal for a wide range of solid, liquid, and gaseous wastes. It constitutes a special case of combustion that can result in a much broader range of pollutant compounds than ordinary combustion, as a result of the volatilization and destructive oxidation of the material being incinerated. Efficient incineration requires the complete oxidation of all molecular species to their theoretical limits at the temperature of the combustion chamber. In practice, this requires first the evaporation of any moisture in the material, followed by volatilization and combustion of the components boiling below the incineration temperature. Only then can the nonvolatile residue attain a high-enough temperature to be oxidized. This process requires a finite amount of time, and it is a challenge to the incinerator designer to provide enough residency time in the combustion chamber to achieve complete combustion. In practice, it rarely is completely achieved; therefore, incineration emissions usually include some fractions of volatiles, partially oxidized solids, and ash, in addition to the fuel-generated combustion products.

Even when incineration achieves complete combustion, undesirable oxidation products may result from some toxic constituents of the waste. An example is the incineration of waste vinyl chloride polymer or monomer, which forms hydrogen chloride in addition to carbon dioxide and water. Wastes containing phosphorus, halogens, and heavy metals even at low concentrations may generate toxic emissions. Because of the breadth in the spectrum of materials that are candidates for disposal through incineration, the consideration of toxic or corrosive by-products attains paramount importance. The result is that, from a practical standpoint, carefully screened petroleum- or cellulose-based wastes are the only materials that can safely be incinerated unless the facility has emissions control equipment capable of eliminating any toxic emissions.

Combustion for the purpose of waste disposal is generally regulated according to the material being burned and the purpose of the combustion unit. If the unit is intended to provide process heat and the waste has useful fuel value without toxic contamination, most agencies regulate it as a combustion source. The operating permit will have to stipulate the fuel type, but generally the same requirements apply for all fuels. Co-combustion of wastes with ordinary fuels, and the mixing of wastes with fuels before combustion when the purpose is to produce process heat, are similarly permitted. Co-combustion, in which, for example, a liquid or solid waste is injected into a gas-fueled combustion unit, is useful when variations in fuel value might cause difficulties in maintaining stable combustion conditions. It can also be used to bring down the overall fuel percentage of sulfur when the waste might be high in that element. This can also be accomplished by mixing the waste with a low-sulfur fuel before combustion.

Many state agencies regulate waste combustion by considering it to be waste incineration, which must comply with specific combustion criteria. At a minimum, residence time and combustion temperature are defined. In addition, analyses of the wastes or stack tests or both are generally required. Some form of control device may be necessary if toxic emissions are predicted from the waste analysis, or, more likely, the waste would be considered hazardous and the source would not be permitted at all without a hazardous waste incineration license from EPA.

Incineration for air pollution control is often the only way to achieve complete control of highly odorous or volatile emissions. It is usually very costly because fuel must be mixed with the exhaust stream to attain the required combustion temperature. This temperature should be checked by the auditor and compared with the permit or design conditions. Flares constitute a special case of pollution incineration, used only in emergency situations. They generally do not meet emission limits, but they do provide a safer means of rapidly disposing of volatile materials in comparison to uncontrolled venting. The afterburner is another special case of incineration for pollution control, involving partial combustion of an exhaust stream by a low-temperature flame. It is useful in cases where the uncontrolled emissions do not quite meet the state's standards for hydrocarbons, and odors are not a problem. In this case, as with incinerators, the auditor should check the combustion temperature against the design temperature.

Materials Storage and Transport and Fugitive Sources

Finely divided solids and volatile liquids have very similar storage requirements in that they must be completely enclosed in impervious containers of sufficient strength to withstand the static pressure of full loading. Solids are stored in silos or bins and liquids in tanks. The emissions from these containers while standing are usually minimal. Exceptions would be heated tanks that cannot be safely pressurized,

Figure 3-10. A source of fugitive emissions—dusty material accumulations on the roof.

or containers in which inert gas blanketing is used to protect the contents from oxidation. In these cases, pollution control equipment must be kept in operation at all times.

Tank and silo filling produces emissions. In the case of tanks, the quantity of air that is displaced during filling from inside the empty tank is usually saturated with vapors. Some oxidant nonattainment areas require vapor balance filling for hydrocarbons with appreciable vapor pressures. This is accomplished by means of a second pipe parallel to the fill pipe, which returns the displaced vapors from the tank being filled to the tanker or barge being emptied. Vapor balance automotive refueling is also common at service stations in these areas. Very volatile hydrocarbons such as gasoline, however, demonstrate "vapor growth" during pumping and therefore cannot be completely controlled by vapor balancing. In addition, vapor balance transfer requires pressure-tight connections, whereas a vapor collection system that exerts a slight negative pressure on the tanks may be easier to maintain. Disposal of the collected vapors can be accomplished by absorption, adsorption, condensation, or incineration. Very often ducting flammable vapors to a heater or the plant boiler is the most economical approach to vapor control. More often, in less stringent areas of the country, the vapors can simply be vented. These control systems or vents should be noted by the auditor as emission points.

Silo filling with dusty solids produces visible emissions due to the turbulent suspension of particulate in the displaced air. Additional emissions result when pressurized air is used to convey the solids to the silo. These emissions are most often controlled with a small baghouse mounted on top of the silo. Several silos can be served by a single baghouse through the use of a crossover pipe. These baghouses may operate on the pressure of the displaced air, releasing their catch back into the silo once the flow has stopped and the bags have collapsed. Others may require shakers set to operate after each fill cycle.

Solids can be conveyed to the silo and throughout the plant by vacuum as well as by pressure. In either case, the termination point must be suitably filtered to eliminate visible emissions to the atmosphere and, in the case of vacuum conveying, to protect the pump. One problem that the auditor should check for in pressure conveying is that of silo overfilling. Maintenance of level alarms is often neglected. Alarm failure can result in solids being blown through relief hatches and then coating the roofs and surrounding areas of the plant. While regulatory agencies may be tolerant of these unplanned upsets, management should consider the cost of wasted materials and manpower.

Solids are also conveyed by moving belts, bucket elevators, screw conveyors, or other mechanical devices. These often create dust in the plant, particularly when the material transfers from one device to another. One of these transfers might be the point at which the material is incorporated into the manufacturing process. The device could be a mixer, heater, kiln, or coater, and if vented, it too may be a dust source. These dusts, when liberated inside a work area, create haze and may violate OSHA standards for nuisance dust. To counteract this, roof and wall ventilators or open windows and clerestories are often designed to transfer the dust to the atmosphere outside the building. Here the dust becomes fugitive emissions. The auditor must be alert for these situations and recommend better dust control procedures if warranted.

Liquid transfer systems can also be a source of fugitive emissions of volatile hydrocarbons. These are caused by leaking flanges, pumps, and valves and are very difficult to locate because the emissions cannot be seen. On the other hand, they are most likely to be a problem only of refineries or large chemical plants, which usually have well-established programs for surveying and correcting piping leaks. The survey tools are hand-held detectors for specific contaminants. They can be calibrated with known concentration standards so that the leakage rates can be estimated from tests made at specific distances from the fittings.

In addition to material transport systems, fugitive emissions can also derive from processes such as melting and casting operations, spray painting, and sandblasting, or from plant facilities such as waste storage areas and unpaved parking areas. The auditor must try to identify these sources by several means. He should look for likely sources, note dust clouds around the plant, and look for evidence of dusty emissions on roofs or walls. In the latter two cases, he should track the evidence and try to identify the source of the dust. Regulatory agencies may cite a plant for visible dust emitting from any location or for an increase in the air mass dust loading as evidenced by upwind and downwind sampling.

PLANT AIR POLLUTION AUDIT

Preparation

As pointed out earlier in this chapter, most plants will be sources of air pollution to some extent. Therefore, almost all audits will include a review of air pollution sources. The amount of preparation the auditor needs is a function of the nature of the industry being audited. If it is known to have processes that produce air emissions, the auditor should familiarize himself with the techniques common in that industry for pollution control before making the plant visit. Likewise, he should review the NSPS for the industry, if promulgated, and obtain an up-to-date copy of any state or regional regulations covering the pollutants or processes. The latter may not be possible before the audit, and compliance may have to be judged after reviewing the sources and permits on file at the plant. If problems are then apparent, a follow-up review with the state agency to obtain the regulations may be necessary.

Data Forms

Air pollution data can best be compiled by describing each source on a separate inventory form. One advantage to this is that permit data can be easily verified, as most agencies inventory plant emissions on a source-by-source basis. Each source inventory form should include the following:

Source description
Location
Rated capacity
Normal capacity
Operation schedule
Fuel
Control equipment
Flow
Temperature
Pollutants
Permit number
Expiration date

Source test results
Comments

Plenty of room should be left for remarks based on observations made during the audit. The auditor may want to use several different formats, depending on whether the source involves fuel combustion or not, or to take into account information relating specifically to different types of processes.

Figure 3–11 shows an air pollution inventory form that was designed to be flexible enough to cover all types of air pollution sources. It has room for up to three control devices and provides generous space for remarks. Note that space is allowed for installation dates for both the source and the control equipment. These dates are useful in placing the source and its control equipment in perspective with other equipment at the plant and with the evolving network of regulations.

More detailed forms may be useful for plants with large numbers of sources that are similar to each other, such as paint spray booths or drying ovens. The auditor may want to design specific forms for each type of process equipment. No matter how detailed the forms are, however, some sources inevitably will not "fit." For this reason, all forms should include enough room for remarks and, in addition, have copious margins and space between the lines for annotating the data when more detail is necessary to fully describe the equipment.

If a large number of sources are present at a plant, the auditor may have to prepare a summary sheet (Figure 3–12) listing each source by number. In addition, it may be desirable to place source numbers on a copy of the plot plan in the case of large or complex facilities, to relate each inventory form to a specific location. This is particularly useful if there are similar or identical sources that the auditor wants to keep separate. The summary sheet and the annotated plot plan can be prepared as part of the final report, but the inventory forms should be filled out during the audit.

Plant Data

Once he is familiar with the general layout of the plant and the locations of the major sources, the auditor should review the air permit file. Depending on how well-organized the plant files are, this may re-

ENVIRONMENTAL AUDIT
PLANT________________
DATE________________

AIR POLLUTION SYSTEM NO. _______

SOURCE DESCRIPTION ____

____

LOCATION______________________________ DATE OF OPERATION____________

FUEL__________________________________ RATE____________________

OPERATION__________ HR./DAY______ DAYS/WK. PRODUCTION__________ ____/___

EXHAUST__________ CFM@________°F OF POLLUTANT____________________

CONTROL #1____

LOCATION______________________ DATE OF OPERATION______________

CONTROL #2____

LOCATION______________________ DATE OF OPERATION______________

CONTROL #3____

LOCATION______________________ DATE OF OPERATION______________

EMISSION POINT LOCATION__________ HT.__________ DIAM______________

EMISSION TEST DATA DATE__________ TEAM__________________________

RESULTS____

____

PERMITS____

REMARKS____

____

____

____

____

____

RECOMMENDATIONS____

____

____

Figure 3-11. Example of an air pollution inventory form.

quire reviewing all pollution correspondence dating back several years. If so, the first pass should attempt to locate all current permits, recent (within a year) notices of violation (NOVs), agency inspection reports, and source test reports. In addition, there will often be source

ENVIRONMENTAL AUDIT
PLANT________________
DATE________________

AIR POLLUTION SUMMARY (PAGE____

___SOURCE________________
CONTROL________________
PERMIT________________

___SOURCE________________
CONTROL________________
PERMIT________________

___SOURCE________________
CONTROL________________
PERMIT________________

___SOURCE________________
CONTROL________________
PERMIT________________

___SOURCE________________
CONTROL________________
PERMIT________________

___SOURCE________________
CONTROL________________
PERMIT________________

___SOURCE________________
CONTROL________________
PERMIT________________

___SOURCE________________
CONTROL________________
PERMIT________________

___SOURCE________________
CONTROL________________
PERMIT________________

___SOURCE________________
CONTROL________________
PERMIT________________

___SOURCE________________
CONTROL________________
PERMIT________________

Figure 3-12. Example of an air pollution equipment summary form.

inventories, either filled out by the plant for submission to the agency or copies of the agency's computer file. The latest of these should be reviewed.

An air pollution source data inventory form should be started for each source for which a current permit exists or that is listed on an agency or plant inventory. All the available data should be recorded on the form. This will usually consist of a source description, normal and peak capacities, fuel and BTU rate, control equipment, emission rate, emission point, and permit number and expiration date. Other information may include emission factors for various pollutants and installation dates. If the source has a continuous emission monitoring device, the latest average and peak readings should be recorded. These data may be useful at some later time, and it is far better to note them now on the inventory form than to try to remember where they were at a later date. In this way, the inventory forms become a single location for all the data concerning a source. In future audits it is only necessary to note where changes have taken place.

The information contained in recent NOVs or test results can be added to the inventory forms as remarks, once the basic information is in place. Of particular interest are any compliance requirements imposed by either the source permit or as a result of an NOV. Examples might include an upper limit on the process, periodic source testing, or monthly submission to the agency of the control device operating log. Other information from the file should also be reviewed and added if it increases understanding of the sources; but this could be done more efficiently after completing the plant tour, to avoid spending time on documents relating to sources proposed but never built or equipment out of service. Similarly, the auditor's observations after inspecting each source and piece of control equipment should be added to the forms, and new forms started for sources discovered on the tour for which there are no permits.

Plant Tour

On the detailed tour of the plant, the auditor should accomplish the following tasks for the purposes of the air pollution part of the audit:

- Inspect each major source and estimate whether its control device (if any) is operating properly. This may be done by observing the opacity of the stack or reading an indicator such as a manometer.
- Identify the sources of all other stacks and vents.
- Fill out inventory forms for any unpermitted emission sources and make evaluations of their operation and control.

- Note any apparent problems with the plant's air pollution control system.
- Note potential or actual fugitive emission sources such as raw material piles, powder conveyors, or dusty in-plant conditions.

To achieve these goals, the auditor must find and identify every emission point in the plant. That means every stack, ventilator, clerestory, wall fan, and exhaust port. Each must be inventoried and related to its emission source. One way of accomplishing this is by photographing every roof on which there are stacks and every wall that has fans or vents. Exhaust points on tankage and in chemical processes will be trickier to locate, and the effort will be aided by the auditor's experience with the specific process involved. Without such experience, he should request the assistance of a process operator or supervisor to explain the process and point out the emission controls and vents.

It is advantageous to have a familiarity with pollution control devices. Some of them may have been fabricated at the plant or have obsolete designs; therefore, they may not be readily recognizable as control equipment. Large baghouses, cyclones, and precipitators have distinctive shapes and are easy to identify. Smaller baghouses, scrubbers, high-energy filters, and incinerators could be almost any shape, depending on the manufacturer and the age. Nevertheless, a guess based on knowledge of pollution control technology will usually ascertain the function of a unit. A photograph of the device can then be used in the follow-up discussion with the environmental coordinator to confirm or revise the identification.

The auditor cannot judge the appropriateness of each piece of control equipment for the source on which it is installed without evaluating accurate emissions data for the source. This is obviously beyond the scope of an audit. Rather, the auditor must assume that the equipment is appropriate for the source, that its size is adequate, and that it was installed properly. Compelling evidence to the contrary, however, should be noted on the inventory form. In the absence of such evidence, the auditor should try to convince himself that the equipment is operating properly at the time of the audit, and, further, that it has been operating properly. If either of these conditions is not met, the auditor should note the facts and discuss them with the environmental coordinator.

Every piece of control equipment has some means of determining whether or not it is operating. However, determining whether it is operating properly may require more equipment or time than is available to the auditor. For example, the sound of the rappers and sparking are indications of operation in an EP. A high voltage probe is necessary, however, to tell if it is operating properly. This could not be done by the auditor although he may request that the voltages be checked by the maintenance department during his audit. Likewise, the auditor would not conduct a stack test for compliance or efficiency (although he will check the plume). These factors must be assumed to be correct.

The photographs should show all unknown stacks on building roofs as well as the major source emission points. Using these as reference points inside a plant building, it should be possible to follow the other vent ducts from their sources to the points where they penetrate the roof. Once the major source emission point to the roof is located inside the building, the other vent ducts can be identified by their location relative to the major emission point.

Photography of the sources inside the building will generally be unsuccessful, at least with an automatic camera. Either the light will be so poor as to obscure any useful details (even when using a flash), or the proximity will be such that only a very wide angle lens will work. Fortunately, a photograph is not necessary once the identity of the unit has been determined.

Stacks and vents traced from the roof will lead either to process equipment or to control devices. In the case of process equipment, an inventory form can be started, with notes relating it to the numbered photograph showing its stack. Very little information will be available at the unit except its location and any data shown on a builder's plate such as model number and capacity. This information is useful to note even when it is duplicated in plant files because errors that have crept into emission inventories over the years can sometimes be weeded out in this way. If the vent leads to a control device, the source may not be obvious. In this case, the auditor should record the location, size, manufacturer, and any other available data, referencing them to the rooftop photograph so that the source can be identified by the environmental coordinator.

Particular attention should be paid to the stacks themselves. Some

Figure 3-13. A stack with facilities for source testing: port, platform, and monorail for supporting equipment.

may be set up for source testing, indicated by the presence of welded nipples on a plenum or on the stack itself. There may also be a test platform and monorails. This should be noted on the inventory form, both for future reference and because there is a good chance that source tests have already been run. Permanently mounted stack probes or monitors should also be noted and every effort made to locate the data readout device. Recent test reports from either continuous monitors or stack tests should be reviewed as part of the audit.

The auditor may not be able to identify some stacks during the plant tour. He then must rely on the environmental coordinator for identification. Some will turn out to be remains of discontinued operations or obsolete control equipment. Others may be vents from space heaters or sanitary plumbing or simply roof ventilators. The latter along with wall fans, clerestories, and even windows must be looked at carefully during the plant tour. Is there any evidence of visible emissions from these points? Is the surrounding wall or roof area stained any differently from the rest of the building? Is a lower roof near a wall vent covered in dust? These are all evidences of fugitive emissions.

Figure 3-14. Possible fugitive emission source indicated by dust deposit on roof below the wall vent.

If any evidence of fugitive emissions is seen, the immediate vicinity of the vent inside the plant building must be investigated. Is there an apparent dust source? If so, it should be noted on an inventory form and the vent listed as an emission point. In many cases, exhaust fans or hoods installed to bring a work area into compliance with OSHA regulations create an air pollution source that may require a control device.

Follow-up Data

Once the plant tour is completed, all the plant files concerning permits or pollution control should be reviewed for additional information that might help explain the history, operation, or purpose of the equipment. At this time, installation dates, manufacturer specifications, and agency inspection comments can be reviewed. Compliance test reports will show the original flows and efficiencies of the control equipment. Where monitoring equipment was noted, the monitoring data logs should be reviewed to determine the frequency of data collection, the original operating range, the latest operating range, the percentage of outage time, and the method of reporting the data.

Numerous questions will arise during the plant tour, many of them involving identification of equipment or stacks or information on the operation of plant equipment. Generally the environmental coordinator will be best suited to answer these questions. If he is new to the plant, however, he may require the help of someone with more experience there, perhaps a process or maintenance supervisor. In any case, the photographs will be particularly useful because they will eliminate any possible confusion about the location of a source or denial of an existing condition (such as high opacity).

The maintenance supervisor should be interviewed with respect to his program for maintaining pollution control equipment. The auditor should determine whether the maintenance program is reactive or proactive. That is, is maintenance scheduled and accomplished only after a breakdown occurs, or is there a regularly scheduled program of periodic inspections and servicing? In the former case, the operating condition of the control equipment both at the time of the audit and as indicated by the historical record in the files will usually show the need for the latter program. One problem with a reactive maintenance program is that maintenance of pollution control equipment is always secondary to process equipment maintenance. Therefore, delays often occur before needed repairs are made. For this reason, any plant with major pollution control equipment, especially if the permits require reporting of upsets, should have a proactive maintenance program, including daily operation checks and periodic service such as lubrication or belt replacement. Internal inspections are important for some control equipment such as EPs. Finally, a store of spare equipment is important to minimize downtime. Such a program will require that a maintenance log be kept on each piece of control equipment. This should be reviewed by the auditor and an evaluation made on the reliability of the program. The auditor's opinion of the maintenance program for environmental control equipment should be included in the audit report.

The plant's reporting system for breakdowns of control equipment is important. Generally, the maintenance supervisor will know of an outage first. He should relay the information to the environmental coordinator immediately so that any obligation to notify the agency can be met. The plant manager should also be informed because it is his ultimate responsibility to comply with regulations governing air emissions. The status of the air pollution control system should be a subject for routine plant staff meetings.

Agency Visit

A visit to the local agency is not a requirement of an initial audit. It may turn out to be convenient, however, because of the auditor's travel schedule or for some other reason. In that case, the value of the audit report can be enhanced by adding the agency's view of the plant's compliance.

Most state or regional agencies have a computer system listing all industrial air pollution sources within their jurisdiction that exceed some minimum size. This will be organized by company and will contain a lot of the information supplied during the permitting process. In addition, there may be estimates of emissions based on emission factors or test data.

The auditor should request a printout of the latest version of the computer inventory data so that it can be reviewed for inaccuracies.

Errors are likely because the inventory probably evolved over the years as permits were filed by the plant. Thus, the terminology for process equipment might have changed as different engineers filed for permits, and obsolete equipment might still be listed long after it was replaced at the plant. Similarly, equipment derating or fuel conversions may not have been reported to the agency. The plant would be well advised to return a corrected copy of the printout to the agency to eliminate any possibility of misunderstanding during a future inspection and to demonstrate a spirit of cooperation with the agency.

A review should also be made of the agency's inspection reports. The auditor may not be allowed to copy them, but can quickly get an idea of the inspectors' general attitude about the plant. It may even be possible to discuss items on the reports with an inspector who is familiar with the plant. In many cases, the low turnover of personnel at state agencies might mean that an inspector is more knowledgeable of the compliance history of the plant than anyone at the plant. The auditor is advised to assume an attitude of seeking information and not be defensive or argumentative about the plant. This is especially important if litigation is pending between the plant and the agency.

A discussion of regulations with agency personnel will be very helpful in preparation of the final audit report. Not only can agency personnel provide definitive interpretations of current regulations affecting the plant; they can also provide insight on the direction in which the regulations are heading.

AIR POLLUTION REPORT

The air pollution section of the audit report should group the emission sources at the plant into four categories:

1. Permitted sources with control equipment
2. Permitted sources without control equipment
3. Nonpermitted sources
4. Fugitive sources

The first group probably includes the sources that have cost the plant the most money (and aggravation) to bring into compliance. A brief description of past control efforts on the large sources at older plants may help to put the present equipment into proper perspective. This would be particularly valuable if previous control equipment was removed because it was incapable of providing adequate emissions reduction. Occasionally these lessons are forgotten, and a reminder may reduce the chance that a new engineer will specify a control device that has already been shown to be ineffective for a particular type of emission.

The narrative should highlight any operating problems with the present control equipment, and if possible, suggest their cause. Examples of causes might be improper sizing or specification, inadequate routine maintenance, worn-out or leaking structures, or overdue element replacement. The report should include a recommendation to correct the situation. Moreover, the auditor should recommend whatever maintenance changes are necessary to prevent recurrences of the problems. Most often, this will involve changes in the maintenance procedures. In these cases, the report may include the elements of a proactive maintenance program as an appendix.

Permitted sources without control devices, for example, boilers and heaters, require little mention in the narrative section of the report unless there are obvious problems such as opacity. These sources are usually regulated only with regard to fuel type and rate or capacity. Nonpermitted sources, however, should be covered on a case-by-case basis. Some may require control equipment and permitting. If the auditor feels this may be the case, he must review the state regulations and cite chapter and verse supporting his recommendation. He may wish to suggest a particular type of control equipment if he is aware of technology that the plant engineer may not know of. Conversely, if the source does not need to be controlled owing to a de minimus exclusion, the regulation stating this should also be cited to provide assurance of this status.

Fugitive sources should be reviewed in the narrative section of the report even though they may pose no pollution problem. They may be useful as offsets in the future, to obtain permits for new sources at the plant. They may also come under future regulations and require reduction. Plant management must be aware of all such opportunities or pitfalls. Some fugitive sources may be due to plant upsets or sloppy housekeeping. These can be covered under a general recommendation to eliminate dusty material accumulations, but photographs showing the specific examples should be reviewed with the environmental coordinator so that there is no misunderstanding about the recommendation.

Some fugitive sources may derive from process emissions that have been vented outside a manufacturing building. Tests and, if necessary, new control equipment should be recommended if the auditor observed visible emissions or noted evidence of emissions such as staining on nearby surfaces. Again, photographs may help in the review with plant personnel.

All recommendations should be listed in order of priority. Recommendations to achieve compliance such as repairing or adjusting control equipment should be listed first. Improvements to the plant's compliance status should follow. These include permitting and, if necessary, providing control equipment for sources not presently listed on the agency inventory. Recommendations for improvements in the plant's air pollution control system should be made where the auditor feels that energy or maintenance reduction may be possible or that by-product recovery could be improved. Finally, the auditor should provide information on proper maintenance procedures and a schedule for assuring that compliance is continued.

4
Water Pollution

Unlike some forms of industrial pollution, the contamination of a waterway is a distinctly visible phenomenon, often resulting in significant public awareness. Because all industrial plants, regardless of size, use water, it is clear that its proper management is an important concern. Further highlighting this concern over water pollution is the relatively recent recognition that clean water is not an inexhaustable resource available for the taking. In some industrial applications, the extent of required treatment is more a function of the need to recycle rather than discharge. Given the reality of future usage restrictions as

Figure 4-1. Plants located along rivers deserve special attention during water pollution audits.

well as more stringent discharge standards, the subject of water pollution prevention, control, and treatment promises to garner additional attention.

The introduction of pollutants into the nation's waterways has been the subject of federal attention at least since the 1950s. The current regulatory program for industry is largely a result of legislation enacted by Congress in 1972 and 1977. These legislative efforts, and their attendant regulations, have created a network of effluent standards, permitting requirements, and other regulations. Although these rules can be complex, a water pollution audit of an industrial plant can be designed and implemented in a direct fashion. For auditing purposes, our attention will focus upon several major portions of the federal water pollution control effort: standards for existing sources of water pollution, performance standards for new or modified sources, pretreatment standards, and National Pollutant Discharge Elimination System (NPDES) permits.

LEGISLATIVE BACKGROUND

In 1977, the United States Congress enacted major amendments to the existing Federal Water Pollution Control Act of 1972, now known as the Clean Water Act. With these amendments, the federal government effectively assumed overall responsibility for addressing water pollution. This overall responsibility was complemented by provisions for the delegation of several programs to the states. The act established aggressive national goals to eliminate pollutant discharges by 1985, attain "fishable, swimmable" water quality in 1983, and prohibit the discharge of toxic pollutants in toxic amounts. Although attainment of these goals has not been achieved, the act has created many regulatory programs to achieve these objectives. For the most part, the act and its regulations divide all sources of water pollution into one of three categories for control: existing sources, new or modified sources, and sources of toxic pollutants. In addition, the discharge of pollutants to local Publicly Owned Treatment Works (POTWs) is regulated. Although the act addresses the subject of nonpoint sources of pollution, it is clear that this effort has become secondary to the control of direct discharges.

Existing Sources

In addition to reaffirming the use of water quality standards to protect the nation's waters, the act reaffirms the use of technology-based effluent standards. The act now empowers the United States Environmental Protection Agency (EPA) to set industry-by-industry effluent limitations that apply to all members of the industry class described in the regulations. Using this process, Congress intended these discharge limits to become progressively more stringent, resulting in progressively cleaner water. Table 4–1 lists the industry categories included in this effort to date. Those effluent standards are imposed on individual facilities through the NPDES permits, which all direct dischargers are required to apply for and receive.

The act requires existing sources eventually to achieve compliance with several levels of technology-based standards. These include: best practicable control technology (BPT), originally required by July 1, 1977; best conventional technology (BCT); and best available

TABLE 4–1. Effluent Standards by Industrial Category.

INDUSTRY	40 CFR PART	INDUSTRY	40 CFR PART
Dairy products	405	Glass manufacturing	426
Grain mills	406	Asbestos manufacturing	427
Canned and preserved fruits / vegetables	407	Rubber manufacturing	428
Canned and preserved seafood	408	Timber products processing	429
Sugar processing	409	Pulp, paper and paperboard	430
Textile industry	410	Builders paper and roofing felt	431
Cement manufacturing	411	Meat products	432
Feedlots	412	Coal mining	434
Electroplating	413	Oil and gas extraction	435
Organic chemicals manufacturing	414	Mineral mining and processing	436
Inorganic chemicals manufacturing	415	Pharmaceutical manufacturing	439
Plastics and synthetics	416	Ore mining and dressing	440
Soap and detergent manufacturing	417	Paving and roofing materials	443
Fertilizer manufacturing	418	Paint formulating	446
Petroleum refining	419	Ink formulating	447
Iron and steel manufacturing	420	Gum and wood chemicals	454
Nonferrous metals manufacturing	421	Pesticide chemicals	455
Phosphate manufacturing	422	Explosives manufacturing	457
Steam electric power generating	423	Carbon black manufacturing	458
Ferroalloy manufacturing	424	Photographic materials	459
Leather tanning and finishing	425	Hospitals	460

technology economically achievable (BAT), originally required by July 1, 1983. The Clean Water Act amendments enacted in 1977 modified these standards by providing for a BPT extension to 1979, by adding BCT and providing for its extension to 1984 and 1987.

EPA has delegated authority to a number of states for overall management and enforcement, yet, in all cases, retains authority to establish national effluent standards. As a result of this delegation, individual plants must be especially cognizant of any national standards that regulate their effluent, any more stringent state regulations that may apply, and the specific agency charged with enforcement. Some plants that discharge into heavily polluted waters may be subject to effluent limitations even more stringent than national standards. In these cases, EPA has the authority to establish smaller effluent limitations than those under best available technology to achieve the act's "swimmable, fishable" goals. The agency must consider economic factors when establishing these more stringent limits.

New or Modified Sources

The Clean Water Act, in Section 306, requires the EPA to establish limits for water pollution from new sources in 27 listed industrial categories. At its discretion, the agency may set New Source Performance Standards (NSPS) for industries other than those listed. NSPS are based upon best available demonstrated control technology, which is closely related to best available technology for existing sources. A source is considered new if construction began after proposal of the applicable standard (as long as the standard is eventually promulgated). NSPS apply to all new sources throughout the country and may require complete recycle of wastewater. The act establishes a ten-year "grace" period for new sources, during which more stringent standards may not be applied. This protection does not apply to toxic pollutants. Standards for new sources without established NSPS are determined on a case-by-case basis and normally approximate BAT.

Toxic Pollutants

Under the Clean Water Act, EPA has the authority to establish effluent standards for toxic water pollutants. The act initially defined a group of 65 pollutants (Table 4–2) as toxic, and gave EPA authority to expand the list as necessary. Standards for their discharge are set on an industry-by-industry basis, and the agency may ban their discharge entirely. Enforcement authority for toxic pollutants is not delegated to state agencies, but, as always, states may establish and enforce standards more stringent than EPA's. Plants that discharge toxic pollutants for which no standards have been established are regulated on a case-by-case basis. For certain highly toxic pollutants, the act em-

TABLE 4–2. Toxic Pollutants.

Acenaphthene	Endrin and metabolites
Acrolein	Ethylbenzene
Acrylonitrile	Fluoranthene
Aldrin / Dieldrin	Haloethers
Antimony and compounds	Halomethanes
Arsenic and compounds	Heptachlor and metabolites
Asbestos	Hexachlorobutadiene
Benzene	Hexachlorocyclohexane
Benzidine	Hexachlorocyclopentadiene
Beryllium and compounds	Isophorone
Cadmium and compounds	Lead and compounds
Carbon tetrachloride	Mercury and compounds
Chlordane	Naphthalene
Chlorinated benzenes	Nickel and compounds
Chlorinated ethanes	Nitrobenzene
Chloroalkyl ethers	Nitrophenols
Chlorinated naphthalene	Nitrosamines
Chlorinated phenols	Pentachlorophenol
Chloroform	Phenol
Chlorophenol	Phthalate esters
Chromium and compounds	Polychlorinated biphenyls
Copper and compounds	Polynuclear aromatic hydrocarbons
Cyanides	Selenium and compounds
DDT and metabolites	Silver and compounds
Dichlorobenzenes	2,3,7,8-Tetrachlorodibenzo-*p*-dioxin
Dichlorobenzidine	Tetrachloroethylene
Dichloroethylenes	Thallium and compounds
2,4-Dichlorophenol	Toluene
Dichloropropane and dichloropropene	Toxaphene
2,4-Dimethylphenol	Trichloroethylene
Dinitrotoluene	Vinyl chloride
Diphenylhydrazine	Zinc and compounds
Endosulfan and metabolites	

powers EPA to set even stricter effluent limits. Under this provision, EPA has regulated six pollutants: Aldrin, Benzidine, DDT, Endrin, Toxaphene, and PCB.

Pretreatment Standards

In addition to regulating the direct introduction of pollutants into the nation's waters, the Clean Water Act also regulates the discharge of pollutants into POTWs. These "indirect" discharges typically occur using city sewers or other similar conveyances and do not require a specific permit under the NPDES. Indirect discharges must comply with any pretreatment standards in effect as well as any contractual limits or regulations imposed by the POTW. Pretreatment limits may take the form of general standards, which apply to all indirect discharge, or categorial standards, which apply to certain industrial categories. These limitations are intended to ensure that the eventual discharge of water by the POTW is in compliance with its NPDES permit conditions. In addition, these standards are intended to prohibit the discharge of pollutants that interfere with or pass through the POTW.

Regulations appearing at 40 CFR Part 403 contain five major pretreatment criteria, with which all indirect discharges must comply. These regulations prohibit:

- The introduction of pollutants that can cause a fire or an explosion hazard.
- Discharges that are corrosive.
- Discharges that are viscous in nature to the point of causing an obstruction.
- The discharge of pollutant "slugs."
- The discharge of heat sufficient to interfere with biological activities.

In addition to these general pretreatment standards, the EPA may set categorical standards on an industry-by-industry basis. These national pretreatment standards are similar to other industry limitations such as NSPS and toxic pollutants, and, in fact, are often promulgated simultaneously. Existing sources within an industrial category must comply with these standards within three years of passage, and new sources must comply before beginning to discharge. In addition to complying with these pretreatment rules, individual discharges must pay certain user fees and may also be required to contribute to new facility construction and debt service costs. Generally, the decision to use a POTW to treat a plant's wastewater is based on economic rather than environmental concerns. Nonetheless, compliance with applicable federal, state, and local POTW rules is mandatory. The risk of failure in this area can be astronomical because noncompliant discharges can cause POTW upsets, permit violations, and, at the extreme, biomass contamination.

NPDES Permits

Section 402 of the Clean Water Act established a National Pollutant Discharge Elimination System (NPDES) that encompasses all water pollution control regulations. The system consists of a basic permitting mechanism for all discharges from "point sources" into virtually any surface water in the nation. Discharges to groundwater are regulated by the Underground Injection System, its regulations and permits. NPDES permits may be issued to a plant directly by the EPA, or by a state agency with an approved permit program. These permits impose specific effluent limitations, compliance schedules (where applicable), and monitoring and reporting requirements. To establish a specific effluent limit, the agency will use existing general or categorical standards. If specific standards do not exist, BPT, BAT, NSPS, and toxic pollutant limits will be determined on a case-by-case basis, largely through negotiation and by consideration of the general quality of the proposed receiving water. NPDES permits may also contain nonnumerical standards to limit the introduction of pollutants. These standards, known as "best management practices," may include maintenance and operating procedures used to control the impact of a facility's operations as well as prohibited activities. Best management practices are established on an industry-by-industry basis and will often be published with the industry's effluent standards.

Good Management Practices

The term "best management practices" has a specific regulatory definition under Clean Water Act rules. It generally refers to maintenance or operating procedures designed to reduce a plant's impact on local ground or surface waters. It connotes a requirement to take any reasonable actions necessary to manage operations well. Although it is not always specifically required by rule, well-managed plants show evidence of commitment to the following areas:

Knowledge. Plant personnel, including operators, are aware of wastewater sources, flow patterns, control points, and final dispositions. In addition, personnel are aware of effluent limits, sampling requirements, and other pertinent rules. Specific contributors to each wastewater system have been identified and recorded. Sewer prints and flow diagrams are maintained that differentiate between contaminated water systems, sanitary systems, water supply networks, and noncontaminated discharges. Some plants go so far as to color-key individual manholes or post warning signs near noncontaminated sewers. Revisions to piping and flow diagrams are promptly recorded.

Communications. Upset conditions are effectively communicated to downstream discharge points including on-site treatment plants and local POTWs. Specific procedures have been implemented to control nontypical discharges. Procedures for bypassing treatment plants are well known and include proper notification of government agencies and downstream water users. Drainage of containment structures is well managed with prior notification given. Operating instructions are posted in wastewater treatment plants that specify additives used, mix ratios, and contact times. Emergency numbers are posted throughout. Active liaison with local POTWs and agencies is evident.

Sampling and Analysis. All discharge points are routinely sampled and analyzed pursuant to NPDES or POTW self-monitoring provisions. Some plants have installed continuous "upset" monitors to guard against catastrophic discharges. Samples for analysis are taken using proper sampling, flow proportioning, and chemical fixing methods. Composite samplers are routinely maintained and cleaned. The laboratory used is either state-certified (if required) or subscribes to the USEPA Quality Assurance Program. Periodic spikes and duplicates are used to spot-check the laboratories' accuracy and precision. Plants with complex water flow patterns use computer-based data management systems to generate current wastewater flow and quality information. This information is routed through the environmental coordinator for monitoring.

Maintenance. All on-site water treatment systems are maintained under a well-designed preventive maintenance program. Some plants use microprocessors to identify required maintenance activities pursuant to the manufacturer's recommendation. Frequent inspections are conducted by operating personnel to assure on-line efficiency. Settling basins, guard boxes, and separators are cleaned periodically to maintain their efficiency. Clean-out material is managed and disposed of properly. Conveyance systems are monitored to detect spurious leaks, in-flows, or out-flows.

Water Management. All consumptive uses of water are documented and monitored. If required, this information is periodically communicated to local water management agencies. Wastewater recycle opportunities have been investigated and implemented when feasible. Once-through or noncontact water is monitored closely to minimize its use and effect on local water bodies. Stormwater run-off is segregated into potentially contaminated and noncontaminated for proper management. Water draw-offs from tanks, vessels, or process units are routed to contaminated sewers using conveyance systems that eliminate contact with the ground.

Self-Monitoring

Section 308 of the Clean Water Act empowers EPA to require the owner/operator of any "point source" to establish and maintain appropriate monitoring systems for each effluent discharge. These monitoring programs may include the installation and maintenance of specific sampling equipment, the use of approved analytical methods, and the filing of certain reports. Any required monitoring activities are included as a condition of the NPDES permit, which usually also requires the periodic submission of a Discharge Monitoring Report. In addition to periodic reports, the act also requires dischargers to notify the agency immediately of bypasses, upsets, and permit violations.

The act further stipulates that all reports and information required under this section can be made available to the public unless the company demonstrates that doing so would divulge trade secrets. Authorized state or EPA inspectors are empowered to enter the plant to inspect monitoring equipment, sample effluents, and review and copy records. It should be noted that company representatives can usually "split" any samples taken by the agency and have duplicate analysis conducted as a check on the agency's effort. This is frequently a useful exercise for plants to conduct, largely because the analysis of small concentrations of pollutants is frequently inexact. By conducting duplicate analysis, the company may be able to show that an effluent is in compliance when agency results suggest otherwise. In any event, duplicate analysis will further confirm agency results.

WATER POLLUTION SOURCES AND CONTROLS

The sources of water pollution at industrial plants can be broadly described as any acts or processes that use water, and by its use, degrade its quality. This degradation may be small and consist only of added heat (noncontact cooling water) or may be large and consist of gross contamination by chemicals, raw materials, or finished products (process wastewater). In reality, the number of possible ways to degrade water are almost as infinite as the number of unique manufacturing processes employed. Although plants, and their ability to generate wastewater, vary greatly, the types of wastewater generated can be loosely grouped into five major categories: sanitary wastewater, stormwater, cooling water, blowdown, and process water.

At most industrial plants that generate wastewater, measures have been taken to reduce its environmental impact. These measures vary and may range from complete recycle (after appropriate treatment) to simple conveyance to remote treatment plants. In many cases, complex facilities have been constructed on-site to treat all waters prior to release through a permitted discharge point. Although the number of unit operations used to treat polluted waters varies, they too can be loosely classified for description into four major categories: pretreatment, physical treatment, chemical treatment, and biological treatment. Although space limitations preclude complete descriptions of all processes used, the goal here is to provide a general overview. It should be noted that few cases exist in which an auditor can be expected to judge specific equipment applications. This important function should be left to qualified experts or consultants. The auditor's role is to help judge the overall effectiveness of pollution abatement activities, so he generally only needs an overall understanding of pollution control equipment.

Sanitary Wastewater

All industrial plants manage wastewater that is generated by the personnel they employ. This wastewater is typically composed of human wastes from on-site locker rooms and lavatories, food-related wastes from cafeterias and break rooms, and in some cases laboratory wastewater. Sanitary waste contains 80 to 90% water, with 20% to less than 10% total organic and inorganic solids. In small plants the various components of this waste stream may simply be collected and conveyed to a local POTW for treatment. Plants located in remote areas or in areas without POTW service connections may operate a

Figure 4-2. A package sanitary wastewater treatment plant.

small "package" treatment plant and discharge this water to a local stream under the auspices of an NPDES permit. Although it is less common, some plants may use a local "honey dipper" periodically to remove collected waste for subsequent land treatment or shipment to a nearby POTW. At some plants, septic tanks and tile fields are also used to dispose of sanitary wastes.

Typically the greatest motivation for properly managing sanitary wastewater is the potential threat to human health from disease. The literature is replete with evidence that large numbers of disease-carrying organisms can be found in sanitary waste. For this reason the proper collection, conveyance, treatment, and discharge of sanitary waste is mandatory. In addition to this concern for human health, sanitary wastewater has been identified as a potentially uncontrolled source of chemical contamination. In many plants, introduction of waste chemicals, laboratory reagents, and quality control samples into sanitary systems is common. Although specific exemptions exist under federal hazardous waste regulations, the mixing of large quantities of chemicals can severely impact treatment plant operations, or they may simply "pass through" untreated. Some plants have made efforts to minimize this occurrence by segregating potentially contaminated sources from the sanitary system. In other cases, special chemical waste containers are located at potential contamination points to encourage segregation. In any event, it is important for the auditor to remain aware of this cross-contamination potential.

Stormwater

All industrial plants must provide for the proper collection, treatment (if necessary), and discharge of stormwater run-on and run-off. For many plants this requirement is easily accomplished using simple surface drains, ditches, and impoundment basins. For many other plants, however, a real potential exists for stormwater to become contaminated with various chemicals from shipping and receiving areas, "open" process areas, and raw material storage areas. In these cases, it may be necessary to collect potentially contaminated water separately and subject it to appropriate treatment prior to discharge through an NPDES point.

The treatment of run-off merely contaminated with higher levels of solids may be achieved by use of a simple settling basin. Similarly, run-off potentially contaminated with oil may be treated using a common oil/water separator. Plants that have a significant quantity of contaminated run-off may route this stormwater through their wastewater treatment plant prior to discharge. In these cases, provisions must be made to prevent excess flow during storms. This is often accomplished by using surge basins designed to accommodate a five-year storm. In this fashion abnormal stormwater flows are evened out over several days to prevent washout of the treatment plant.

Perhaps the greatest difficulty associated with stormwater management is in the design and maintenance of systems to segregate potentially contaminated from uncontaminated water. On the one hand, the amount of contaminated water slated for treatment should be held to a minimum for simple cost considerations. In the other, all contaminated waters should be collected to prevent untreated discharge and its impact on local streams. This balance can be amazingly difficult to achieve for plants with many potential contamination points or plants that cover a large area. In these cases, it is common for a veritable labyrinth of contaminated and uncontaminated sewers and conveyances to exist.

Blowdown

Blowdown represents a portion of water purposely wasted from a water system to help control the buildup of solids or minerals. Two common examples are blowdown from cooling towers and that from boilers. This wasting of poor-quality water from a system is accompanied by the addition of higher-quality water as makeup. In some cases, the volume of blowdown generated by an individual plant is significant, and it may require treatment prior to discharge. More frequently however, contributions of blowdown are very small, and it is merely combined with other wastewater prior to treatment or discharge.

The water used in cooling towers or boilers is often subjected to a complex treatment scheme designed to control corrosion and scale formation. In most cases, chemical agents such as zinc or sodium chromate, caustics, and acids are used for these purposes. Usually a regular analysis program is followed to ensure treatment effectiveness. Frequently a specific blowdown rate is stipulated to control solids. Although the auditor cannot be an expert in cooling or boiler water treatment, he should recognize the existence of these waste streams. In addition, measures should be taken to ensure that their discharge complies with permit limits or POTW rules, and that changes in the treatment schedule or chemicals do not cause violations.

Noncontact Cooling Water

As the name implies, noncontact cooling water is used to cool products or raw materials without mixing or intimate contact. Typically, water is withdrawn from a nearby stream, circulated through sealed exchangers or manifolds, and discharged downstream of the original withdraw. In some cases, the quality of the discharged water is greater than its original quality because incoming water is frequently treated prior to use. The fact that this water may have little chance to become grossly polluted does not preclude the need for a discharge permit—unless it is conveyed to a POTW, in which case pretreatment standards or POTW rules may apply. In particularly severe applications (where the chance for exchanger leakage exists), cooling water is frequently treated prior to discharge, normally using simple unit operations such as settling basins or separators. In some cases the continuous reuse of cooling water, by employing towers or ponds, is receiving impetus from water management agencies to reduce the number of large-scale withdraws from water bodies. It is important for the auditor to note that this encouragement may create another wastewater source in the form of blowdown, discussed previously.

Process Water

This single category of wastewater is usually responsible for the most significant discharge from many industrial plants. Additionally, this category represents the greatest variety of wastewater that environmental auditors will encounter. The amount and the quality of process-related wastewater generated by a specific plant are functions of the manufacturing process employed, raw materials used, finished products produced, and throughput. Process water may be generated as a result of various washing steps (as in the canning industry) or cooling and heating (as in petroleum refining), or by air pollution control equipment in which water is used to scrub or strip entrained pollutants from process air. Water is often used in manufacturing processes as a carrying agent for the transmission of raw materials to finished products. Examples include the use of coatings, adhesives, paints, and binders. In any event, it is important for the auditor to gain a basic understanding of the process technology used at the plant, its ability to generate contaminated water, and the pollutants present.

Process wastewaters can contain dissolved solids such as salts and minerals, suspended particles such as silt and finished products, as well as any number of soluble chemicals. It is these constituents that

Figure 4-3. Discharge point to a process sewer.

usually dictate the treatment process to be used. Although many unit operations used to treat process water are basically physical methods, biological treatment has been found effective in many applications. For many processes, it is first necessary to pretreat incoming water to make it more amenable to subsequent treatment. Some of these pretreatment methods are discussed in the following paragraphs.

Pretreatment Methods

As used here, pretreatment refers to the initial unit operations that wastewater is frequently subjected to prior to subsequent treatment and discharge. These steps may be taken to make the wastewater more compatible with downstream unit operations, or may be used to help mitigate wide variations in wastewater flow or quality. Although many unit operations exist that may be considered pretreatment steps, four particularly common categories deserve review here: screening, equalization, pH control, and mixing.

Screening. Often the first step used in treating a specific wastewater is a screening operation. Its purpose is to remove large debris such as rags, metal, and other solids that can damage pumps and other equipment. This operation can be conducted using screens (wire cloths or perforated plates) or a parallel-bar arrangement. The size of the openings specified largely depends on the raw wastewater, its ability to plug or blind screens, and the nature of the solids expected to be retained. A wide variety of specific equipment arrangements exist, relying on natural or mechanical forces to impinge on and remove solids. Screening equipment may be hand-cleaned on an as-needed basis, or more likely may be automatically cleaned using scrapers or traveling rakes. Independently of the specific equipment used, it is important to ensure that solids are removed promptly and are properly managed, including their disposal. Incomplete or infrequent cleaning may cause blinding, tremendous head loss, and overflow of wastewater.

Equalization. Most processes employed to treat wastewater chemically or biologically rely on a more or less constant flow of water to be effective. Although downstream operations can absorb some variations in flow and quality, their efficiency is often enhanced by a steady state condition. Flow equalization is often the method used to mitigate wide variations in the supply of raw water. Equalization can be accomplished by using large in-line basins to accumulate incoming wastewater, resulting in a constant, or nearly constant, effluent. Although less effective, some measure of equalization can be achieved using an off-line basin that receives only those flows above a predetermined level. These higher flows are held for subsequent "trickling" back to the original influent. The design of equalization basins must provide for both dry- and wet-weather flows, as well as variations in manufacturing cycles. It is often necessary to provide mixing in equalization basins to help prevent solids deposition and septicity. Supernatant or filtrate generated from downstream unit operations is often returned to the equalization basin for treatment.

pH Control. Unlike most municipal wastewaters, industrial process water is often subject to wide variations in pH due to process upsets, spills, or the manufacture of off-spec products. Because treatment plants are often pH-sensitive, it is important to provide for the monitoring and positive control of wastewater pH. The system used should provide for both coarse and fine pH control, and should permit diversion of flow as an emergency measure. Any variations outside a predetermined range are corrected with the addition of caustic or acid. An ability to divert flow to an emergency basin may not be necessary in plants that experience only minor pH variations. This monitoring and control of pH can sometimes be complicated by the need for proper maintenance of appropriate instrumentation, including pH probes which often foul and give erroneous readings. In many cases, pH systems are entirely computerized to minimize operator error and ensure consistent operation.

Mixing. Pretreatment schemes that specify the addition of chemicals to the wastewater or that use an equalization basin for flow control often require a mixing operation to ensure proper combination. Examples include the addition of polymers to promote settling, caustics or acids for pH control, or other chemicals to treat specific constituents. Even pretreatment schemes that do not rely on the addition of chemicals often use a mixing operation to ensure uniform water quality. Mixing can be carried out using a number of specific equipment arrangements, including hydraulic jumps, venturis, and mechanical mixers. In each case, it is important to minimize vortexing and "dead spaces," which decrease effectiveness. Depending on the specific application, mixing may be done using slow, nonturbulent paddles, or it may be vigorous enough to result in some aeration.

Physical Treatment Methods

Water pollution treatment units that rely on the application or use of physical forces to remove pollutants are commonly defined as physical treatment methods. The unit operations previously described as pretreatment methods are sometimes classified as physical treatment. For the purposes of conducting an audit, our interest will be focused on three common unit operations: flocculation, separation, and filtration.

Flocculation. Many wastewaters contain solid particles that must be removed prior to downstream treatment or discharge. In some cases, the density, size, and character of these particles do not permit simple settling in a basin. In other applications, the space and equipment necessary to operate large basins are not available, so quick settling is needed. This is often accomplished by the addition of a specific agent to attract and bind small particles together, thereby increasing their mass and tendency to settle. This chemical addition must be closely controlled and accompanied by stirring, mixing, or agitation to promote contact (i.e. flocculation).

Flocculation is accomplished by providing for mixing at a rate gentle enough to avoid the imposition of shear forces which would serve to break up bound particles. Manufacturers of flocculants and wastewater equipment typically specify a mixing rate and equipment configuration to achieve mixing without breakup. In many cases, the unit consists of a tank or basin in which several paddles are submerged, driven by a small-horsepower motor. Although paddle and stationary baffle configurations may vary, their intent remains the same: the gentle mixing of wastewater and added flocculants.

Separation. Separation is a broad term used to describe the settling, sedimentation, or flotation of various constituents from a wastewater. Separation is often considered for the removal of solids (perhaps after the addition of a flocculant) and oil (perhaps in a specially designed oil separator). It is often combined with the addition of air, which attaches itself to small particles or oil droplets and forces them to float to the surface. In either case, settling or flotation, the goal is the same: to reduce water flow to a velocity small enough to permit entrained constituents to separate out for removal.

In practice, most separators are similar and consist of a pit or basin with appropriate baffling to reduce turbulence and provide for a clean effluent. If material is collected on the surface, the effluent leaves the chamber below the water level to reduce overflow of separated oil or solids. Some units, such as clarifiers, are essentially large cone-shaped tanks that collect solids on the bottom for subsequent removal by suction. A common problem associated with separating equipment is the need to ensure that design flow rates are not greatly exceeded. If large increases in water flow are experienced after construction, velocity through the unit may become too great for effective separation of materials from the flow. Likewise, large increases in solids or oil content may overtax the collection and removal systems. All separating devices require cleaning to remove solids and minimize reentrainment. Cleaning is often performed continuously by pumping captured sludge or oil as it accumulates. In some applications it may be possible to clean separators on a "campaign" basis according to anticipated accumulation rates. In either case, some provision must be made for flow diversion so that maintenance and cleaning operations are possible.

Filtration. In some industrial applications, the use of simple settling devices is insufficient to achieve desired solids removal. In these cases, a supplemental filtering step is called for. Although the use of granular bed filters has been common in treating potable water, their use in industrial wastewater treatment is recent. The typical filtration operation involves two distinct process steps: filtration and backwash. Filtration occurs by passing the incoming wastewater through a bed of suitable granular material. The bed may be composed of two different media (sand and gravel) or may use three different media for improved efficiency (sand, gravel, and anthracite). The removal action associated with filtration is generally a complex process using several physical phenomena such as straining, sedimentation, impaction, and adsorption. The filtering step may be complemented by the addition of chemicals such as flocculants. Filtering continues until solids begin showing up in the effluent or until available head loss is exceeded.

When these conditions exist, filtering ceases, and the filter bed is backwashed to remove accumulated particles. Backwashing usually occurs by reversing the flow of water, essentially "fluidizing" the media bed and washing up accumulated solids. This washwater can be returned to the primary settling device for treatment. Plants with large washwater flows may employ several filter beds in parallel so that treatment is not interrupted by backwashing.

Chemical Treatment Methods

Chemical treatment processes, by definition, are unit operations that rely upon a chemical reaction to reduce the level of pollutants in a wastewater. Few chemical processes are used alone; more often, chemical unit operations are used in conjunction with other physical or biological systems. In some respects, the development of new or modified chemical and biological systems represents the future of wastewater treatment. As the discharge of toxic pollutants from industrial operations is subjected to regulation, the need for additional treatment options will grow. Some believe these options reside in the use of specific chemical processes, in some cases similar to the manufacturing process that generated the wastewater.

Chemical treatment methods suffer one distinct disadvantage over physical or biological processes, in that chemical methods rely on the addition of material to affect change. This chemical usage is often expensive, and in some cases the chemicals used are energy-intensive. Although this disadvantage is real, the use of certain chemical unit operations is common and can be expected to remain so. Here we will review two categories of chemical treatment methods: precipitation and adsorption. Although two general operations are reviewed here, the environmental auditor should recognize that a large number of specific chemical treatment methods may be encountered at individual plants. Examples include the use of hydrogen peroxide to oxidize phenol prior to biological treatment, the use of stripping towers to remove hydrogen sulfide, and any number of disinfection methods. In each case the auditor should understand the chemicals added, the methods used to specify and control this addition, and procedures used to monitor its success.

Precipitation. In the application of wastewater treatment, chemical precipitation is the addition of certain agents (chemicals) to a wastewater to help facilitate the removal of pollutants by sedimentation. The use of this unit operation has grown since the advent of tighter effluent limits for organic nutrients and suspended solids. Although a large number of potential agents exist, common chemicals in use include lime, ferric sulfate, ferric chloride, alum, and ferrous sulfate. The ability of this method to clarify wastewater is largely a function of the quantity of chemicals used and the ability to control the process to maintain optimum conditions. With chemical precipitation, solids, biological oxygen demand (BOD), and bacteria removal rates can exceed 70% and, in some cases, approach 90%. Both the rate of chemical addition and the exact precipitate used are largely specified by the results of bench scale studies. If the wastewater to be treated is acidic, it must be neutralized before precipitation takes place, thereby increasing chemical usage. For the most part, the equipment associated with precipitation processes is simple and consists of chemical storage and delivery, a mixing operation, and a sedimentation basin. Care must be used in handling the chemicals because many are corrosive, and provisions must be made for sludge removal, dewatering, and disposal. Depending on the characteristics of the original wastewater, this sludge may pose disposal problems due to the presence of heavy metals or organic solids.

Adsorption. Adsorption is a unit operation that collects soluble materials in a wastewater on a suitable surface for removal. Although not always considered a true chemical treatment process, it is described here because it entails the addition of a substance to affect change. Adsorption can occur at any interface between two phases (air–liquid, liquid–liquid, and liquid–solid). The liquid–solid application, which is the most common, is described here.

Any number of solids can be used to remove pollutants from wastewater; generally, each has a large surface area per unit of mass. This large surface area is due to the network of small pores making up the structure of the particle. Specific adsorbents may include activated alumina, molecular sieves, and activated carbon, carbon being the most common. Treatment with activated carbon often occurs using a fixed bed through which water is passed. Although carbon treatment is sometimes considered a polishing step after other unit operations, some solids removal can occur in the bed. This removal, in fact, can cause serious operating problems if provisions for backwash and surface cleaning are not made.

Some treatment plants use activated carbon in a powder form by direct addition to the wastewater flow. At least one firm has patented a process in which activated carbon is added directly to a biological reactor. This process is said to result in higher removal of biodegradable and nonbiodegradable agents than either biological or carbon treatment alone. Independent of the exact point of addition, provisions must be made for the subsequent removal of the powdered carbon. This usually occurs in a clarifier or settling chamber. Here, a carbon slurry is continuously removed, dewatered by a thickener or filter press, and prepared for regeneration.

Economical use of carbon in wastewater treatment requires a method of regeneration to reduce chemical costs. This is easily accomplished in a furnace where organic material is oxidized and regenerated carbon returned to service. The adsorptive capacity of regenerated carbon is generally less than that of fresh material, and some fraction is usually lost during the regenerating cycle. This loss must be made up on a continuous basis. For specific applications, the amount of makeup required is estimated by bench scale studies and empirical data.

Biological Treatment Methods

Biological treatment methods are used to reduce complex molecules of pollutants into simple products and biomass for removal. This conversion takes place by using a culture of microorganisms that are usually well acclimated to a specific wastewater. Because the organic and inorganic pollutants present in industrial wastewaters are often toxic, some measure of pretreatment is sometimes necessary. Few wastewaters exist that cannot be effectively treated with biological methods, provided proper care is taken in operating the system. The role of biological unit operations in treating industrial wastewaters is expanding and represents an opportunity to treat difficult materials in an effective way. The effectiveness of biological treatment systems is a function of several variables, including residence time in the unit, the concentration of pollutants in the wastewater (and its variability), and the concentration of biomass and its age. In most cases, the success of biological activity is directly related to consistent influent quality and the ability to operate the system in a steady state condition. Although most systems can absorb a certain level of shock loadings, each should have design provisions included to equalize loads and reduce upsets. Common biological treatment processes can be grouped into two general categories: activated sludge and anaerobic digestion.

Activated Sludge. Activated sludge treatment systems make use of microorganisms to oxidize organic constituents of a wastewater to carbon dioxide, water, and new biomass. They operate in the presence of oxygen and rely on a recycling of a fraction of microorganisms to "seed" raw influent. Although a number of specific systems exist using this operation, most are basically similar.

Activated sludge treatment occurs by introducing the organic wastewater into a reactor (perhaps a tank, basin, or vessel) where a suitable mixture of aerobic microorganisms is maintained. This mixture of wastewater and organisms present in the reactor is referred to as the mixed liquor. The microorganisms in the reactor convert complex molecules to simple products by biological activity, and in the process grow to form new biomass.

Aerobic conditions are maintained by the addition of oxygen via aeration or diffused air. This aeration also results in maintenance of a completely mixed system. After an appropriate reaction time, which is usually specified by operating conditions such as flow and wastewater quality, the mixture is sent to a settling tank or basin where biomass is separated from treated water. A fraction of this biomass is recycled to incoming wastewater to maintain the level of microorganisms in the reactor, while the balance is wasted. In a steady state condition the amount of biomass wasted roughly corresponds to the growth of new cells, and is usually a function of the original wastewater type and quality. Wasted biomass is usually dewatered for subsequent incineration or disposal.

Anaerobic Digestion. Anaerobic digestion is commonly used to stabilize wasted biological sludges, in order to reduce subsequent biological activity and provide a stable, or nearly so, end product. Digestion is a complex process, generally thought of as consisting of two steps, in which anaerobic and facultative microorganisms are used to break down complex organic molecules. The first step in the process is conversion of complex organics to volatile acids, such as acetic and propionic acid, by acid-forming bacteria. Methane-producing bacteria next convert these acids to methane and carbon dioxide in a reaction that is recognized as the overall rate-limiting step. The rate of biomass formation is generally less than in aerobic systems, which is often an advantage for industrial wastes because nutrient requirements are reduced. This slow reaction rate usually requires the use of elevated temperatures (85–100°F) in the reactor to reduce space and time requirements. Anaerobic digestion is sensitive to the pH of the reactor, ammonia concentration, and temperature, thereby requiring the close monitoring of several important parameters.

The equipment arrangement used to conduct anaerobic digestion is generally one of two types: (1) conventional digestion; and (2) two-stage, high-rate digestion. Conventional digestion consists of a single tank, in which influent is added, and digestion, thickening, and gas evolution take place. Several stratified layers are present in a conventional digester, such as gas, scum, supernatant, digesting sludge, and stabilized sludge. Mixing and/or heating takes place in the digestion layer, with solids removal at the bottom and gas removal at the top. To provide for better mixing and temperature control, the two-stage process was developed. In this arrangement, two separate vessels are used; the first contains the active digesting sludge, while the second receives digested material from the first for separation into sludge, supernatant, scum, and gas. Mixing and heating occur in the first stage.

THE PLANT AUDIT

The water pollution audit is a systematic review process designed to examine each regulated area of the plant and compare these areas with current standards. It consists of several steps, each focusing on a separate concern. These steps begin with an examination of obvious water-related areas, then expand to include the more subtle potential impacts.

For purposes of organization, the water pollution audit can be divided into six major areas of attention:

1. Pre-audit preparations
2. Initial plant tour
3. Review of currently regulated discharges
   (a) NPDES discharges
   (b) POTW discharges
   (c) Stormwater run-off
4. Wastewater inventory and overview
   (a) On-site treatment plant review
5. File and records review
6. Final plant tour and summary

Although the areas are listed separately here, these distinctions often blur during the actual plant audit. As long as each area is adequately addressed during the audit, the exact order of implementation can be flexible.

Pre-audit Preparations

Prior to visiting the plant site, it is important that the auditor first review the applicable water pollution regulations that govern the facility's operations. This review should focus on the industry effluent standards as well as any specific pretreatment standards and best management practices that apply. Since enforcement and permitting authority is often vested in local or state agencies, it is important to review their requirements as well.

During pre-audit preparations, the auditor will attempt to gain at least a general understanding of the manufacturing process employed at the plant, its equipment, and the type of wastewater generated. This nominal understanding of the process will be complemented by the

Figure 4–4. Holding tank for process wastewater.

general plant tour conducted by the environmental coordinator of the facility. If the plant to be audited discharges a significant amount of process water to a local POTW, it may be beneficial to secure a copy of the POTW regulations for review beforehand. In addition, any contractual arrangement with the POTW may be reviewed, as well as test schedules and results. Pre-audit preparations may include a review of all NPDES permits held by the plant, the sampling and analytical requirements they specify, and even a sample of several test results.

Initial Plant Tour

The auditor's first exposure to the plant's wastewater management system comes during the initial tour with the environmental coordinator. In addition to gaining a nominal understanding of the plant's layout and process (discussed in Chapter 2), the tour should include at least a cursory examination of wastewater generation points, flow patterns, and discharge locations. This examination is frequently complicated by the fact that many discharge points are not obvious (e.g., underground sewer lines). In any event, a basic understanding of their location and use is necessary. At this stage of the audit, the auditor begins "marking up" the facility plot plan with notes for future reference regarding water sources, flows, and discharge locations. If the plant uses an on-site wastewater facility for treatment prior to discharge, the auditor should specifically receive a tour and description of its operation. In addition, the auditor should receive a general understanding of run-on and run-off patterns around the plant. Flow patterns and directions toward any local bodies of water should also be noted on the plot plan.

Review of Currently Regulated Discharges

A convenient and logical way to begin the water pollution audit is with a review of each currently regulated discharge point. These points may include direct discharges through NPDES points or indirect discharges through a local POTW. In either case, the goal is to characterize each discharge adequately and compare this information with permit standards or POTW limits. The audit now becomes an ef-

Figure 4-5. Some discharge points are hidden and easily missed.

fort to determine whether each discharge is in compliance with its applicable limits.

NPDES Discharges. In the case of NPDES discharges, the actual permit is the basis for comparison. The auditor should secure and review copies of all current NPDES permits issued to the plant. Any expired permits, or permits with expiration dates within 180 days, should be noted for action by the plant. In some cases, regulatory agencies have allowed plants to operate with "old" permits until new effluent standards have been promulgated. If this is the case, documentation should exist to confirm this permission.

In addition to actual numerical limits, NPDES permits may contain specific effluent limitations for variables such as flow, temperature, biological oxygen demand (BOD), chemical oxygen demand (COD), solids, turbidity, and specific chemical constituents. In addition, the permit will specify sampling requirements, routine reporting requirements, and perhaps certain best management practices. The plant should have a file containing the test data and reports sent to the agency in compliance with permit conditions. The auditor should review this information to compare the plant's actual effluent quality with that required by the permit. If the plant has several NPDES outfalls, it may be beneficial to organize this information using a standard format such as that presented in Table 4–3. By listing permit limitations with current effluent data, problem areas become apparent.

Table 4–3. Water Pollution Discharge Data: Direct Discharges.

Plant: ______________________ Date: ______________

Plant contact: ________________ Auditor(s): ______________

Discharge point No.:[1] __________ Receiving water: ________________

Describe process area served:[2] ______________________________

____

____

Is discharge covered by an NPDES permit? ____________ If no, why not? _____

____

NPDES permit no.:[3] ______________ Expiration date: ____________

Issuing agency: ________________ Agency contact: ____________

[1]Enter each number on facility plot plan.
[2]For example, process water, sanitary water, cooling water, boiler blowdown, etc.
[3]Attach copy.

(Continued)

Table 4-3. (*Cont.*)

Flow Data		Is water treated prior to discharge? ________
Daily	max: ____________	Describe: ____________
Ave.	daily: ____________	____________
Min.	daily: ____________	____________

Parameter	Limit	Permit Limits Test Frequency	Latest Test	Lab.[4]

Do best management practices (BMP) regulations apply? ____________

Have any consent orders or decrees been issued for this point? ____________

Describe agency reporting requirements: ____________

____

____

____

[4]Certain state agencies require the use of state-certified laboratories.

For discharge points that frequently exceed their permit limits, an additional step is necessary. In these cases, a short history of these exceedences should be prepared to help document the nature and extent of the problem. Table 4-4 is an example of such an effort. By listing all parameters with their exceedence history, the auditor can quickly define what is and is not the problem. This information and any facts gained from plant contacts form the basis for auditor recommendations.

Table 4-4. Water Pollution Discharge Data: Exceedence History.

Plant: ______________________ Date: ______________________

Plant contact: ______________________ Auditor(s): ______________________

Discharge point no.: ______________________ Test frequency: ______________________

Wastewater Parameter	Discharge Limit	Last Exceedence	No. of Exceedences in last 12 mos.
BOD			
COD			
TOC			
TSS			
Oil and grease			
Ammonia			
pH			
Sulfide			
Sulfate			
Hexavalent chromium			

(Continued)

Table 4-4. *(Cont.)*

Total chromium
Lead
Mercury
Zinc
Copper
Iron
Phenol(s)
Others:
NOTES:

POTW Discharges. The next major class of discharge points is those involving POTWs. The delivery of contaminated water to a remote POTW may be governed by three distinct bodies of rules:

1. General pretreatment standards
2. Categorical pretreatment standards
3. POTW contract limits or POTW regulations

Most plants that discharge to a POTW combine their individual wastewater flows prior to transport to the facility. Here, the auditor is usually concerned with one discharge point whose character may vary greatly, depending on individual wastewater stream contributions. Once again, it is beneficial to organize a data summary for this discharge that compares the POTW limit with the actual discharge. Table 4–5 is an example of this organization. For small facilities with minor process flows, an actual contract with the POTW may not be involved. In these cases, it is important at least to review the POTW rules briefly to determine the parameters of greatest concern. In all cases, it is important to determine the nature of the discharge and its quality. Facilities that lack this information should be encouraged to perform the sampling and analysis necessary to characterize their discharge adequately. This information is becoming increasingly important as more POTWs are required to institute pretreatment programs.

Table 4–5. Water Pollution Discharge Data: Indirect Discharges.

Plant: ______________________ Date: ______________________

Plant contact: ______________________ Auditor(s): ______________________

Discharge point no.:[1] __________ Name of POTW: ______________________

Final receiving water: ______________ POTW contact: ______________________

Describe process/area served:[2] ______________________________________

____

____

Is this discharge covered by a POTW contract?[3] ________________________

Has POTW instituted a pretreatment program? ________________________

[1]Enter each number on facility plot plan.
[2]For example, process water, sanitary water, cooling water, boiler blowdown, etc.
[3]Attach copies.

(Continued)

Table 4-5. (*Cont.*)

Flow Data

Daily max: ______________________

Ave. daily: ______________________

Min. daily: ______________________

Describe POTW treatment: ______________________

CONTRACT LIMITS/POTW LIMITS

Parameter	Limit	Test Frequency	Latest Data	Lab.

NOTES: ______________________

In some cases, these POTW pretreatment programs have required industrial users to perform this analysis as a first step. For a small plant, the total cost to secure a representative composite sample and analyze it for a variety of parameters including priority pollutants can range from $1,500 to $3,500. Even in the absence of an actual regulatory or POTW requirement, these surveys are extremely useful tools to help protect the plant's interest. Without knowledge of its own discharge, the plant may be unable to prove its innocence in a POTW upset or other discharge problem.

In cases where the subject plant discharges a significant flow to the local POTW, it may be beneficial to schedule a meeting and tour with the POTW plant engineer. This opportunity may be used to gain insight from the POTW on the plant's operation. The meeting could be used to discuss the status of the POTW's pretreatment program and any difficulties the POTW experiences with the plant, and to receive a copy of the POTW's NPDES discharge permit. Since this permit contains the POTW's actual discharge limits, an industrial customer should be interested in its content.

Stormwater run-off. The last major class of discharge that deserves particular attention is stormwater run-off. Uncontaminated run-off from parking lots, roofs, and other areas of the plant rarely requires specific permitting. Where the potential for contamination exists, as with storage piles, loading areas, and other process areas, best management practices may apply. Normally these requirements are specifically referred to in any NPDES permits issued to the facility. The absence of specific regulations should not be interpreted as a license to contaminate. Because all facilities are responsible for their discharges, common sense and prudent management should govern these "gray" areas.

The most straightforward way to review the run-off situation of a plant is to look for signs of water flow during the tour of the property. If obvious streams and swales exist, simple inspection will indicate the potential for contamination. Any obvious signs of contamination such as discolored soil or dying vegetation should be noted so that the source may be identified and mitigated. As with other discharges, it is recommended that a standard format be used to record the results of these simple inspections. Table 4–6 is an example of a format used to organize this information.

Wastewater Inventory and Overview

After the obvious regulated discharges are examined for compliance, it is necessary to review the plant for any discharges that have escaped attention. These may be minor ones such as seal water leaks, or may

Table 4–6. Water Pollution Discharge Data: Facility Run-off.

Plant: ____________________ Date: ____________________

Plant contact: ____________________ Auditor(s): ____________________

Describe area of facility contributing to this run-off point: ____________________

Potential Run-off Character

Description of Source	Contamination Potential	Receiving Water	Water Treatment
Parking lots			
Shipping areas			
Receiving areas			
Roof drains			
Other areas:			

Table 4-6. (*Cont.*)

Note drainage patterns on facility plot plan.
Describe any evidence of contamination: ______

have large potential impacts such as process water releases. Although there is no easy way to ferret out these instances, one way to begin this effort is to compile a comprehensive inventory of wastewater sources present at the plant. Table 4–7 lists many common wastewaters found in industrial plants. By tracking the flow of these individual contributors, the auditor will confirm their eventual discharge through permitted points. Cases of discrepancies may become the basis for auditor recommendations.

For each type of wastewater present at the plant, the auditor will list its source, flow, treatment, and eventual discharge. For small- to medium-size plants, this step is relatively straightforward and culminates in the preparation of an actual field diagram of the plant wastewater system. An example field diagram appears as Figure 4–6.

Table 4-7. Typical Wastewater Sources Found in Industrial Plants.

Process water	Ballast water
• Wash water	Plant floor drains
• Spray booths	Warehouse drains
• Clarifier water	Air pollution control equipment
Sanitary wastewater	Compressor blowdown
• Employee lunchrooms	Loading area drainage
• Locker rooms	Roof drains
• Rest rooms	Condensate water
Cooling water	• Autoclaves
• Noncontact	• Steam traps
• Blowdown	Quench tanks
Boiler blowdown	Spray booths
Stormwater	Storage pile run-off
Tank farm drainage	Fire water
Containment area drainage	Seal water

Even for relatively large plants, a simplified block diagram will help the auditor appreciate the plant's water system, its complexity, and its potential impact on the local environment. Since the purpose of the diagram is a broad overview, it is not necessary to list every valve or pipe. However, it should show major control points, all discharge points, and any sample points currently in use. The facility's plot plan may be convenient for this use.

On-Site Treatment Plant Review. If the facility employs an on-site wastewater treatment plant, the auditor will next review its operation and maintenance. This review begins with a simple overview of the facility itself, the sources of treated wastewater, equipment used, and its discharge point. Lack of time and specific expertise usually prevents the auditor from performing an in-depth review of the treatment plant design and operation. However, operator interviews and visual examinations will indicate any gross problems. The presence of many persistent operating or maintenance problems may give rise to an auditor recommendation that the facility be reviewed by a competent professional.

A special note applies to plants with their own wastewater treatment facility. The subject of toxic pollutants promises to receive additional attention from both the public and regulatory agencies in the future. This is especially true for certain industries such as chemical manufac-

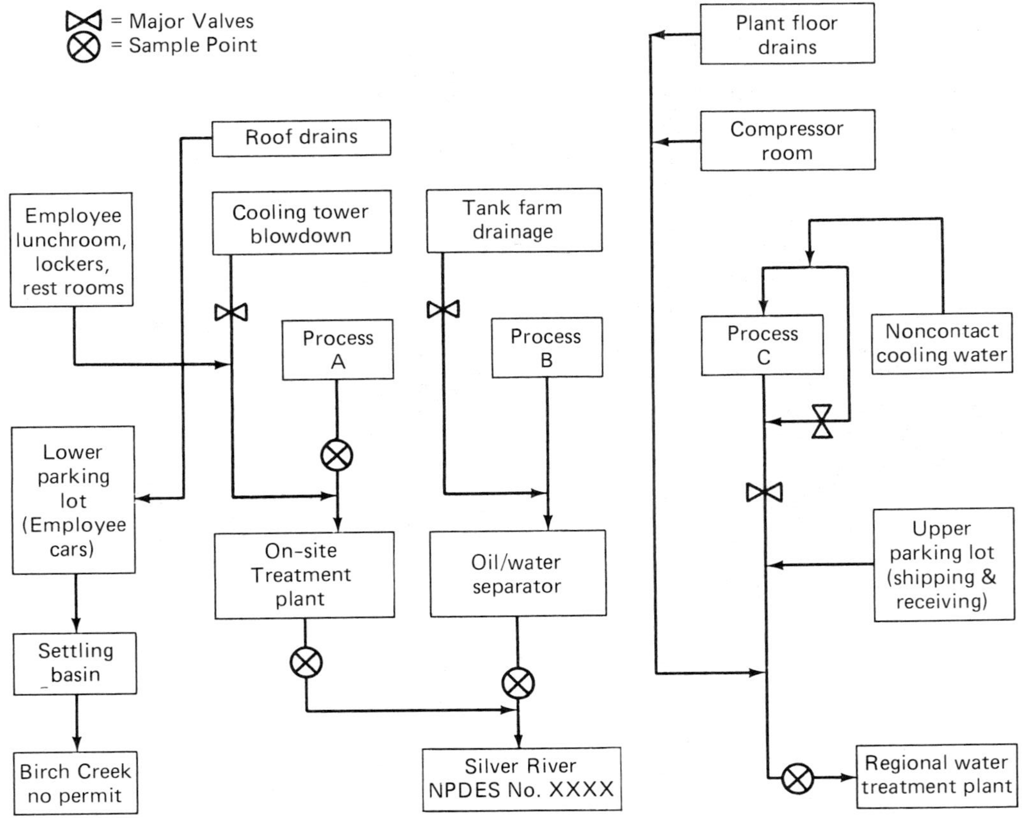

Figure 4-6. Example field diagram: plant wastewater system.

Figure 4–7. Discharge point into a river. Note weir arrangement to measure flow.

turing, petroleum refining, and the metals industries. As specific effluent standards are promulgated incorporating limitations on these pollutants, on-site plants may face the prospect of tighter effluent limits. Such limits can easily require additional treatment capacity or equipment. If resources permit it during the audit, a useful planning tool may be a complete priority pollutant analysis of the wastewater.

File and Records Review

At this point in the water pollution audit, the plant's various wastewaters have been characterized, and their flow, treatment, and discharge examined and evaluated for compliance. These steps have been accomplished by conducting various interviews and by touring the facilities. Prior to conducting the final, comprehensive plant tour, it is necessary for the auditor to perform a complete review of the water-pollution-related files and records. This step, although time-consuming, is beneficial for several reasons. It helps highlight any voids that otherwise may have gone unnoticed, it confirms much of the information previously received, and it helps prepare the environmental coordinator for the next "official" agency inspection.

During this review, all copies of NPDES permits and POTW contracts should be specifically compared against the information previously given for accuracy and completeness. Any deficiencies should be noted and resolved. Copies of any consent orders, decrees, or compliance schedules should be reviewed closely. Often such documents supersede "normal" agency rules and require additional compliance measures. The plant's compliance with each condition should be specifically evaluated. Any status or progress reports required by these documents should be readily available.

Plant files can contain much information concerning the local POTW pretreatment program. Frequently these programs are implemented by first conducting surveys of each industrial user. The forms or information packets used to conduct these surveys will be helpful to confirm the pretreatment information received from the plant contact. Any basic differences between the versions should be resolved.

If the subject facility has ever applied for or received an Army Corps of Engineers dredge or fill permit, it too should be reviewed. This environmental program is outlined in the Appendix.

Certainly one of the most important areas of records review is the examination of the several reports and notifications specifically required by government agencies. Facilities with NPDES permits are required to file periodic Discharge Monitoring Reports with the issuing agency. This file should be complete and up-to-date.

In addition, all permit noncompliances and exceedences must be reported to the agency within five days of their occurrence. Although there is some dispute on exactly when the five-day clock begins, it is clear the agencies place much importance on this reporting tool. Likewise this file should be complete and up-to-date.

All analysis results performed under an NPDES permit must be kept on hand. The results of any additional tests above the minimum requirements must also be reported and kept on file. Emergency situations such as bypassing or upsets must be immediately reported. Information on each such condition should be kept on hand for future reference. The presence of such reports in the environmental file confirms the plant's compliance with these requirements.

In addition to these records, the auditor should pay particular attention to any past agency inspection reports contained in the file. These "official" reports often list a summary of water pollution problems noted by the agency. Particular attention should be focused on any corrective actions required. Any situations that remain unresolved may result in auditor recommendations.

Any construction or operating permits issued for on-site treatment facilities should be closely examined for operating and maintenance requirements. Often, such permits contain specific requirements that may be overlooked. Compliance with each permit term should be assured.

Final Plant Tour and Summary

Before finishing the water pollution audit and presenting its results to the plant manager, it is important that the auditor conduct a final, comprehensive tour of the facility. The major purpose of this tour is to resolve any problems or deficiencies noted during the records and file review step. In general, the final plant tour is an opportunity for the auditor properly to summarize the water-related problems noted at the plant. These problems may range from simple permit exceedences to full-blown fish kills or upsets. The conditions that caused these situations must be well understood, as must the actions taken to prevent their recurrence. Any lack of corrective measures, or their failure, must be noted for improvement. The presence of discharges without a permit certainly falls into this category.

The final plant tour is also a convenient opportunity for the auditors to discuss your preliminary findings with the environmental coordinator prior to meeting with his boss, the plant manager. Such courtesy is usually much appreciated by the coordinator and helps generate support for the findings. The coordinator now has the opportunity to begin outlining potential corrective actions and, in doing so, to be better prepared to implement them.

Summary. A water pollution audit of an industrial plant is essentially an effort to construct a water balance of the facility. All sources of wastewater, their flow, and characteristics are listed. The final disposition of each flow is identified and classified as either direct (NPDES), indirect (POTW), or run-off (best management practices). For each type of discharge, the applicable standards are identified and listed. The quality of each discharge is compared against these limits to determine compliance. Finally, comprehensive record reviews and plant tours are conducted to assure that no major areas are missed. All results, conclusions, and recommendations are reviewed with the environmental coordinator for accuracy.

5
Solid and Hazardous Waste

For most industrial facilities, the proper management of solid and hazardous waste represents an increasingly important aspect of environmental compliance. Examples of failure in this area are illustrated almost daily in local and national publications. The ramifications of such cases on a facility's operations are often devastating and can impact everyone from employees and customers to shareholders. It is clear that facility managers must ensure that all wastes generated by their operations are properly handled and disposed of. An environmental audit of a facility's waste-handling practices can fulfill this need.

The purpose of this chapter is to provide a framework for evaluating a plant's waste management system. This evaluation compares the current practices employed at an individual plant against a number of standards for compliance. These standards consist of corporate policies and procedures as well as laws and agency regulations. It is important to note that the risk associated with waste management transcends agency regulations and includes several avenues of public suit. For this reason, government regulations should not be the only standard used for comparison. Many examples exist in which a company's activities were technically within the bounds of regulation, yet their operations suffered because of public opinion. Therefore, facility performance must be evaluated with an eye toward common sense and good management practices.

A well structured and implemented audit will give a comprehensive picture of a plant's waste-related activities. At a minimum, the audit will document each individual waste generated at the facility and its approximate generation rate, management technique, and eventual disposal method. In most cases, the audit report will identify a list of actions that must be taken to bring the facility into total compliance with current regulations. If properly planned, the audit can be used to identify the effect of future or proposed regulations as well. To be effective, a waste-related audit should be structured to generate a list of potential actions aimed at reducing the facility's overall related liability and exposure. Although environmental audits are not typically conducted for this purpose, obvious liability-limiting activities should be identified for subsequent consideration. An example may be the incineration of a particularly hazardous waste in lieu of land disposal. Because incineration results in total destruction, it is often the preferred disposal technique from a risk standpoint. When the cost differences between these two alternatives approach parity (taking all costs into consideration), incineration is especially attractive.

Good Management Practices

A well-managed waste program shows evidence of attention in each of the following areas:

Systematic Supervision. The waste program should show evidence of being thorough and well-planned. All wastes should be addressed. Elements of this system include good records, logs, and reports. Other examples are written procedures and policies that are distributed and followed throughout the organization.

Effective Control. Efforts should be expended to control the wastes that are generated from the point of generation to final disposal. This concept is closely linked to "tracking." The plant should know how much is generated, when it is generated, and where it goes. Contracts, manifests, and invoices are all used to track and control these movements. Extremely well-managed operations attempt to determine why the waste is generated and how can it be reduced or eliminated.

Close Monitoring. The plant's waste management program should be designed to include several monitoring points. These could be inspection reports, incident reports, monthly summaries, and disposal site visits. The wastes should be analyzed periodically to make sure their character does not change. This monitoring system is useless, however, if no provision is made for feedback. Inspection reports must be read, not just filed. Comments, notes, and reports that indicate budding problems should be acted upon, not just noted. The plant with an effective monitoring and feedback system already has the foundation for effective communication.

Personnel Training. The RCRA regulations specifically require training for all "handlers" of hazardous waste. This regulation is the minimum necessary to meet the definition of good management practices. "Nonhandlers" such as maintenance workers, contractors, foremen, and staff need to be informed as well. An effective program shows signs of these "awareness" sessions in addition to training programs.

Effect on the Environment. In some respects, the effect a plant has on the environment is the only appropriate criterion for judgment. The fact that it complies with the "letter of the law" is meaningless if its operations degrade. Any degradation is a liability that should be addressed. Good housekeeping, "destructive" disposal techniques, and proper handling procedures all help limit this exposure.

Contingency Efforts. All plants experience emergencies at one time or another. The program's efforts to plan for these emergencies determines their effect. The plant and its facilities should be constructed to minimize the effects of leaks or spills. When it is impossible to "engineer" for this purpose, procedures and arrangements should be made to limit their occurrence and effect. Many companies have all capital appropriation requests reviewed by their environmental department to be sure this important area is not overlooked on retrofits or new construction. In some cases, the fire and safety departments should also have input. Contingency efforts should extend to the point of arranging for alternate disposal options for each major waste stream.

REGULATORY BACKGROUND

The major regulatory standards regarding waste management practices are largely a result of passage of the Resource Conservation and Recovery Act in 1976 (RCRA). In it, Congress recognized that the continued growth and progress of the United States had created a waste disposal problem worthy of attention at the national level. Congress directed the United States Environmental Protection Agency (EPA) to promulgate the regulations necessary for the proper management of both solid and hazardous waste. Since that time most states have promulgated similar rules regarding waste management. Subtitle D, concerning solid waste management, essentially encourages state and regional governments to promote the proper disposal of solid, nonhazardous waste. It specifically prohibits the use of "open dumps" and provides for the eventual closure or upgrading of all such sites. The specific regulatory requirements for an individual plant are embodied in state regulations. Because each program is unique, the treatment of solid, nonhazardous waste in this chapter will be limited to general discussion and guidance.

The greatest interest and concern associated with RCRA lies with Subtitle C, entitled "Hazardous Waste Management." Here, Congress gave EPA specific directions to write regulations to identify, store, treat, transport, and dispose of hazardous waste properly. In this area, most state agencies have closely modeled EPA efforts. In fact, specific provisions exist in the law requiring each state program to be substantially equivalent to EPA's. Owing to this requirement, some assurances exist that program similarities will remain for some time. The law does provide, however, that individual state programs may be more strict than EPA's. For this reason, a review of state requirements is in order during the pre-audit preparation stage. Several states (e.g., California, New Jersey, and Texas) are already significantly more stringent than EPA. The differences can be as basic as the definition of hazardous waste itself. Some states (e.g., California) go so far as to ban altogether the land disposal of certain very hazardous wastes.

In order to implement the various requirements stipulated by Congress in Subtitle C of RCRA, the EPA promulgated a body of regulations in Title 40 of the Code of Federal Regulations. The major subdivisions are listed in Table 5-1. The majority of these rules were

Table 5-1. Federal Hazardous Waste Management Regulations.

CITE	TITLE
40 CFR 260	Hazardous Waste Management System: General
40 CFR 261	Identification and Listing of Hazardous Waste
40 CFR 262	Standards Applicable to Generators of Hazardous Waste
40 CFR 263	Standards Applicable to Transporters of Hazardous Waste
40 CFR 264	Standards of Owners and Operators of Hazardous Waste Treatment, Storage and Disposal Facilities
40 CFR 265	Interim Status Standards for Owners and Operators of Hazardous Waste Treatment, Storage and Disposal Facilities
40 CFR 267	Interim Standards for Owners and Operators of New Hazardous Waste Land Disposal Facilities
40 CFR 270	Permit Requirements

Table 5-2. Major *Federal Register* Publications Implementing RCRA Regulations.

DATE	FEDERAL REGISTER CITE	DESCRIPTION
5/19/80	45 FR 33066	Parts 260-263 and 265, general provisions of 264 and Parts 122-124
7/16/80	45 FR 47832	Additional wastes listed in 261
1/12/81	46 FR 2804	Parts 264 and 122, standards for storage and treatment facilities; and Parts 264, 265 and 122, standards for closure, postclosure care and financial responsibility
1/23/81	46 FR 7666	Parts 264 and 122, standards for incinerators
2/13/81	46 FR 12414	Part 267, interim permitting standards for four classes of new land disposal facilities
7/26/82	47 FR 32274	Part 264, standards for land disposal facilities; also changes in Parts 260, 265, 122, and 123

published in the *Federal Register* on May 19, 1980. Additional major provisions were published in five separate issues of the *Federal Register* up to July 26, 1982. Table 5-2 lists these publications. It is often beneficial to refer to the original *Federal Register* notices in cases where interpretation of a specific rule is necessary because they usually contain a preamble outlining the agency's original intentions and thoughts. Although the preamble does not have the authority associated with regulation, it often supplies meaningful insight into the rule-making process.

FEDERAL HAZARDOUS WASTE REGULATIONS

Part 260—General

Section 260.10 contains the definitions of major terms used throughout the remaining rules. A common mistake in interpreting environmental rules is to be ignorant of regulatory definitions. Commonsense or dictionary meanings of terms should not be used in evaluating compliance. The exact regulatory meaning is the standard by which each facility will be judged. For example, it would be impossible to know without referring to the definition section that the term "sludge" as used in the regulations includes any waste generated from a wastewater treatment plant exclusive of the effluent.

Section 260.20 contains the procedures to be used by any party in filing a rule-making petition. Of primary significance are the specific provisions for equivalent test methods and the delisting of a particular hazardous waste. The EPA publication entitled "Test Methods for the Evaluation of Solid Waste: Physical/Chemical Methods" (Publication No. SW846) specifies the exact analytical methods generators must use to evaluate their wastes. If, for any reason, a generator believes an alternate method is available and wishes to use it in lieu of the "official" test, he must first petition the agency for equivalency. These petitions must demonstrate that the alternate method is equal or superior to the corresponding method in terms of sensitivity, accuracy, and precision. If the auditor determines that the facility has used analytical or testing methods different from those in SW846, he must then determine whether an "equivalency petition" has been filed and approved. If not, the generator's determination is technically noncompliant, and the auditor should so note it in his report.

A "delisting" petition is an effort by a generator to prove to the agency that a particular "listed" waste generated at his facility is not hazardous. If the determination is correct and approved, significant savings in disposal costs and/or permitting requirements can be realized. Section 260.22 details the exact information requirements and steps necessary to file such a petition. The environmental auditor is not in a position to evaluate the delisting petition filed for compliance with 260.22. This determination rests solely with the agency, and the results of their review should be noted. The auditor can, however, recommend that a facility evaluate its listed hazardous wastes for delisting potential. It is important to note that the approval of a federal delisting petition may not be recognized under individual state rules. In any case where a facility has filed under the federal program, the auditor must determine if a similar filing is necessary under the individual state rules. Similarly, a state-approved delisting petition only has the authority of law in that specific state. Interstate management of a particular waste may require delisting petitions from each state agency as well as the EPA.

Part 260 also contains a potentially useful appendix, entitled "Overview of Subtitle C Regulations." This appendix is a step-by-step procedure any generator can use to determine if his activities are regulated under RCRA, and, if so, under what sections. The auditor may find this appendix particularly helpful for facility contacts unfamiliar with hazardous waste rules. Included here, as Figures 5-1 through 5-4, are the block diagrams contained in that appendix.

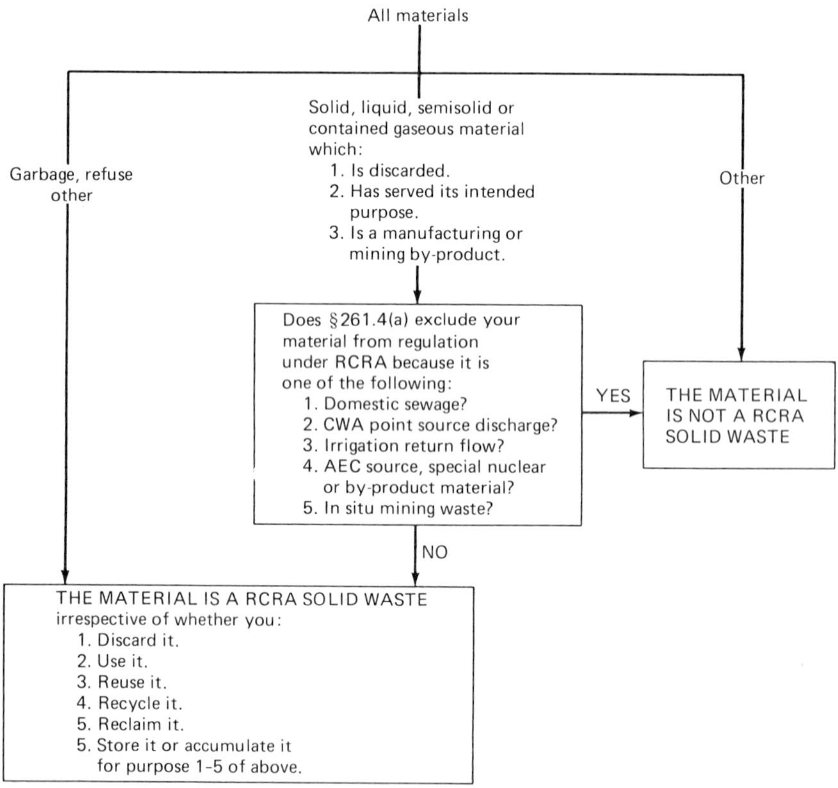

Figure 5-1. Definition of a solid waste.

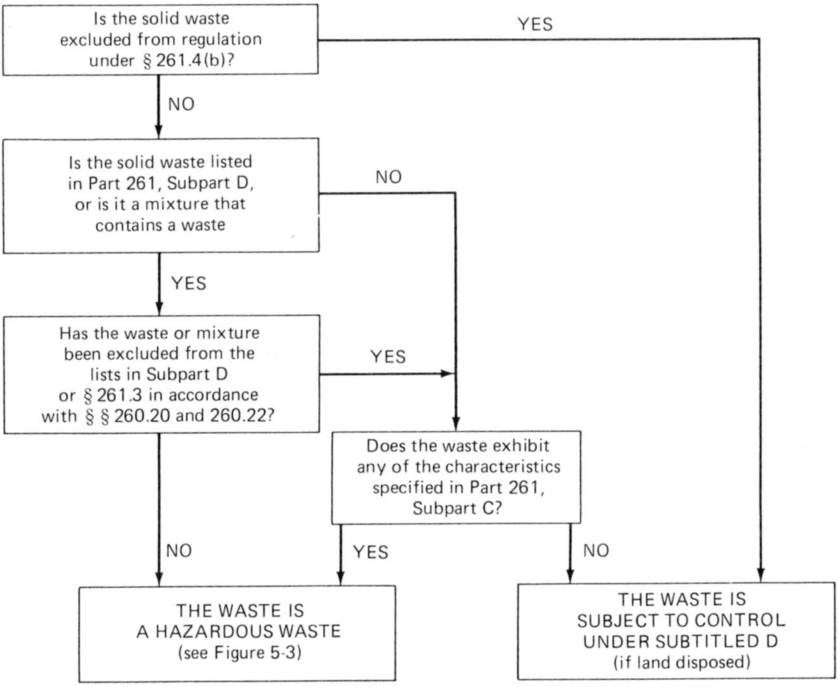

Figure 5-2. Definition of a hazardous waste.

Part 261—Identification and Listing of Hazardous Waste

The heart of any hazardous waste management program is the criteria used to define which wastes are hazardous. This determination specifies exactly which wastes that a facility generates or handles are subject to regulation. Because this is a critical step in determining compliance, it is important for the auditor to be familiar with these rules. A waste is considered hazardous only if it meets the definition contained in this section. A particular company or facility may voluntarily choose to manage a particular material very carefully (as if it were a hazardous waste), but this in no way causes the material to be a hazardous waste in the regulatory sense. It is important for the auditor to keep this distinction in mind so that regulatory standards are not needlessly applied to unregulated materials or activities.

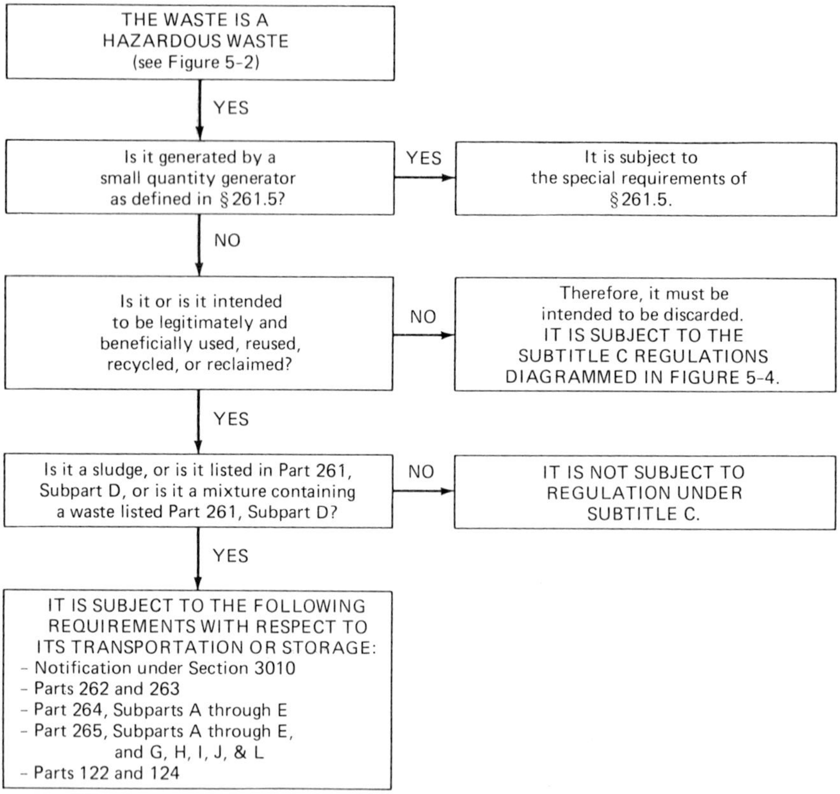

Figure 5-3. Special provisions for certain hazardous wastes.

Part 261, which identifies and lists the materials subject to hazardous waste regulation, is divided into four subparts:

A—General
B—Criteria for Identifying the Characteristics of Hazardous Waste and for Testing Hazardous Wastes
C—Characteristics of Hazardous Wastes
D—Lists of Hazardous Wastes

Also included in 261 are several appendixes that detail specific sampling, testing, and analytical methods. Part 261 is the focal point of the hazardous waste management system.

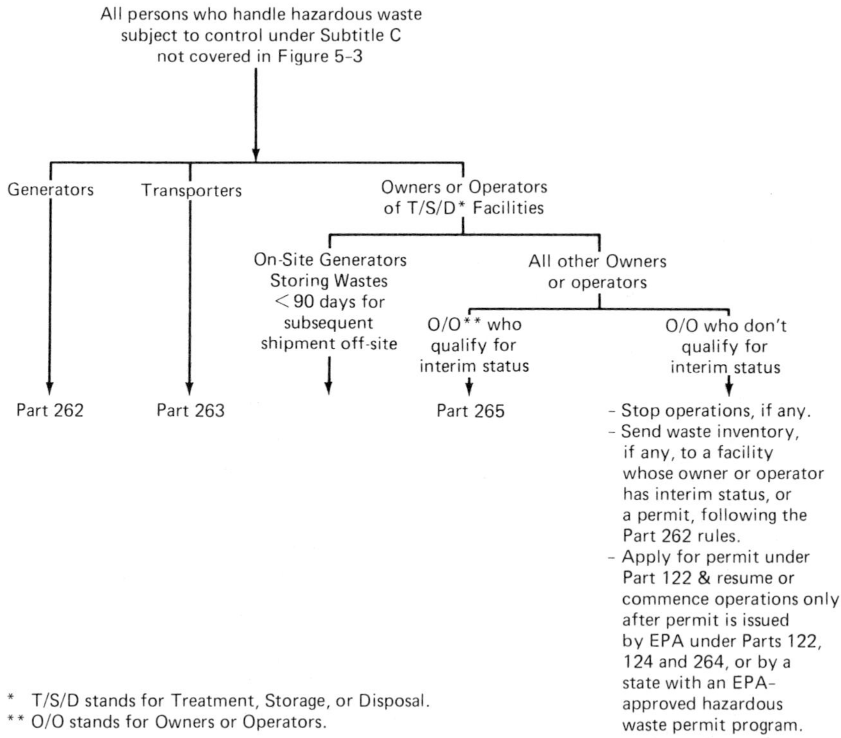

Figure 5–4. Regulations for hazardous waste not covered in Figure 5–3.

Subpart A. In order to determine whether a particular waste is hazardous under RCRA, a generator must first determine if it meets the definition of solid waste. For the most part, any material that has served its originally intended use and is sometimes discarded is considered a solid waste. The term "solid waste" includes solids, liquids, semisolids, and contained gaseous materials. Most materials that are discarded meet the definition of solid waste. Figure 5–1 is a graphic representation of this determination.

After determining that a particular material is a solid waste, the generator must refer to 261.3 to determine if it meets the definition of hazardous waste. In general, a solid waste is hazardous if it exhibits any of the criteria in Subpart C, if it is specifically listed in Subpart D, or if it is a mixture of solid and hazardous waste. If the mixture is composed of "criteria" hazardous waste (Subpart C) and solid waste, and it no longer exhibits any criterion of hazardous waste, it can be considered nonhazardous. However, a mixture of a "listed" hazardous waste (Subpart D) and a solid waste remains a hazardous waste regardless of test results. If the mixture consists of wastewater subject to Clean Water Act requirements and several listed solvents or chemical products, certain exclusions exist (261.3(iv)). If the facility that is subject to the audit relies on one of these exclusions, the auditor should note this and determine if their interpretation is correct. Such facilities should have proper documentation on file to prove compliance with the requirements.

Section 261.3 defines when a solid waste becomes a hazardous waste and hence subject to regulation. In some cases, this determination is important because a facility may not be properly managing the material soon enough in its generation-to-disposal cycle. This section also stipulates that any solid waste generated from the storage, treatment, or disposal of a hazardous waste is also a hazardous waste. This provision is frequently ignored in plants that have waste management facilities.

Section 261.4 details several materials specifically excluded from the definition of solid waste or hazardous waste. Examples include mixtures of domestic sewage and other wastes that pass through a publicly owned treatment works. These are not considered solid wastes and hence cannot be hazardous. However, this exclusion only applies to the actual discharge; it does not apply to wastewater mixtures being stored, collected, or treated prior to discharge. This exclusion is frequently misunderstood, and a close review of the regulations is in order for cases in which it is relied upon.

Fly ash, bottom ash, slag, and emission control solids generated from the combustion of fossil fuels are excluded as hazardous wastes. For industrial plants with large boilers or powerhouses, this exclusion can be important. Wastes that are hazardous solely because they fail the test for chromium have a specific exclusion available if the process generating it exclusively uses trivalent chromium. This exclusion may be important for leather tanneries and finishing facilities. Once again, facilities relying on the exclusion should have proper documentation. Many state agencies have not adopted this chromium exclusion.

Also excluded under 261.4 as hazardous wastes are the following materials:

- Mining wastes.
- Cement kiln dust waste.
- Certain wood wastes that fail the characteristic for arsenic.
- Certain sludges from TiO_2 manufacture.
- Drilling fluids, produced waters, and other wastes from the exploration and production of oil, natural gas, or geothermal energy.

Section 261.4 also exempts wastes generated in product or raw material storage tanks or other non-waste-treatment manufacturing units until they are removed from the unit. In addition, samples that are collected for the purpose of testing to determine a material's characteristics or composition are excluded from regulation. This exemption does not relieve the generator from complying with Department of Transportation or U.S. Postal Service regulations.

Subpart A contains the requirements for small-quantity generators of hazardous waste. Although this section is the agency's attempt to minimize the effect of federal regulation on small businesses, its real utility is very limited. Many state agencies have not adopted a small-quantity generator exclusion in their regulations. In other states, the "threshold" of hazardous waste generation is only 100 kg/mo. rather than the EPA's 1000 kg/mo. In addition, there is considerable public pressure on the EPA to lower its threshold also. For certain wastes, the threshold level is as low as 1 kg/mo. under current regulations. Because this exclusion is so limited, it is important for the auditor to examine facilities relying on it in detail. The first step in this process is to review the applicable state regulations to determine if such an exclusion exists in the first place.

Section 261.7, entitled "Residues of Hazardous Waste in Empty Containers," outlines a specific exclusion that is important for virtually all industrial plants. During the plant tour the auditor will become aware of the facility's purchase, use, and disposition of drummed (or similarly contained) materials. If the plant is cognizant of the exclusion in 261.7, the proper management of the resulting "empties" can be simplified, making it unnecessary to accumulate large numbers in a plant "bone yard" for lack of a suitable disposal alternative. The presence of bone yards at a plant should warn the auditor to examine the facility in greater depth. The "empties" rule provides that any container (or inner liner from a container) that held hazardous waste is a hazardous waste unless it meets the definition of empty. This rule provides significant motivation to manage all containers so that only "empties" are generated. Table 5-3 summarizes the criteria various containers must meet to be considered empty.

In evaluating a facility's ability to manage its empty containers effectively, the auditor should keep several important points in mind:

- A container that is empty by EPA definition might still be regulated by the Department of Transportation (DOT). Any over-the-road transportation of containers ("empties" or not) should be reviewed for compliance with DOT marking, placardings, or other requirements.
- Given a choice, the preferred method of managing containers is to return them to the original supplier for reuse or refill under contract.
- If the supplier will not take "empties," the plant could consider triple-rinsing them. This process is straightforward for certain chemicals such as cooling water additives where the rinsate (a hazardous waste) can be managed by using it in the cooling water system.
- For containers in which the residue is more difficult to rinse (e.g., an adhesive), the plant may want to set up a drum dumping station for transferring as much product as possible from the old drum into the next full drum for use.
- For containers in which the residue cannot be reused at all, the plant may contact suppliers to request that an inner liner be added to the packaging. It is usually much easier to accumulate contaminated inner liners for eventual disposal than empty drums.
- Commercial drum reconditioning services should be monitored closely. The drums must be "empty" prior to shipment (unless the firm is a licensed and permitted hazardous waste treatment facility). In addition, the drums should have all markings and references to the original plant removed. *Note:* DOT regulations may require that certain markings remain. It is not uncommon for reconditioners to have an enormous inventory of drums on site which could reflect poorly on the original plant.

Subpart B. Subpart B of Part 261 lists the criteria that EPA will use to establish new characteristics for determining hazardous waste and the criteria to be used for listing additional wastes. Many firms have

Table 5-3. Criteria for Empty Containers/Inner Liners, 40 CFR 261.7.

WASTE	CAPACITY	CRITERIA
If the container or inner liner was used to hold . . .	and has the following capacity . . .	then it must meet these criteria to be considered empty . . .
Commercial chemical products (see 261.33 (e) and (f) for lists)	Any size	1) It has been triple-rinsed with appropriate solvent(s), *or,* 2) It has been cleaned with an equally effective method, *or,* 3) For containers only, the inner liner has been removed.
Compressed gases	Any size	1) Pressure in container approaches atmospheric.
Any other hazardous waste	≤ 110 gallons	1) All wastes are removed using common methods such as: pumping, pouring or aspirating, *and,* 2) No more than one inch of residue remains, *or,* 3) No more than 3% (by weight) of the total capacity remains.
Any other hazardous waste	> 110 gallons	1) All wastes are removed using common methods such as pumping, pouring, or aspirating, *and,* 2) No more than one inch of residue remains, *or,* 3) No more than 0.3% of the total capacity remains.

mistakenly used Subpart B to make hazard determinations. Similarly, firms have looked to Appendix VIII (list of toxic constituents) for the same reason. In both cases, companies may be needlessly complicating their operations. Although firms may voluntarily manage specific materials carefully (including recordkeeping and proper disposal) as a risk management action, it should be recognized as a conscious liability-limiting activity, not a legal requirement.

EPA originally proposed including the characteristics of radioactivity and infectiousness as hazardous characteristics. Through public and industry comment, it was found that reliable test methods were not yet available for these criteria. In addition, radioactive materials may already be adequately regulated by the Nuclear Regulatory Commission. EPA does anticipate eventually regulating these wastes, and the auditor should pay particular attention to wastes that could meet these descriptions, including a note concerning possible future regulations in the audit report.

Subpart C. This section describes the four characteristics currently used by the agency to determine the hazardous class of a waste. Additionally it prescribes the use of certain sampling and analytical methods and gives each waste a unique EPA identification number. The specified characteristics are ignitability, corrosivity, reactivity, and extraction procedure toxicity (EP toxicity).

Ignitability. A solid waste is "ignitable" if it exhibits any of the following properties:

- For liquids, it has a flash point less than 140°F.
- For nonliquids, it is capable of causing fires through friction, absorption of water, or spontaneous chemical changes under standard conditions.
- For gases, it is an ignitable compressed gas as described in DOT regulation 49 CFR 173.300.
- It is an oxidizer as described in DOT regulation 173.151.

Corrosivity. A solid waste is corrosive if it exhibits either of the following properties:

- It is aqueous and has a pH less than or equal to 2.0 or greater than or equal to 12.5.
- It is a liquid and corrodes steel at a rate greater than 0.250 inch per year.

Reactivity. A solid waste is reactive if it exhibits any of the following properties:

- It is normally unstable.
- It forms potentially explosive mixtures with water.
- It reacts violently with water.

- It generates toxic gases, vapors, or fumes when mixed with water.
- It is a cyanide- or sulfide-bearing waste that, when exposed to a pH between 2 and 12.5, can generate toxic gases, vapors, or fumes.
- It is capable of detonation or an explosive reaction.
- It is a forbidden explosive, Class A explosive, or Class B explosive as defined in DOT regulations.

EP Toxicity. A solid waste is EP-toxic if the "leachate" from the waste contains any contaminant listed in Table 5-4 at a concentration greater than specified. The "leachate" from the solid waste sample is generated in a specific test method outlined in regulations. EPA is considering revising the list in Table 5-4 to replace total chromium concentration with hexavalent chromium as the determining contaminant. Many state agencies may not adopt this change.

Subpart D. Another means of determining whether a solid waste is hazardous is by reference to the lists of wastes promulgated by EPA in Subpart D. The wastes in this section are organized into four separate lists:

Table 5-4. Maximum Concentration of Contaminants for Characteristic of EP Toxicity.

CONTAMINANT	MAXIMUM CONCENTRATION (MILLIGRAMS PER LITER)
Arsenic	5.0
Barium	100.0
Cadmium	1.0
Chromium	5.0
Lead	5.0
Mercury	0.2
Selenium	1.0
Silver	5.0
Endrin	0.02
Lindane	0.4
Methoxychlor	10.0
Toxaphene	0.5
2,4-D	10.0
2,4,5-TP Silvex	1.0

261.31. Hazardous Waste from Non-Specific Sources. This list contains approximately 13 wastes that could be generated by any number of industrial facilities. The list is not industry-specific and includes many spent solvents and cleaning solutions.

261.32 Hazardous Waste from Specific Sources. This list contains approximately 80 waste streams that are generated by certain industrial processes. The list covers 24 different industry classes from wood preservation to petroleum refining.

261.33(e) Acutely Hazardous Commercial Chemical Products. This list contains approximately 120 different chemical products that, if discarded, must be considered acutely hazardous. The list is not industry-specific.

261.33(f) Hazardous Commercial Chemical Products. This list contains approximately 240 chemical products that if discarded must be considered hazardous. The list is not industry-specific.

Each waste on these lists has its own unique EPA Hazardous Waste Number. These numbers appear in each table and must be used to identify the waste on all recordkeeping, reporting, and manifests required by the regulations. Mixtures of "listed" hazardous wastes and other solid wastes are defined as hazardous by the regulations; therefore, segregation of listed wastes from other plant wastes is advisable. For certain listed wastes, the corresponding small-quantity generator exclusion levels are significantly lower than 1000 kg/mo. Perhaps the largest area of potential misinterpretation concerning listed wastes occurs within the commercial chemical products lists (261.33(e) and (f)). These lists are intended to regulate the disposal of hazardous chemical products and do not refer to process wastes that may contain contaminants appearing on these lists. It is important to make this distinction so that relatively innocuous process wastes are not needlessly managed as if they were pure chemicals.

Part 262—Standards Applicable to Generators of Hazardous Waste

Part 262 of the RCRA regulations contains standards that all generators of hazardous waste must meet. For the most part these requirements are straightforward and easy to understand. In summary, all waste generators are required to:

• Determine whether the wastes they generate are in fact hazardous by EPA definition. The determination can be made by either testing the waste or applying the generator's knowledge of the process and materials that generated the waste.

• Apply for and obtain an EPA Identification Number prior to storing, treating, transporting, or disposing of hazardous waste. This number is a facility identification number that permits the agency to identify all generators and facilities in the country. It is received by filing a Notification of Hazardous Waste Activity form with EPA (Figure 5-5).

• Use only transporters, treatment, storage, and disposal facilities that have EPA hazardous waste identification numbers.

• Initiate hazardous waste manifests for all off-site shipments of hazardous waste. The information contained on the manifest must comply with certain requirements (262.21) and include sufficient copies so that each party will receive a signed manifest. Special requirements apply to rail or water shipments.

• Properly package, label, mark, and placard all shipments of hazardous waste according to DOT regulations. In addition to DOT requirements, all containers of less than 110 gallons must be marked with the information below:

> HAZARDOUS WASTE—Federal Law Prohibits improper Disposal.
> If found, contact the nearest police or public safety authority or the U.S. Environmental Protection Agency.
> Generator's Name and Address ______________________________
> ____
> Manifest Document Number ________________________________

• Obtain a storage permit if hazardous wastes are accumulated on-site for greater than 90 days. *Note:* Even generators who accumulate for less than 90 days are required to meet certain facility standards such as contingency plans, inspections, and arrangements with local authorities. In addition, the date on which accumulation began must be clearly marked on each container.

• Generate and maintain certain records (for a period of three years) regarding hazardous waste. Included among these are copies of:

Please print or type with ELITE type *(12 characters/inch)* in the unshaded areas only.

Form Approved OMB No. 158-S79016
GSA No. 0246-EPA-OT

EPA

U.S. ENVIRONMENTAL PROTECTION AGENCY

NOTIFICATION OF HAZARDOUS WASTE ACTIVITY

INSTALLATION'S EPA I.D. NO.

NAME OF INSTALLATION

II. INSTALLATION MAILING ADDRESS

III. LOCATION OF INSTALLATION

PLEASE PLACE LABEL IN THIS SPACE

INSTRUCTIONS: If you received a preprinted label, affix it in the space at left. If any of the information on the label is incorrect, draw a line through it and supply the correct information in the appropriate section below. If the label is complete and correct, leave Items I, II, and III below blank. If you did not receive a preprinted label, complete all items. "Installation" means a single site where hazardous waste is generated, treated, stored and/or disposed of, or a transporter's principal place of business. Please refer to the INSTRUCTIONS FOR FILING NOTIFICATION before completing this form. The information requested herein is required by law *(Section 3010 of the Resource Conservation and Recovery Act).*

DETACH

FOR OFFICIAL USE ONLY

COMMENTS

C C 15 16 55

INSTALLATION'S EPA I.D. NUMBER | APPROVED | DATE RECEIVED *(yr., mo., & day)*

F T/A C 1 — 1 2 13 14 15 16 17 22

I. NAME OF INSTALLATION

30 67

II. INSTALLATION MAILING ADDRESS

STREET OR P.O. BOX

C 3 15 16 45

CITY OR TOWN | ST. | ZIP CODE

C 4 15 16 40 41 42 47 51

III. LOCATION OF INSTALLATION

STREET OR ROUTE NUMBER

C 5 15 16 45

CITY OR TOWN | ST. | ZIP CODE

C 6 15 16 40 41 42 47 51

IV. INSTALLATION CONTACT

NAME AND TITLE *(last, first, & job title)* | PHONE NO. *(area code & no.)*

C 2 15 16 45 46 48 49 51 52 55

V. OWNERSHIP

A. NAME OF INSTALLATION'S LEGAL OWNER

C 8 15 16 55

DETACH

B. TYPE OF OWNERSHIP *(enter the appropriate letter into box)*

F = FEDERAL
M = NON–FEDERAL

56

VI. TYPE OF HAZARDOUS WASTE ACTIVITY *(enter "X" in the appropriate box(es))*

☐ A. GENERATION (57)
☐ B. TRANSPORTATION *(complete item VII)* (58)
☐ C. TREAT/STORE/DISPOSE (59)
☐ D. UNDERGROUND INJECTION (60)

VII. MODE OF TRANSPORTATION *(transporters only – enter "X" in the appropriate box(es))*

☐ A. AIR (61) ☐ B. RAIL (62) ☐ C. HIGHWAY (63) ☐ D. WATER (64) ☐ E. OTHER *(specify):* (65)

VIII. FIRST OR SUBSEQUENT NOTIFICATION

Mark "X" in the appropriate box to indicate whether this is your installation's first notification of hazardous waste activity or a subsequent notification. If this is not your first notification, enter your Installation's EPA I.D. Number in the space provided below.

☐ A. FIRST NOTIFICATION ☐ B. SUBSEQUENT NOTIFICATION *(complete item C)*

C. INSTALLATION'S EPA I.D. NO.

IX. DESCRIPTION OF HAZARDOUS WASTES

Please go to the reverse of this form and provide the requested information.

EPA Form 8700-12 (6-80) CONTINUE ON REVERSE

Figure 5-5. Notification of Hazardous Waste Activity: EPA Form 8700-12.

I.D. – FOR OFFICIAL USE ONLY

S W | | T/A C 1

IX. DESCRIPTION OF HAZARDOUS WASTES *(continued from front)*

A. HAZARDOUS WASTES FROM NON–SPECIFIC SOURCES. Enter the four–digit number from 40 CFR Part 261.31 for each listed hazardous waste from non–specific sources your installation handles. Use additional sheets if necessary.

1	2	3	4	5	6
7	8	9	10	11	12

B. HAZARDOUS WASTES FROM SPECIFIC SOURCES. Enter the four–digit number from 40 CFR Part 261.32 for each listed hazardous waste from specific industrial sources your installation handles. Use additional sheets if necessary.

13	14	15	16	17	18
19	20	21	22	23	24
25	26	27	28	29	30

C. COMMERCIAL CHEMICAL PRODUCT HAZARDOUS WASTES. Enter the four–digit number from 40 CFR Part 261.33 for each chemical substance your installation handles which may be a hazardous waste. Use additional sheets if necessary.

31	32	33	34	35	36
37	38	39	40	41	42
43	44	45	46	47	48

D. LISTED INFECTIOUS WASTES. Enter the four–digit number from 40 CFR Part 261.34 for each listed hazardous waste from hospitals, veterinary hospitals, medical and research laboratories your installation handles. Use additional sheets if necessary.

49	50	51	52	53	54

E. CHARACTERISTICS OF NON–LISTED HAZARDOUS WASTES. Mark "X" in the boxes corresponding to the characteristics of non–listed hazardous wastes your installation handles. *(See 40 CFR Parts 261.21 – 261.24.)*

☐ 1. IGNITABLE (D001) ☐ 2. CORROSIVE (D002) ☐ 3. REACTIVE (D003) ☐ 4. TOXIC (D000)

DETACH

X. CERTIFICATION

I certify under penalty of law that I have personally examined and am familiar with the information submitted in this and all attached documents, and that based on my inquiry of those individuals immediately responsible for obtaining the information, I believe that the submitted information is true, accurate, and complete. I am aware that there are significant penalties for submitting false information, including the possibility of fine and imprisonment.

SIGNATURE	NAME & OFFICIAL TITLE *(type or print)*	DATE SIGNED

EPA Form 8700-12 (6-80) REVERSE

DETACH

Figure 5-5. *(Continued)*

- All manifests
- Biennial reports
- Waste analysis reports
- Exception reports

Part 263—Standards Applicable to Transporters of Hazardous Waste

It is important to understand Part 263 rules so that the auditor may determine if the plant is using a permitted transporter for removing its hazardous waste. In summary, a transporter of hazardous waste must:

- Obtain an EPA Identification Number similar to that required of generators.
- Comply with the manifest system for each shipment of hazardous waste. In general, transporters may not accept shipments of hazardous waste unless they are accompanied by a manifest.
- Deliver the entire shipment to the facility designated by the generator. If unable to do so, he must contact the generator for additional instructions or return the shipment.
- Maintain certain records such as manifests and shipping papers for a period of three years.
- Take immediate response action in the event of a discharge of hazardous waste during transportation. Such actions must include:

  - Immediate notification to the National Response Center (if required) by DOT regulation 49 CFR 171.15.
  - A written report to DOT according to 49 CFR 171.15.
  - Cleanup of any hazardous waste discharged, or other such actions as specified by federal, state, or local authorities.

Transporters who operate transfer facilities for hazardous waste may also be required to receive a storage facility permit under 263.12. A permit is required if the waste is kept at the transfer facility for more than ten days.

The federal permitting standards for transporters of hazardous waste are the minimum standards that must be met. In many cases, state agencies have required additional permitting and licensing for these firms, which may include a bonding and insurance requirement. If the facility to be audited transports hazardous waste itself, the auditor must be aware of any additional requirements. In any event, assurances must be received that the transporters used by the plant are properly licensed and permitted according to both federal and state provisions.

Parts 264, 265, 266, 267—Standards Applicable to Owners and Operators of Hazardous Waste Treatment, Storage, and Disposal Facilities (TSDFs)

Several parts of the RCRA regulations contain the standards to be met by all facilities that store, treat, or dispose of hazardous waste. Although the specific technical and administrative requirements are very similar among the various parts, each part is applicable to a certain class of facilities. This applicability is summarized as follows:

- Part 264: applies to all treatment, storage, and disposal facilities that have received a *final* permit from the agency.
- Part 265: applies to all TSDFs that are operating under *interim status. Note:* Congress in Section 3005(e) of RCRA permitted the continued operation of "existing" TSDFs until EPA issues or denies a final permit. Part 265 contains the conditions interim status facilities must meet to continue operating.
- Part 266 (proposed). On November 17, 1980, the EPA proposed establishing specific standards applicable to certain wastes and certain types of waste management facilities. Currently the proposal covers only elementary neutralization units and wastewater treatment units. Although still in the proposal stage, these regulations can give meaningful insight to generators with such units. A facility auditor may likewise find them useful as a guide to the effective management of such units.
- Part 267 (expired). On February 13, 1981, the EPA established interim standards for new hazardous waste land disposal facilities. These standards applied only to facilities that were yet to be constructed, and in fact expired on February 13, 1983. These standards have limited applicability for environmental audits.

As Parts 266 and 267 have limited applicability for auditing purposes, the remaining discussion of TSDF standards will focus on Parts 264 and 265. Taken together, these portions of the RCRA regulations encompass approximately three hundred pages of federal standards. Because of the sheer volume of detailed requirements that must be evaluated, the auditor is forced to adopt a checklist format in order to review the facility. For the most part, the majority of standards in Parts 264 and 265 are identical. This is particularly true for the administration and record-keeping requirements. Because the majority of TSD facilities in the United States are operating under interim status (Part 265), those standards will be addressed in detail.

Subpart A—General. This section of the Part 265 regulations outlines its purpose, scope, and applicability. More important, 265.1(c) lists 13 activities that do not require compliance with Part 265:

1. The disposal of hazardous waste by means of ocean disposal subject to a permit under the Marine Protection, Research and Sanctuaries Act.
2. The disposal of hazardous waste by means of underground injection subject to a permit under the Underground Injection Control Program.
3. The treatment, storage, or disposal of hazardous waste by a Publicly Owned Treatment Works (POTW). *Note:* Certain sections of Part 264 may apply under the permit-by-rule provisions of Part 270.
4. The treatment, storage, or disposal of hazardous waste in states with approved programs. *Note:* In these cases the states' rules apply.
5. Permitted, licensed, or registered facilities for the management of municipal or industial solid waste, provided any hazardous wastes received are excluded under 261.5.
6. The recovery or recycle of hazardous waste as specified in 261.6(a).
7. Generators accumulating hazardous wastes on site pursuant to 262.34.

8. Farmers disposing of waste pesticides in compliance with 262.51.
9. Totally Enclosed Treatment facilities as defined in 260.10.
10. Elementary neutralization units as defined in 260.10.
11. Activities taken in immediate response to a spill situation.
12. The storage of hazardous waste by a transporter at a transfer facility in DOT-approved containers for ten days or less.
13. The addition of absorbent material to a waste in a container, provided it occurs when the waste is first introduced to the container. *Note:* Sections 265.17(b), 265.171, and 265.172 still apply.

Subpart B—General Facility Standards. Subpart B of Part 265 outlines seven general facility standards that apply to all facilities that store, treat, or dispose of hazardous waste.

- 265.11: Every facility must have an EPA identification number in accordance with the EPA notification procedures that appeared in the *Federal Register,* 45 FR 12746.
- 265.12: (a) Receipt of hazardous waste from a foreign source must not occur without prior written notice given to the agency at least four weeks in advance.
  (b) Before transferring ownership or operation of a facility, the existing owner or operator must inform the new party of the requirements contained in Part 265 in writing.
- 265.13: Before accepting any hazardous waste for storage, treatment, or disposal, a facility must conduct analysis sufficient to manage the waste properly. In addition, the facility must:
  - Repeat this analysis often enough to ensure that it is accurate.
  - Inspect (and analyze, if necessary) every shipment of hazardous waste to ensure that it meets the description.
  - Prepare and follow a written waste analysis plan that specifies the parameters, test methods, and sampling methods to be used.
- 265.14: Facilities must prevent access and unauthorized entry to the active portions of the facility unless contact with the waste or

the facility poses no harm to the public. In addition all facilities must have:

- A 24-hour surveillance system.
- An artificial or natural barrier.
- Controlled entry.
- Signs with the legend "Danger . . . Unauthorized Personnel Keep Out."

- 265.15: Facilities must be regularly inspected for signs of malfunction, deterioration, errors, or discharges that may cause release of hazardous waste or threats to human health. In addition, the facility must follow a written inspection plan specifying the equipment and areas to be inspected, their frequency, the types of problems to look for, and corrective actions to be taken. Inspections and results must be recorded in a log maintained for this purpose.
- 265.16: Facility personnel must successfully complete a program of classroom or on-the-job training that teaches them to perform their duties to ensure compliance with the regulations. The program must be taught by a person trained in hazardous waste management. The program must familiarize all personnel with emergency response procedures, equipment, and systems. Employees must be trained within six months of employment and must participate in annual reviews. The following training-related records must be kept at the facility:
    - Job titles for each position and the names of each employee.
    - Job descriptions.
    - Written description of the training to be given to each employee.
    - Records to document that training has been given.
- 265.17: Facilities that manage ignitable or reactive hazardous wastes must take precautions to prevent their accidental ignition or reaction. These precautions can include protection from sources of ignition and restrictions on smoking, welding, and other "hot work." "No Smoking" signs must be conspicuously placed wherever there is a hazard.

Several notes apply to the subject of employee training for audit purposes. EPA does not define the qualifications necessary for the training director. As a result, wide variations exist in the experience, background, and training such "teachers" have. It is difficult for an auditor to pass judgment on the qualifications of the training director without better guidelines from the agency. EPA has made it very clear that on compliance inspections, the documentation required under training will receive significant attention. In order to best prepare for inspections, all such records should be organized in a central location. It is recommended that a training record be prepared for each employee at the facility, detailing each session attended and completed. An example appears in Figure 5-6. Similarly, attendance sheets for every training session given should be maintained (Figure 5-7). As further guidance on the subject of employee hazardous waste training, EPA published a draft Training Manual in September 1980. This publication (SW-915) should be recommended to any plant environmental coordinator who is unsure of this requirement.

Subpart C—Preparedness and Prevention. Subpart C applies to all hazardous waste management facilities and requires that they be operated and maintained to minimize the possibility of fire, explosion, or other releases. It requires all facilities to have internal communications or alarm systems, equipment capable of summoning emergency assistance such as fire and police, portable fire extinguishers and control equipment, and water at adequate volume and pressure. All emergency equipment must be inspected and maintained regularly. Facility personnel must always have immediate access to communication equipment whenever hazardous waste is being handled. Adequate aisle space must be maintained so that emergency equipment and personnel have unobstructed access to the facility. Subpart C also requires all facilities to enter into arrangements with local emergency response authorities appropriate for the type of waste handled at the facility. Such authorities can include local fire companies, police departments, hospitals, and spill contractors. If any emergency authorities decline to enter into such arrangements, the facility must document this refusal in its operating record.

Subpart D—Contingency Plan and Emergency Procedures. All hazardous waste management facilities must prepare and maintain a contingency plan for their facility to minimize the health or en-

Employee Name: ______________________________

Job Title: ___________________________________

TRAINING DATE	SUBJECT OF TRAINING	INITIAL TRAINING OR	REVIEW TRAINING

Figure 5-6. Example individual hazardous waste training form.

vironmental hazards arising from emergencies. The plan must be carried out whenever there is a fire, explosion, or release, and it must describe the actions to be taken by facility personnel. *Note:* Facilities with an existing Spill Prevention, Control and Countermeasure (SPCC) plan may amend the plan to include hazardous waste. The plan must describe arrangements made with local authorities and must list names, addresses, and phone numbers of all emergency coordinators. It must include a list of emergency equipment available and

Training Session ______________________ Date ____________________

Plant Location ______________________ Time ____________________

Instructor ______________

NAME	JOB CLASSIFICATION

Figure 5-7. Example hazardous waste training attendance sheet.

an evacuation plan for facility personnel. Copies of the contingency plan must be maintained at the facility and submitted to all local authorities that may be called upon. The plan must be updated whenever the facility, regulations, or list of emergency coordinators changes. At all times, an emergency coordinator must be on-site or on call available for response. In case of emergency, he must activate facility alarms, notify authorities, characterize the emergency, and assess possible hazards and response. After the emergency has been brought under control, the coordinator must file a written report with the agency that includes the:

1. Name, address, and telephone number of the owner and operator of the facility.
2. Name, address, and telephone number of the facility.
3. Date, time, and type of incident.
4. Name and quantity of material(s) involved.
5. Extent of injuries.
6. Assessment of actual or potential hazards to human health or the environment.
7. Estimated quantity and disposition of residual material from the incident.

Many state regulatory programs require greater efforts at contingency planning. For example, the State of Pennsylvania requires that a Preparedness, Prevention and Contingency (PPC) plan be prepared for all industrial plants. This plan must incorporate the contingency plans required under all environmental programs such as oil spills, best management practices, and RCRA. The auditor should be aware of state program requirements before the plan audit.

Subpart E—Manifest System, Record-keeping, and Reporting. *Manifests.* Subpart E requires that facilities that receive shipments of hazardous waste accompanied by a manifest sign and date each manifest and note any discrepancies concerning the shipment. The transporter must be given at least one copy of the signed manifest, and the generator must be sent one copy within 30 days. Slightly different provisions exist for facilities that receive wastes by rail or water. Manifest discrepancies are defined as differences in quantity or type of waste received from that identified on the manifest. Significant discrepancies are defined as either of the following:

- For bulk waste, variations greater than 10%.
- For batch waste, variations in piece count.

Upon discovering a significant discrepancy, the facility must immediately attempt to reconcile the difference with the generator. If unable to do so within 15 days, the facility must file a written discrepancy report with the agency, detailing the shipment involved and actions taken and include a copy of the manifest at issue.

The entire issue of manifest preparation and handling is currently under review at the federal level. It appears that EPA will attempt to issue a uniform manifest form for use throughout the country. Currently most agencies require the use of their particular manifest on all shipments originating within their borders. For interstate shipments it may be necessary to complete several different manifests for the same shipment. In any case, the state's manifest rules should be reviewed during the audit. Special attention should be paid to any shipments destined for out-of-state sites.

Operating Record. All facilities are required to maintain a written operating record at the facility. The following information must be recorded as it becomes available, and maintained until facility closure:

1. Description and quantity of each waste received and the treatment, storage, and disposal methods used.
2. The location of each hazardous waste at the facility, especially disposal facilities.
3. Waste analysis and "treatability" results.
4. Summaries of all emergency incidents.
5. Inspection records and results.
6. Monitoring, testing, or analytical results.
7. Closure cost estimates.

Biennial Report. Facilities must prepare and submit a summary report of their activities once every two years. This report is due by March 1 of each even-numbered year and details the wastes received, handling methods used, and other information regarding their operation. *Note:* Many state agencies have retained their original annual report requirement and several, such as Pennsylvania, have even instituted a more frequent reporting format.

Unmanifested Waste Report. If a facility accepts for treatment, storage, or disposal any hazardous waste from an off-site source without a manifest, it must file a written report to the agency within 15 days. This requirement does not apply to wastes excluded under the small-quantity generator rule. The report includes information on the facility, generator, transporter, waste, and handling method.

Subpart F—Groundwater Monitoring. Hazardous waste management facilities that consist of surface impoundments, landfills, or land treatment units must implement a groundwater monitoring program capable of determining the facility's impact on the quality of groundwater in the uppermost aquifer. This program must be carried out during the active life of the facility as well as its post-closure care period. Waivers from this requirement are available, provided the facility can demonstrate a low potential for migration of hazardous waste or its constituents. This demonstration must be in writing, kept at the facility, and certified by a qualified geologist or geotechnical engineer. An alternative groundwater monitoring program may be used for an individual facility, provided a certified plan is submitted to the agency, and groundwater quality assessments are conducted every quarter until facility closure. The groundwater monitoring requirement may also be waived for facilities using surface impoundments to neutralize wastes that are hazardous solely because of corrosivity. The facility must demonstrate that there is no potential for migration of hazardous waste. This demonstration must be in writing and must be certified by a qualified professional. During an audit, the auditor will determine if goundwater monitoring is required at the subject facility. In addition, the auditor may briefly review whether the potential exists to receive a waiver from some or all of these requirements, and if so, note it in the audit report. In this way the audit serves to identify opportunity for regulatory relief.

Groundwater Monitoring System. The groundwater monitoring system required by the regulations consists of upgradient wells (at least one) and downgradient wells (at least three), designed and installed to be able to detect significant changes in groundwater quality. Specific requirements apply to the construction and placement of each well. It should be noted that in certain areas, such as near tidal water, the determination of upgradient and downgradient is not as straightforward as it appears. For this reason, most firms retain qualified professionals to help place, design, and install their monitoring systems.

Sampling and Analysis. Facilities must prepare and maintain a groundwater sampling and analysis plan, which must include procedures and techniques for sample collection, sample preservation, analytical methods, and chain of custody. In the regulations, the agency refers to two EPA publications for guidance: "Procedures Manual for Groundwater Monitoring at Solid Waste Dispoasl Facilities" (EPA-530/SW-611) and "Methods for Chemical Analysis of Water and Wastes" (EPA-600/4-79-020). Groundwater monitoring samples must be analyzed for the following parameters:

1. EPA Interim Primary Drinking Water Standards (see Table 5-5).
2. The following groundwater quality parameters: chloride, iron, manganese, phenols, sodium, and sulfate.
3. The following groundwater contamination indicators: pH, specific conductance, total organic carbon (TOC), and total organic halogen (TOX).

These parameters must be determined quarterly for all wells for one year to establish background concentrations. For pH, specific conductance, TOC, and TOX, four replicate samples must be analyzed from all upgradient wells during the first year. The initial background arithmetic mean and variance must be determined. Samples of groundwater must be analyzed at least annually for the groundwater quality parameters and at least semiannually for the groundwater contamination indicators. Elevation of the groundwater surface at each well must be determined each time a sample is obtained.

Preparation, Evaluation, and Response. All facilities that are required to monitor groundwater must prepare an outline of a groundwater quality assessment program. This program must be capable of determining:

Table 5-5. EPA Interim Primary Drinking Water Standards.

PARAMETER	MAXIMUM LEVEL (MILLIGRAMS PER LITER)
Arsenic	0.05
Barium	1.0
Cadmium	0.01
Chromium	0.05
Fluoride	1.4–2.4
Lead	0.05
Mercury	0.002
Nitrate (as N)	10
Selenium	0.01
Silver	0.05
Endrin	0.0002
Lindane	0.004
Methoxychlor	0.1
Toxaphene	0.005
2,4-D	0.1
2,4,5-TP silver	0.01
Radium	5 pCi/l
Gross alpha	15 pCi/l
Gross beta	4 millirem/yr
Turbidity	1/TU
Coliform bacteria	1/100 ml

Comment: Turbidity is applicable only to surface water supplies.

- Whether wastes or constituents have entered the groundwater.
- The rate and extent of their migration.
- Their concentrations.

For each indicator parameter, the arithmetic mean and variance of four replicate samples must be compared with the background levels previously obtained. If this comparison for upgradient wells (by the Student's t-test at the 0.01 level of significance) shows a statistically significant increase over background, the facility must notify the agency. If the comparison for downgradient wells shows a statistically significant change, the facility must immediately obtain additional samples to confirm these results. If the results are confirmed, the facility must notify the agency within seven days that it may be affecting the groundwater quality. Within 15 days of notification, the facility must submit a detailed plan for a groundwater quality assessment program. This detailed plan must specify:

- The number, depth, and location of wells.
- The sampling and analytical methods.
- The evaluation procedures to be used.
- A schedule of implementation.

In addition, the facility must determine:

- The rate and extent of migration.
- The concentrations of wastes or constituents in the groundwater.

If these determinations indicate that wastes or constituents from the facility have not entered the groundwater, then the facility may reinstate the indicator evaluation program. If the results show the facility has impacted the groundwater, then these determinations must be continued on a quarterly basis until facility closure.

Record-keeping and Reporting. Facilities that are required to implement a groundwater assessment program must keep records of the analysis and evaluations made under the program during the facility's active life and post-closure period (for disposal facilities). In addition, an annual report of the assessment program must be filed with EPA. Facilities that have not been required to institute an assessment program must also keep records of all analyses and evaluations for their active life. During the first year of the groundwater monitoring program, facilities must report the concentration of all EPA Interim Primary Drinking Water Standards in each well within 15 days of each quarterly testing. On an annual basis the concentrations of pH, specific conductance, TOC, and TOX must be reported, along with the results of all evaluations required. Each calendar year, a summary of the groundwater surface evaluations is required.

An auditor concerned with the compliance status of an individual facility is not in a position to evaluate the technical merits of a groundwater monitoring program. The auditor can only determine that the facility is maintaining and filing the required reports and conducting the necessary analysis and evaluations. Any problems the facility experiences in this regard should be noted for action. The agency has made it clear that it considers the groundwater monitoring requirement a central point in the proper management of hazardous waste. Similarly, the auditor must place significant importance on this aspect of the RCRA regulations.

Subpart G—Closure and Post-Closure. *Closure.* All hazardous waste management facilities must close their operations in a way that minimizes the need for further maintenance and minimizes the post-closure escape of hazardous waste, waste constituents, or by-products. A written plan describing how and when the facility will be closed must be prepared and maintained at the facility. The plan must include an estimate of the facility's maximum inventory of hazardous waste, a description of the steps necessary to decontaminate the facility, and the estimated year of closure and closure schedule. This plan may be updated at any time during the facility's active life and must be updated whenever changes affecting closure occur at the facility. The plan must be submitted to the agency at least 180 days prior to facility closure. The agency will evaluate the plan, solicit public comment, and request modifications to the plan (if necessary) within 30 days. Within 90 days of receiving the final shipment of waste, the facility must process or dispose of all inventory. All closure activities must be complete within 180 days after receipt of the final shipment. Longer closure periods may be approved for reasons specified in the regulations. When closure is complete, facility equipment must be disposed of or decontaminated, and a certification (sealed by an independent registered professional engineer) must be submitted to the agency.

Post-Closure. All hazardous waste disposal facilities must care for their installations at least 30 years after closure. This post-closure care must be specified in a written post-closure plan and include provisions for groundwater monitoring, maintenance of the facility, and the name, address, and phone number of the facility contact. This post-closure plan may be amended at any time during the facility's active life and must be amended whenever changes affecting post-closure occur. The plan must be submitted to the agency at least 180 days before the facility "expects to begin closure." The agency will evaluate the plan, solicit public comment, and request modifications to the plan (if necessary) within 30 days. This plan may be amended during post-closure by the facility or agency, based on cause. The regulations contain specific procedures and criteria for plan amendments. Within 90 days after closure is complete, hazardous waste disposal facilities must submit to the local land authority and agency a survey plan indicating the locations and dimensions of disposal areas, complete with a record of the type and quantity of wastes disposed of. In addition, hazardous waste disposal facilities must record, in accordance with state law, a notice of the need for the property that will notify any potential purchaser that the land was used to manage hazardous waste, and that its use is restricted under federal regulation (Section 265.117(c)).

Subpart H—Financial Requirements. Subpart H of the RCRA regulations specifies in detail the requirements that hazardous waste management facilities must meet to assure that money is available to adequately close and care for each facility. These requirements are very complex and well beyond an auditor's effort to evaluate in detail. In general, the regulations are divided into several sections (each with specific provisions):

- 265.142: All facilities must prepare, maintain, and update annually an estimate for the cost of closing the facility.
- 265.143: All facilities must establish financial assurance for the closure costs. This assurance can take the form of:
    - Closure trust fund.
    - Surety bond guaranteeing payment into a closure trust fund.
    - Closure letter of credit.
    - Closure insurance.
    - Financial test and corporate guarantee for closure.
    - Use of multiple financial mechanisms.
    - Use of a financial mechanism for multiple facilities.
- 265.144: All hazardous waste disposal facilities must prepare, maintain, and update annually an estimate for the cost of post-closure care.
- 265.145: All disposal facilities must establish financial assurance for these post-closure costs. This assurance can take the form of:

  - Post-closure trust fund.
  - Surety bond guaranteeing payment into a post-closure trust fund.
  - Post-closure letter of credit.
  - Post-closure insurance.
  - Financial test and corporate guarantee for post-closure care.
  - Use of multiple financial mechanisms.
  - Use of a financial mechanism for multiple facilities.
- 265.146: A facility may satisfy both the closure and post-closure financial assurance requirement using one of the following methods:
  - Trust fund.
  - Surety bond.
  - Letter of credit.
  - Insurance.
  - Financial test.
  - Corporate guarantee.
- 265.147: All facilities must demonstrate financial responsibility for bodily injury and property damage caused by sudden accidental occurrences. The limits must be at least in the amounts of $1 million per occurrence, with an annual aggregate of at least $2 million. In addition, facilities with surface impoundments, landfills, or land treatment units must demonstrate financial responsibility for bodily injury and property damage caused by nonsudden accidental occurrences. The limits of coverage must be at least in the amounts of $4 million per occurrence with an annual aggregate of at least $6 million. Both the sudden and nonsudden coverages may be demonstrated by means of the financial test and insurance outlined in this regulation.
- 265.148: Facilities must notify the agency within ten days of the commencement of a voluntary or involuntary proceeding under Title II of the U.S. Code (Bankruptcy) that names the facility as a debtor.
- 265.149: Facilities located in states that have their own financial requirements may use methods specified in these regulations to meet the federal requirements if the EPA determines the state mechanisms are at least equivalent to the federal.
- 265.150: A state may assume legal responsibility for a facility's

financial requirements, provided the EPA makes a determination that this assumption is at least equivalent to the federal requirements.

Specific Technical Requirements, Subparts I through R. The remaining portion of the Part 265 regulations is composed of specific technical requirements for individual hazardous waste management facilities. These rules are organized in the following subparts:

I : Use and Management of Containers
J : Tanks
K: Surface Impoundments
L: Waste Piles
M: Land Treatment
N: Landfills
O: Incinerators
P : Thermal Treatment
Q: Chemical, Physical, and Biological Treatment
R: Underground Injection

Each subpart contains detailed administrative and technical requirements that apply in addition to the requirements contained in Subparts A through H. The presence of a hazardous waste management facility on plant property triggers the need for detailed review of the appropriate subpart by the auditor. The auditor should note that EPA (and many states) interpret "treatment" very broadly and include many common waste management techniques.

THE WASTE AUDIT

The waste-related section of an environmental audit can be organized into several general areas of effort, as follows:

- Pre-audit preparations
- Waste inventory
- Waste classification
- Waste management
- Waste disposal

- File review
- Plant tour
- Audit report

Although these areas of effort are presented here as separate and distinct steps, overlap occurs in the practical implementation of the audit.

Pre-audit Preparations

The subject of general audit preparations is covered in depth in Chapter 2. Several items specific to wastes deserve review here. In the case of solid and hazardous waste requirements, it is beneficial to review the state and federal regulations that apply to the plant. Because all plants, regardless of industry, must comply with essentially the same body of rules, this review is straightforward. In states with well-developed waste management regulations, it may be necessary to contact the agency to determine the major areas of difference between the federal and state programs. If possible, it would be useful to review a copy of the checklist used by state inspectors during their compliance visits.

Of special importance during the review of hazardous waste regulations is a good understanding of the waste streams listed under the title "Hazardous Wastes from Specific Sources." This section appears in the federal rules at 46 CFR 261.33, and most state rules contain similar listings. If the audit team is unfamiliar with the specific industry to be audited, it may be necessary to review the EPA background documents on these wastes. These documents contain complete descriptions of each listed waste, the agency's rationale in listing it, and other data relative to the process generating the waste. These background documents are available at regional EPA offices.

In addition to the specific waste stream background documents, many industries themselves have been the subject of in-depth contractor studies for EPA. These studies, conducted prior to the promulgation of RCRA rules, characterize the hazardous waste practices of individual industries. They can be very useful to the auditor as a general introduction to the industry, the processes employed, and the wastes generated. A partial listing of the documents available through the National Technical Information Service (NTIS) appears in Table 5-6.

Table 5-6. Selected Industry Background Documents Available through NTIS.

TITLE	ACCESSION NUMBER
Assessment of Industrial Hazardous Waste Practices, Rubber and Plastics Industry. Appendices.	PB-282 073/6SL
Assessment of Industrial Hazardous Waste Practices, Rubber and Plastics Industry. Rubber Products Industry.	PB-282 072/8SL
Assessment of Industrial Hazardous Waste Practices, Rubber and Plastics Industry. Plastic Materials and Synthetics Industry.	PB-282 071/0SL
Assessment of Industrial Hazardous Waste Practices, Rubber and Plastics Industry. Executive Summary.	PB-282 070/2SL
Assessment of Industrial Hazardous Waste Practices, Rubber and Plastics Industry.	PB-282 069-SET/SL
Assessment of Industrial Hazardous Waste Practices in the Metal Smelting and Refining Industry. Volume IV. Appendices.	PB-276 172/4SL
Assessment of Industrial Hazardous Waste Practices in the Metal Smelting and Refining Industry. Volume III. Ferrous Smelting and Refining.	PB-276 171/6SL
Assessment of Industrial Hazardous Waste Practices in the Metal Smelting and Refining Industry. Volume II. Primary and Secondary Nonferrous Smelting and Refining.	PB-276 170/8SL
Assessment of Industrial Hazardous Waste Practices in the Metal Smelting and Refining Industry. Volume I. Executive Summary.	PB-276 169/0SL
Assessment of Industrial Hazardous Waste Practices. Special Machinery Manufacturing Industries.	PB-265 981/1SL
Assessment of Industrial Hazardous Waste Practices—Electronic Components Manufacturing Industry.	PB-265 532/2SL
Assessment of Industrial Hazardous Waste Practices. Electroplating and Metal Finishing Industries—Job Shops.	PB-264 349/2SL

(*Continued*)

Table 5-6. (*Cont.*)

TITLE	ACCESSION NUMBER
Assessment of Industrial Hazardous Waste Practices. Leather Tanning and Finishing Industry.	PB-261 018/6SL
Assessment of Hazardous Waste Practices in the Petroleum Refining Industry.	PB-259 097/4SL
Assessment of Industrial Hazardous Waste Practices, Textiles Industry.	PB-258 953/9SL
Assessment of Industrial Hazards Waste Practices, Paint and Allied Products Industry. Contract Solvent Reclaiming Operations, and Factory Application of Coatings.	PB-251 669/8SL
Assessment of Industrial Hazardous Waste Practices. Organic Chemicals, Pesticides, and Explosives Industries.	PB-251 307/5SL
Assessment of Industrial Hazardous Waste Practices, Inorganic Chemicals Industry.	PB-244 832/2SL
Assessment of Industrial Hazardous Waste Practices, Storage and Primary Batteries Industries.	PB-241 204/7SL

In addition to reviewing the applicable regulations and background documents, it is also necessary to define the exact scope of the waste audit prior to visiting the facility. Decisions must be made on whether the audit will focus only on hazardous waste management or will also include examination of nonhazardous waste management. In the latter case, the pre-audit preparations must include an in-depth review of state and local solid waste rules. It must also be determined if any off-site properties will be included in the auditing effort. These might include off-site warehouses owned by the plant or remote tank farms under the plant's control. Some auditing efforts include examination of off-site disposal operations as well. They may be plant-owned or contracted to a commercial vendor. If the audit is to include commercial disposal companies, prior scheduling and arrangements are necessary. The waste-related audit could go so far as to include following transporters from the plant to the disposal site. In any event, a review of transporter operations is useful and can be accomplished through a short meeting with the carrier's representative.

If possible, the audit team can review several plant-related documents prior to the actual visit as further preparation. These may include copies of any hazardous waste permit applications filed by the plant, sample manifests, and prior agency inspection or audit reports. The auditor should also prepare a list of plant personnel to be interviewed. This list can include the environmental coordinator, purchasing agent, health and safety director, training director, personnel director, and a sample of operating employees. This list will be confirmed during the initial meeting with the plant manager, at which time any deletions, additions, and scheduling changes can be made.

Waste Inventory

The first step in performing a waste audit is the preparation of a comprehensive waste inventory. Proper completion of this step should result in an exhaustive list of every waste generated at the plant. Because the waste material itself is the subject of regulation, it is important that the inventory be as complete as possible. A convenient starting point for some facilities may be the EPA Notification Package (EPA form #8700–12) that was required to be filed by all hazardous waste generators by August 18, 1980. Other possible starting points include the RCRA Part A permit application and any waste surveys the plant may have completed. This information will become available during the file review step of the audit.

The waste inventory effort is recorded in the first eight columns of Figure 5–8. It is helpful to assign a waste number (column 1) to each individual waste and identify this number on the plant's plot plan for future use during the tour. The auditor thus begins to have a geographical appreciation of the plant and its waste management practices. For the waste inventory to be as complete as possible, it is desirable to organize this effort according to operational or process divisions at the plant. Using these divisions, the entire plant is split into manageable process-related areas amenable to close review. The division of the entire plant becomes more necessary as the total size of the operation increases. Hence, Figure 5–8 contains space to organize the inventory according to specific process areas.

PLANT ____________________ PAGE ____ of ____
PROCESS AREA ______________ DATE ____________
HAULER ____________________
DISPOSAL SITE _____________

Waste Number	Waste Name	Waste Desc.	Physical form— solid, gas, sludge	Generating Site(s)	Generation Rate T/yr Gal/yr	Accumulation Area(s)	Containers Used to Accumulate	Analysis Performed (Y/N) (attach copy)	Date of Last Analysis	Waste: Hazardous	Waste: Non-Hazardous	Waste: Undetermined	USEPA/State Hazardous Waste I.D. #	NOTES

Figure 5-8. Solid/hazardous waste: inventory and classification.

It is possible to use alternative divisions for an individual facility. For example, plants with many different transporters or disposal facilities may be organized according to these divisions. A special note applies to extremely large or complex industrial plants such as petroleum refineries or chemical plants. These installations may have many possible material flow patterns, which would be difficult to "follow through" from raw material receiving to finished product shipping. In these cases, the entire complex could be divided into geographic areas, with each subject to its own review.

It is even more useful to divide the entire plant according to the same divisions used to organize the plant's management. In this case, the entire facility is divided into the many manufacturing units that make up the total. Table 5-7 lists several typical process divisions

Table 5-7. Sample Process Divisions and Corresponding Waste Streams.

DIVISION	PLANT AREAS	POSSIBLE WASTES
Raw material receiving	Unloading docks, incoming pipelines, receiving areas	Packaging materials, off-spec raw materials; damaged containers; spill residue, transfer line blowdown/drippings.
Raw material storage	Tanks, silos, warehouses, drum storage yards, storerooms	Tank bottoms; empty, damaged, off-spec, or frozen drums and raw materials. Old insulation.
Raw material preparation	Filtering, classifying, blending, preheating	Filtrate, spent filters, cutting scrap, raw material fines.
Manufacturing steps	Melting, curing, baking, distilling, washing	Washwater, solvents, still bottoms, off-spec product, catalysts, containers, sweeping, duct work clean-out, additives.
Support services	Laboratories	Reagents, off-spec chemicals, samples, sample containers.
	Maintenance shops	Solvents, cleaning agents, degreasing sludges, sand-blasting waste, lubes, oils, greases, scrap metal, caustics.
	Warehouses	Off-spec products and raw materials, forklift wastes (oil changes, filters), battery charge station acids.
	Garages	Oils, filters, solvents, cleaning bath sludges.
	Powerhouse/boilers	Fly ash, slag, tube clean-out material.
	Fuel storage	Tank bottoms, spent filters, spill residue, transfer line blowdown
	Cooling towers	Chemical additives, empty containers, cooling tower bottom sediment.
	Medical/nursing offices	Pathological, infectious wastes.

(*Continued*)

Table 5-7. (*Cont.*)

DIVISION	PLANT AREAS	POSSIBLE WASTES
	Office building	Paper waste, copier fluids, empty containers.
	Instrumentation shop	Radioactive materials from level indicators, solvents, PCBs, etc.
	Electric shop	Capacitors, transformers with PCBs.
Water pollution equipment	Separators, clarifiers, settling tanks, filters	Filtrate, sludges, DAF float, treatment chemicals.
Air pollution equipment	Scrubbers, baghouses, electrostatic precipitators	Slurries, baghouse dust, EP dust.
Off-site properties	Warehouses, tank farms, pipelines, terminals, research and development shops, pilot units, laboratories	See above.
General	Plant property	Construction debris, excavation soil, demolition wastes, scrap metal, cleanup debris.

common to most industrial plants, with corresponding sample waste streams. The goal here is to be sure that all property under plant control or ownership is examined. It is important to structure the divisions according to those already existing at the facility. In most cases, this scheme will essentially follow material flow throughout the plant, from incoming raw material through processing to finished product shipment.

Compilation of the waste inventory usually begins with an interview with the plant environmental coordinator. The coordinator will rely on his knowledge of the process and past efforts at characterizing its wastes to provide this information. The goal of this step is to list all wastes generated by the plant, independent of their hazard classification. In most cases, obvious, high-volume process wastes immediately come to mind. The inventory should not stop there, however. Table

5–7 should be used as a guide to solicit information on less obvious, smaller-volume materials. Often these waste streams have escaped detection and proper management, resulting in clear cases of non-compliance.

The interview with the environmental coordinator can be complemented with a tour of the plant. Once again, Table 5–7 can be used as a guide during the tour so that certain areas are not missed. During the tour, the auditor should be prepared to examine each bulk waste receptacle and photograph any areas he has questions about. Columns one through eight in Figure 5–8 summarize the information necessary to prepare a complete waste inventory.

In addition to interviews and plant tours with the environmental coordinator, it is beneficial to obtain a list of all raw materials and chemicals brought into the plant. This information represents one side of the plant's "mass balance," with the waste inventory representing the other. An obvious source of this information is the plant purchasing agent or materials management person. The purchasing agent should have been forewarned of this request to have time to prepare the list. With today's computer-based information systems, it can be relatively easy to generate a list of all materials purchased in the last three, six, or twelve months. This list will prove beneficial for several other areas of environmental review such as Superfund (Chapter 7) and water pollution (Chapter 4). In addition to each raw material and chemical compound purchased, the list should note the corresponding containers used to receive and store them. This is particularly important because containers that held certain commercial chemical products (Section 40 CFR 261.33(e)) are considered "hazardous wastes" unless cleaned. Particularly toxic or hazardous materials deserve close scrutiny throughout the audit.

The interview with the plant purchasing agent should also be used to gain insight into the plant's ordering and purchasing system. It will be helpful to find out who purchases chemicals or cleaners and whether or not the environmental department is informed of purchases. At some facilities, the plant environmental coordinator and safety director must review and approve all new chemical purchases. Needless to say, this procedure institutes a significant level of control over what is introduced into the facility. Material Safety Data Sheets (OSHA Form 20) should be routinely requested for all new chemicals, distributed to the chemical users, and kept on file in the environmental and safety departments. Finally, the purchasing agent should be asked if the plant ever purchases scrap or recycled material for use as a raw material. Although this area of regulation is not clear, in some cases facilities purchasing waste or spent products may be required to obtain a specific RCRA permit.

The plant health and safety supervisor may be another source of information for the waste inventory. Some plants have installed computer systems to track and record employees' exposure to certain chemicals on site. The heart of these systems is a comprehensive list of materials found at the plant, usually complete with geographic location and chemical abstracts service identification number. This list is usually easy to obtain if you have access to the computer. Even if the facility has not implemented such a program, the health and safety supervisor can usually provide a list of chemicals found at the plant that concern the safety function. This information can be used as a check against that provided by the purchasing agent and the environmental coordinator.

Several other notes may apply to preparing the waste inventory:

- All information sources should be asked whether or not any raw materials are changed from time to time. For example, during some seasons of the year some industries may suspend certain operations or may use slightly different raw materials.
- Time permitting, it may be beneficial to interview several operating supervisors while preparing the waste inventory. Supervisors are usually well attuned to their individual operations and may be helpful in reviewing the inventory for completeness and accuracy.
- It should be remembered that everything in the plant is cleaned at one time or another, and thus can generate significant waste streams that require proper management and disposal. Examples include ductwork deposits, tank bottoms, pipeline clean-out wastes, and stripped insulation.
- Under some state regulatory programs, specific permit applications are required for the disposal of all wastes, hazardous and nonhazardous. Examples include the State of Pennsylvania, which requires the submission of a "Module 1" application prior to waste treatment or disposal at a Pennsylvania site.

Waste Classification

In most facilities with an established environmental function, the classification of each waste identified in the waste inventory will be relatively straightforward. At the very least, the major process wastes should already be determined, analyzed, and classified. Most industrial facilities have some idea about which wastes are considered hazardous, and many have well-developed management systems in place. For this step, the environmental coordinator is the obvious information source. Any EPA notification forms and permit applications will be the initial source of information. The proper determination, analysis performed, and appropriate waste identification numbers are recorded in columns 9 through 15 in Figure 5–8.

Although these classifications should already have been determined, it is important to review this step closely to be sure that every waste has been consciously classified. This classification should be based on actual analysis results whenever possible. Although the RCRA regulations permit generators to use their knowledge of the process to make hazard determinations, this alternative can result in significant liability if errors are made. It is recommended that analysis results be used in most cases in lieu of self-determination. During the classification stage of the audit, the environmental coordinator should be questioned on whether a formal procedure exists to identify, classify, and manage new waste streams. Many facilities have instituted an internal manifest or waste disposal request system to encourage compliance in this important area. With these systems in place, an in-plant generator of a new waste stream (e.g., spill residue) must provide the environmental department with a sample and waste description before any material movement occurs. Although such systems normally impose a time lag, they assure that each new or unusual waste is reviewed before disposal. In large, complex facilities these communication systems are almost mandatory for effective management of solid and hazardous wastes.

Waste Management

The next logical step in the waste audit is a close review of the facility's waste management practices. The goal of this section is to record every step and location used by the plant to manage the wastes identified in the inventory. Columns 1 through 5 in Figure 5-9 outline the information necessary for this step. In effect, this section tracks each waste at the plant from the time it is generated to the time it is ultimately disposed of. Appropriate location references should be noted on the facility's plot plan to gain an overall view of waste movement throughout the plant. For this step, it is important actually to tour the various waste-related areas of the facility. Once again, pictures should be taken of any potential problem areas or locations subject to housekeeping problems. During the tour, the auditor should discuss the waste activities with operators and supervisors if possible.

Special attention obviously should be given to all wastes identified as hazardous by agency definition. Hazardous waste regulations govern every conceivable step in the management process, from tem-

PLANT ________________ PAGE ____ of ____
PROCESS AREA ________________ DATE ________
HAULER ________________
DISPOSAL SITE ________________

		Storage (90 days)				Treatment				Transportation				Disposal				Reuse/ Recycle Sale						NOTES
Waste Number	Waste Name	On-Site	Off-Site	Storage Location	Storage Method	On-Site	Off-Site	Location	Method	On-Site	Off-Site	Location	Method	On-Site	Off-Site	Location	Method	On-Site	Off-Site	Location	Method	Was waste included on USEPA notification form	Waste and mgmt. method included on USEPA Part A Permit appl.	

Figure 5-9. Solid/hazardous waste management and disposal.

porary accumulation to off-site final disposal. A good awareness of these areas will be necessary for proper evaluation of the facility's performance during the last stage of the audit. Nonhazardous wastes must not be ignored, however. Many state agencies have "generic" waste regulations that stipulate "proper management" of solid and nonhazardous wastes. Although these regulations are seldom detailed, they are effective in requiring proper management. For these wastes, obvious cases of improper housekeeping, leaking containers, or mismanagement should be noted for inclusion in the audit report.

During facility tours, the locations of all bulk waste receptacles, drum storage areas, waste tanks, and other waste-related units should be marked on the facility plot plan. As these units are marked, each should be examined closely to determine whether its nominal description matches the actual field conditions. Cases in which it does not match indicate either a communications breakdown or noncompliance. But closely examining the contents of each receptacle, the auditor may also reveal cases in which segregation systems or other arrangements are necessary. Segregation is frequently necessary in order to manage the hazardous fraction properly while minimizing the disposal costs of the nonhazardous fraction.

Containers of raw materials or chemicals listed in the RCRA regulations also deserve special attention. Note that the regulations require containers that formerly held certain commercial chemical products to be managed as hazardous wastes unless they are properly decontaminated. Empty drum accumulation areas should be examined closely. Because empty 55-gallon drums are often associated with improper waste management, these areas ideally should be removed from public view. Drum accumulation areas should be examined to determine compliance with the "empties" rule (40 CFR 261.7). Any partially full containers should be noted for removal and proper management of the residue. All bungs and lids should be secure to prevent the accumulation of rainwater, and the area should not exhibit housekeeping problems.

Waste Disposal

In general, the most significant exposure to liability experienced by an industrial plant with regard to waste management is a result of its disposal activities. The first step in evaluating these activities is to list the ultimate disposal method, site, and company for each waste identified on the inventory. In addition, any alternative or infrequent disposal methods should be identified. This effort is recorded in columns 6 and 7 in Figure 5-9. Although this initial step appears straightforward, in many cases the disposal method used for infrequent wastes is not well known by the plant contact. For such wastes, often the only source of meaningful information is the operator or supervisor of the specific area. If the disposal method used for any waste cannot be determined, that fact should be noted for inclusion in the audit report.

Reviewing the disposal of wastes identified as nonhazardous on the waste inventory can be relatively straightforward. An application package (describing the waste) and approval letter from the facility or agency in charge should be available. Although such documentation may not be available for normal trash and office building waste, it should be on file for any process-related or other "industrial" waste disposal. All waste transportation and disposal operations should be conducted under a formal contractual agreement. Ideally, separate agreements should cover transportation services and waste disposal. These agreements should be current and stipulate the materials involved, services rendered, and fees charged. The contract should include a "compliance with laws" section that requires all vendors to comply with applicable state, federal, and local rules. Examples of laws that may be specifically noted in the contract are listed in Table 5-8. The agreement should include provisions for customer indemnity, liability, and emergencies.

Table 5-8. Waste Disposal Contracts: Compliance with Laws.

Civil Rights Act
Clean Air Act
Clean Water Act
Comprehensive Environmental Response, Compensation and Liability Act
Equal Employment Opportunity Act
Fair Labor Standards Act
Occupational Safety and Health Act
Rehabilitation Act
Resource Conservation and Recovery Act
Solid Waste Disposal Act
Transportation Safety Act
Vietnam Era Veterans Readjustment Regulations

The facility should maintain accurate records of the amounts shipped, their dates, and proof of receipt by the disposal site. Although a manifest shipping paper is not required by regulation for nonhazardous wastes, many firms have instituted internal tracking programs to assure the proper disposal of all wastes. The names of any landfills used for the disposal of nonhazardous waste should be compared with the most recent edition of EPA's inventory of "open dumps." This inventory is a list of landfills that do not comply with EPA's "Criteria for Classification of Solid Waste Disposal Facilities and Practices" (40 CFR Part 257). A facility's appearance on this inventory indicates that it does not comply with at least one of these criteria and hence should be scrutinized by the plant. This inventory is available from the National Technical Information Services (NTIS) or may be reviewed at Regional EPA offices.

Obviously the evaluation of hazardous waste disposal practices, sites, and contractors represents a very serious effort. It is in this specific area that most plants will experience their greatest waste-related scrutiny. Once again, the disposal method and contractors used are listed for each hazardous waste identified on the inventory. Many plants use one hazardous waste disposal firm for all hazardous wastes generated. In any event, there is usually only a small number of possible disposal facilities available to the plant. With prior preparations, the auditor can make arrangements to visit each disposal site and conduct a review of their operations. When alternative sites are available, these reviews can be used to compare the sites to help determine the best option for the plant. Such reviews should address a wide range of waste-related issues and attempt to document the facility's compliance with environmental requirements. An example of guidelines for reviewing commercial hazardous waste treatment, storage, and disposal facilities is included as Table 5-9.

Specific application packages, describing each waste, should be on file for each hazardous waste disposed of off site. In addition, approval letters from the appropriate agency and facility should be available. Especially for hazardous waste, all transportation and disposal vendors should be under contract. These agreements should be formal contracts prepared and reviewed by legal counsel. The contract guidelines summarized in the discussion of solid waste disposal contracts are applicable here as well. Every facility used for the treat-

Table 5-9. Guidelines for Review of Commercial Hazardous Waste Facilities

General Information
- —Facility name, location, and mailing address
- —Facility contacts; technical, business, and compliance manager
- —Services rendered; treatment, storage, transport, disposal
- —EPA ID#, state ID#, transporter license #

Company Information
- —Company name, owners, parents
- —Annual sales, publicly traded
- —Former company names, other related divisions, subsidiaries
- —Insurance carrier, limits

Site Information
- —Facility and land owners, operators
- —Distance from plant, roads used, cities traveled
- —Vertical distance to groundwater, soil types
- —Horizontal distance to bodies of water, "buffer" zones
- —Local zoning, neighbors, industries
- —Fences/natural barriers, warning signs
- —Earthquake zone, 100-year flood zone
- —Former land use, owners
- —Third-party suits, agency actions pending
- —Year operations began, major wastes formerly accepted

Permit Information
- —EPA notification form, wastes and activities listed
- —RCRA "Part A" permit application, wastes and processes listed
- —RCRA "Part B" permit application, wastes and processes listed
- —Air pollution permits, NPDES or POTW limits
- —Other special permit terms and conditions

Compliance Information

—Liner(s)	—Agency contact(s)
—Groundwater monitoring	—Employee training
—Waste analysis plan	—Inspection plan and log
—Emergency plan	—Emergency equipment
—Communications	—Emergency arrangements
—Manifests	—Closure cost estimates
—Post-closure cost estimate	—Financial responsibility
—Local community problems	—History of accidents/spills
—General housekeeping	—Drum management

ment, storage, or disposal of hazardous waste must have the proper federal, state, and local permits. Documentation from the facility describing its capabilities and permits should be on file. It may be beneficial for the auditor to contact the local agency representative regarding the current status of the off-site facilities used. Although agency contacts can seldom give an unqualified "vote of confidence" for a particular facility, they can give some meaningful insight regarding the site. Under the heading of waste disposal, the auditor must also be concerned with the final disposition of empty and partially full containers and drums. All commercial reconditioners and reclaimers used should be evaluated. Many firms choose to crush empties and dispose of them as solid waste or sell them as scrap metal. In either case, the likely character of material involved should be reviewed. Plants that handle large quantities of containers should be reviewed very closely for compliance with the EPA "empties" rule and DOT shipping requirements.

The Issue of Land Disposal

Most environmental agencies and public interest groups are viewing the subject of land disposal with increasing scrutiny. This is especially true for hazardous waste disposal. Many are considering landfills long-term storage facilities rather than disposal operations, in recognition of the fact that the wastes remain essentially intact (and potentially hazardous) for many years. It is already clear that the future will dictate less dependence on land disposal options for all wastes. This is particularly true because siting new facilities is already extremely difficult, and the total capacity of existing facilities is limited. As hazardous waste regulations become more stringent and better enforced, additional existing facilities will close, owing to their inability to meet environmental standards. For these and many similar reasons, generators of hazardous waste must evaluate their long-term disposal needs and plan for alternatives to address them in the future.

With this reality in mind, companies must identify the issue of disposal needs much like any other strategic issue and commit resources to provide for it. The greatest resource a company possesses is a thorough knowledge of its operations, materials, wastes, and needs. By systematically defining these needs, the firm can identify the options best suited to meet them. In some ways, a hierarchy of disposal alternatives can be constructed to suit this purpose. From a risk standpoint, this hierarchy may appear similar to that presented here.

Since the issue of future land disposal availability is important to most generators, an auditor should strongly consider recommending that the company commit some resources to studying its options. Although positive results may not be experienced for some time, a systematic review of projected disposal needs and future options will help meet these needs.

Hierarchy of Waste Disposal Options.

RANK	ITEM	DESCRIPTION
1	Waste reduction	Operating or manufacturing changes can result in less volume or weight of waste generated. Less cost, liability and less dependence on landfills is achieved.
2	Waste quality improvement	Raw materials or operations are modified to result in less "hazardous" waste being generated. Less liability, easier "treatability" results.
3	Waste segregation	If possible, hazardous mixtures are separated into hazardous and nonhazardous fractions. Each fraction can be managed accordingly.
4	Waste pretreatment	Very hazardous wastes may be "pretreated" so that subsequent treatment or disposal operations can occur with less risk.
5	Waste destruction	Hazardous wastes and their constituents are completely destroyed, resulting in no (or very little) residuals available to cause problems.
6	Waste treatment	Pretreated or "raw" hazardous wastes are further treated to render them completely "nonhazardous." Process still results in a waste requiring disposal, and in fact may increase the original wastes volume.
7	Land treatment	Natural biological actions are promoted to render wastes nonhazardous or less hazardous. Operation is often slow and still results in materials requiring proper management.
8	Landfills	Hazardous wastes are "interned" for long periods of time. Some natural "treatment" may occur, but material remains "hazardous" for years, resulting in tremendous liability for future problems.

File Review

The purpose of this step in the waste audit is to assure the plant's compliance with the many specific record-keeping, reporting, and retention requirements under the hazardous waste management regulations. The documents required by these rules are a function of the plant's "status" as a waste management facility. As a result, the auditor must first determine which of the following classifications the plant falls under: generator, transporter, storage facility, treatment plant, disposal facility, or a combination thereof. Each class has its own specific requirements and hence record-keeping needs. The auditor should use the appropriate regulations or agency checklists as a guide to determine the extent of compliance. Table 5-10 summarizes the record-keeping requirements associated with hazardous waste

Table 5-10. Summary: RCRA Record-keeping Requirements.

—Notification package
—Part A permit application
—Part B permit application
—Annual/biennial reports
—Manifests
    —Exception reports
    —Unmanifested waste reports
—Waste analysis plan
    —Analysis, test results
—Inspection plan
    —Inspection logs
    —Maintenance repair orders
—Personnel training records
    —Job descriptions
    —Attendance sheets
    —Training outline
—Emergency plans
    —Evacuation route
    —Emergency coordinators
    —Incident reports
    —Equipment inventory
    —DOT spill reports
    —Arrangements with local authorities
—Operating record
—Closure plan
    —Cost estimate
—Post-closure plan
    —Cost estimate
—Groundwater monitoring
    —Plan
    —Test results
—Financial assurance
    —Closure
    —Post-closure
    —Liability insurance
—Small quantity—Generator documentation
—Agency inspection reports

management. The auditor should review appropriate state regulations prior to the audit to determine and note any specific differences. Many state agencies, for example, have extended the required retention times beyond those stipulated by federal rules. The plant should exhibit an organized system for assuring that these record-keeping requirements are met. Ideally, these records should be housed in a single location at the plant for ease of review, especially during agency inspections.

Plant Tour

The final step of the waste audit is an evaluation of the plant's operations to assure compliance with specific waste management rules. This is accomplished by conducting a comprehensive tour of the plant, its facilities, and properties. In some respects, this tour should closely model the efforts of agency inspectors during their compliance visits. One way to conduct this tour is by using the actual agency checklists as a guide. Copies of these checklists may be available from the local agency or may be purchased commercially. Use of these checklists carries the additional benefit of preparing the plant's environmental coordinator for the next agency visit. Independent of the checklists used, this final tour should specifically examine the following areas:

- General plant operating areas, especially waste generation and accumulation sites.
- All on-site waste treatment, storage, or disposal facilities (TSDFs).
- Waste shipping and receiving areas.
- The remaining plant property(ies).

The inspection of the plant's manufacturing areas should note all waste receptacles, bulk storage containers, and generation sites. The waste inventory sheet should be used as a check for completeness. The auditor should review the housekeeping conditions near each site and note any evidence of spills, leaks, or improper storage. Containers used to accumulate hazardous waste should be properly labeled and marked. The auditor should specifically examine sites where wastes

Figure 5-10. All waste receptacles should be examined during the plant tour.

are mixed to assure their compatibility and determine whether segregation is recommended. Each site should be examined for nearby drains or sewers to determine the effects of potential spills and whether containment measures should be recommended. During the tour of manufacturing areas, the auditor should anticipate the generation of various cleanup wastes and assure their proper disposition. Examples include line washes, vessel clean-out materials, contaminated floor sweepings, or other materials listed in Table 5-7.

In addition to the inspection of each waste generation and accumulation area, the auditor must specifically review each treatment, storage, or disposal facility on plant property. These tours should be conducted using the actual regulations as a guide. The auditor should also use as a guide the inspection plan prepared by the plant to meet agency requirements. Inspection plans should assure that all loading and unloading areas are reviewed daily, that tank and surface impoundments are inspected for freeboard and integrity, that containment structures are properly constructed, and that no leaks or spills have occurred. Alarms and waste cutoff systems should be tested periodically. Appropriate internal and external communication equipment should be present. Specific security rules apply to all facilities that require fences or natural barriers, warning signs, controlled access, and setback distances. Although these rules permit some leeway, most facilities opt for tight security as a risk management measure. Any areas specifically designated for the accumulation or storage of drums should be closely inspected for proper stacking, segregation of incompatibles, containment, and labeling. Most plants store waste-containing drums on wooden pallets to reduce corrosion and permit bottoms inspection for leaks. Drum storage areas should be sited to minimize viewing from public property. In addition to inspecting these areas, the auditor should specifically examine all sites where recycle or reuse operations occur. In certain cases (see 40 CFR 261.6), storage and treatment permits are necessary even though the waste is beneficially reclaimed. These rules are frequently misinterpreted by plant personnel.

Up to this point in the waste audit, the plant tour has focused on specific areas and facilities. The next phase of the tour is a general inspection of the remaining plant property and fence line. The plant plot plan should be used as a guide to assure that all areas are examined. This step is strictly a discovery inspection, a search for problems not previously noted. Examples may include areas of unauthorized dumping, unmanaged salvage or scrap piles, and evidence of ground or water contamination. A walk along the fence line completes the plant tour.

At this stage of the waste audit, a comprehensive waste inventory has been prepared, the plant and its facilities have been inspected, and all waste-related files have been reviewed. The final step of the audit is a short review meeting with the environmental coordinator to confirm the accuracy of the auditor's observations. This meeting is used to resolve any remaining discrepancies and discuss any photos the auditor may have taken during the tour. Finally the environmental coordinator should be asked to summarize his own list of major concerns. Often the coordinator is in the best position to witness the plant's vulnerabilities but may not be able to inspire action. The audit report can be viewed as an opportunity to air these concerns or suggestions.

Figure 5-11. Many plants have a "back forty" that has been used for trash disposal.

Audit Report

The completion of the plant tour signals the first opportunity the auditor has to consolidate and review the information gathered. At this point the auditor should be able to "see" the entire "picture" of the plant for the first time. He is now charged with the task of recording his observations and noting any recommendations in the audit report. A concise record of the auditor's activities exists in the form of the data sheets used during the audit. Because these data sheets contain the list of all wastes, transporters, and disposal sites, they should be included in the audit report, probably as an attachment.

More important than these data sheets, however, are the observations, recommendations, and action items the auditor identifies in the body of the report. The auditor's discussion in this section should begin with a summary of the plant's strengths and weaknesses in waste management. Positive observations might include the use of destructive disposal techniques, institution of recycle methods, or use of internal waste-tracking tools. The discussion of the plant's weaknesses should initially focus on high-priority issues that must be resolved. Failure to file properly for a permit and improper storage or disposal are examples. The auditor must be sure to address these weaknesses in an objective, straightforward manner, relying on regulatory citations to support his observation.

After discussing the plant's major strengths and weaknesses, the auditor should proceed to a discussion of "minor" areas that may eventually require attention. These might include minor manifest errors, unorganized record-keeping provisions, or other clerical errors. If the plant experiences systematic or frequent noncompliances, this issue must be highlighted for correction. Included in this section should be a discussion of any areas of waste management whose compliance is uncertain. Examples might be certain reuse or recycle systems or other exemptions under the rules.

During the audit, the auditor may see several opportunities for the plant to limit its waste-related exposure, a short discussion of which may be in order. Examples might include a recommendation to begin using formal contracts for waste-related work or perhaps to establish a better internal waste-tracking program. Many companies have instituted internal manifests for all waste leaving the site. These manifests are tied into the billing system to encourage contractor compliance. The issue of land disposal may deserve mention in the audit report also. This is especially true if the plant has several easy-to-destroy waste streams such as high-BTU solvents or cleaners. In general, the auditor must be sure to address every noncompliant issue while at the same time never losing sight of the total picture.

6
Spill Prevention

Section 311 of the Federal Water Pollution Control Act (the Clean Water Act) lists minimum quantities of 299 materials that, if discharged into the navigable waters of the United States, require an immediate report to the U.S. Coast Guard National Response Center followed by diligent clean-up efforts. This reporting requirement was superseded and considerably expanded by the Comprehensive Environmental Response, Compensation, and Liability Act of 1980 (Superfund). Section 102 of this act requires reporting of releases of any hazardous substance in amounts equal to or exceeding set quantities into any part of the environment, unless the release occurs in accordance with a permit or is otherwise exempt. The reportable quantities for Clean Water Act pollutants are those defined in Section 311 of the Clean Water Act, and one pound, unless otherwise specified in the regulations, for any other hazardous substances including toxic pollutants defined in Section 307 of the Clean Water Act, hazardous wastes defined in Section 3001 of the Resource Conservation and Recovery Act, hazardous air pollutants defined in Section 112 of the Clean Air Act, imminently hazardous chemicals or mixtures defined in Section 7 of the Toxic Substances Control Act, and any additional substances listed in Section 102. Over half of the approximately 700 hazardous substances included in this list have specific reportable quantities. Most of these are larger than one pound, some as high as 5000 pounds. In addition to these requirements, many states have comprehensive spill reporting regulations, sometimes combined with requirements for prevention and countermeasures plans.

Oil is a Clean Water Act pollutant, and Section 311 lists the reportable quantity as: "any amount to cause a sheen or discoloration on the surface of the water or cause a sludge or emulsion to be deposited beneath the surface of the water or upon adjoining shore lines." In addition to spill reporting, the Clean Water Act also requires any plant storing more than minimum quantities of oil to have a comprehensive plan for oil spill prevention, and this requirement has not been superseded by Superfund. In the future, this requirement may be extended to other hazardous substances. The plan is referred to as an SPCC (Spill Prevention Control and Countermeasures) plan, and it must be compiled by any facility meeting the criteria outlined in the regulations developed from the Clean Water Act (40 CFR 109–114).

Specific spill control and countermeasures are also required under federal laws other than the Clean Water Act. For example, the regulations controlling the manufacture, processing, distribution in commerce, and use of PCBs (40 CFR Part 761) issued under the authority of the Toxic Substances Control Act, Section 6(e), require regular inspections and spill control for PCB storage areas (Chapter 7). The Resource Conservation and Recovery Act has specific requirements designed to minimize the possibility of releases during storage, transport, and disposal of hazardous waste (Chapter 5). Previously mentioned were state regulations designed to reduce the risk of hazardous substance spills and to provide contingency planning for spills. Thus, the concept of spill control in federal and state regulations is very broad, and the auditor would be well advised to take a commonsense approach to the storage of any hazardous liquids. That is, consider first the potential impact of a spill, and then evaluate the countermeasures that are present with respect to the risk involved. The rest of this chapter is concerned specifically with the spill prevention and countermeasure requirements and guidelines for oil issued under the Clean Water Act because these are the most highly developed in the federal regulations. They provide useful insight into spill control for all hazardous substances.

REGULATIONS

Section 311 of the Clean Water Act sets two requirements for an oil SPCC plan: (1) oil storage capacity at a facility exceeding defined minimum volumes, and (2) a potential for any oil spill to reach navigable waters. The storage capacity minimums are defined as:

Figure 6-1. An SPCC plan is required if above-ground storage of oil exceeds 1320 gallons, and if the potential exists for oil to reach navigable waters.

- Underground storage capacity totaling over 42,000 gallons.
- Above-ground storage capacity totaling over 1320 gallons or any single container over 660 gallons.

A plant having oil storage capacity exceeding these minimums must have an SPCC plan if it meets the second requirement, concerning navigable waters. In deciding this, it is important to know the following EPA definitions:

''Oil'' means oil of any kind or in any form, including, but not limited to petroleum, fuel oil, sludge, oil refuse and oil mixed with wastes other than dredged spoil.

''Discharge'' includes but is not limited to, any spilling, leaking, pumping, pouring, emitting, emptying or dumping.

''Spill event'' means a discharge of oil into or upon the navigable waters of the United States or adjoining shorelines in harmful quantities, as defined at 40 CFR Part 110. (Part 110.3 states: For purposes of section 311(b) of the Federal Act, discharges of such quantities of oil into or upon the navigable waters of the United States or adjoining shorelines determined to be harmful . . . include discharges which:

(a) Violate applicable water quality standards, or

(b) Cause a film or sheen upon or discoloration of the surface of the water or adjoining shorelines or cause a sludge or emulsion to be deposited beneath the surface of the water or upon adjoining shorelines. "Sheen" means an iridescent appearance on the surface of the water.)

The term "navigable waters" of the United States . . . includes:

(1) all navigable waters of the United States, as defined in judicial decisions prior to passage of the (1972 Federal Water Pollution Control Act Ammendments), and tributaries of such waters;

(2) interstate waters;

(3) intrastate lakes, rivers, and streams which are utilized by interstate travelers for recreational or other purposes; and

(4) intrastate lakes, rivers, and streams from which fish or shellfish are taken and sold in interstate commerce.

Figure 6-2. Improper storage of empty drums can result in a spill if they fill with rainwater.

The regulations refer to totals of above-ground or underground storage capacities rather than individual tanks. Thus, as few as 25 drums of oil exceed the minimum amount of above-ground storage requiring an SPCC plan. Lesser numbers of drums combined with oil-cooled transformers or fuel tanks bring many plants under the regulations that otherwise would not be considered to have oil storage facilities. On the other hand, above-ground storage is not added to underground storage if neither is above the minimum capacity. It should also be noted that the capacities refer to total storage volume and not actual quantities of oil in storage.

The definition of navigable waters is sufficiently broad to include most bodies of water in the United States. It seems apparent that Congress intended to include as many bodies of water as possible under these regulations. By including tributaries with navigable rivers, for example, EPA covered most flowing streams. The majority of lakes and ponds are included because of possible interstate usage for recreation or industry. If there is any doubt about a specific facility, the

Figure 6-3. Proper storage of empty drums.

auditor should check the location on a USC&GS map. A good test would be to trace the route of stormwater run-off. If it does not discharge to navigable water according to the definition, assuming no other nearby surface waters, the plant probably does not require an SPCC plan.

The only type of facility specifically excluded from the regulations is "transportation-related" as defined in the Memorandum of Understanding between the EPA Administrator and the Secretary of Transportation dated November 24, 1971 (36 FR 24080) or in subsequent memoranda. These facilities are regulated by the Department of Transportation.

THE SPCC PLAN

The regulations for oil pollution prevention require a qualifying facility to have a written SPCC plan describing: (1) any reportable spills that have occurred in the previous year, (2) the steps that have been taken to prevent future oil spills from occurring, (3) the physical structures that would control an oil spill once it did occur, and (4) the countermeasures that would be taken to contain and remove the spilled oil. Thus, the SPCC plan must not only list the emergency procedures to be taken in the event of a spill, but also the ways to prevent a spill from occurring. This dual approach is the key to EPA's regulations on oil spill prevention.

All existing plants coming under these regulations were required to prepare SPCC plans within the first six months of 1974 and to implement them by the end of the year. Facilities constructed since 1974 are required to prepare plans within six months of operation and to implement them within one year of operation. Since implementation usually requires some construction, it may not always be possible to complete it within a year. EPA will grant extensions, provided that the request is accompanied by a copy of the proposed plan, an explanation of the delay, and a time schedule of corrective actions.

The SPCC plan must be certified by a registered professional engineer. To provide this certification, the PE must be familiar with the EPA regulations and must examine the facility with them in mind. By his certification, he is attesting that the SPCC plan has been prepared using good engineering practices. This certification, however, does not relieve the plant of any of the requirements of the regulations, one of which is that the SPCC plan be brought up to date and recertified every three years or within six months of any change in the plant's potential for spills.

It is not necessary to send the SPCC plan to EPA for approval under most circumstances. It must be kept on file at the plant, however, where it can be referred to in a spill emergency. It must also be available for on-site review by the EPA regional administrator during normal working hours. The only exception is this: if the plant has had a major spill of more than 1000 gallons or two reportable spills within any 12-month period, the SPCC plan along with other pertinent information must be submitted both to the EPA regional administrator and to the responsible state agency. The regional administrator will review the plan for adequacy and may require amendments. Obviously, the circumstances that led up to the spill(s) will be particularly scrutinized in the course of this review. In fact, the requirement that a description of each recent reportable spill be a part of the SPCC plan, along with the corrective actions taken and the plans for preventing a recurrence, means that the SPCC plan should be rewritten after each major spill.

EPA does not regulate the methods by which oil spills are to be prevented. This would entail an impossible administrative burden in view of the extreme diversity of facilities coming under these rules. Rather, EPA requires the plan to be designed in accordance with good engineering practices and relies on the certification of a registered professional engineer to assure quality. In Section 112.7 of the regulations, EPA does provide extensive guidelines whereby a plant may develop an SPCC plan, using the nonmandatory "should" language rather than "shall." The auditor is advised to be familiar with these guidelines even though it is beyond the scope of an audit to provide a technical review of the SPCC plan. EPA does mandate the sequence in which the plant's conformance with its guidelines is to be presented in the written plan. This sequence is illustrated in the following paraphrased outline of Section 112.7 of the regulations:

(a) Describe spills within the last twelve months, corrective action taken, and plans to prevent recurrence.

(b) Predict the direction, rate of flow, and quantity of oil that could be discharged from a major failure.

(c) Appropriate facilities to prevent a spill from reaching navigable water would consist of:

- (1) For onshore facilities:
  - (i) Impervious dikes, berms, retaining walls
  - (ii) Curbing
  - (iii) Drainage systems
  - (iv) Weirs, booms, or other barriers
  - (v) Spill diversion ponds
  - (vi) Retention ponds
  - (vii) Sorbent materials
- (2) For offshore facilities:
  - (i) Curbing or drip pans
  - (ii) Sumps and collection systems

(d) If the above facilities are not practical then:

- (1) An oil spill contingency plan is required.
- (2) A written commitment of labor and materials must be made.

(e) In addition to (c), describe conformance with the following guidelines where applicable:

- (1) Facility drainage (onshore—excluding production)
  - (i) Free drainage from diked areas should not be permitted.
  - (ii) Valves or pumps used to remove water from diked areas should be manually operated to permit inspection of the water to ensure that no oil will be discharged.
  - (iii) Drainage from undiked areas should flow into containment to allow oil to be removed before discharge. Area should not be subject to flooding.
  - (iv) Drainage leading out of the plant should have diversionary equipment to be used in the event of an uncontrolled spill.
  - (v) If a pump is required in the movement of drainage water, a backup unit should be provided.
- (2) Bulk storage tanks (onshore—excluding production)
  - (i) Tank material and construction should be compatible with the liquid being stored and the storage conditions.
  - (ii) Secondary containment should be provided to hold the contents of the largest tank with allowance for rain water. Material should be impervious to oil.
  - (iii) Draining rain water from the containment directly to surface waters is acceptable if:
    - (A) The drain valve is sealed normally closed.

(B) Accumulated water is inspected for oil.
(C) Drainage from the valve is supervised.
(D) A record is kept of drainages.

(iv) Buried tanks should be protected from corrosion and periodically pressure-tested.

(v) Partially buried tanks should be avoided because of the potential for corrosion at the ground line.

(vi) Above-ground tanks should be periodically tested and visually inspected. Records should be kept of inspections.

(vii) Leakage from internal heating coils should be controlled:

(A) Any oil contained in steam condensate return lines should be prevented from being discharged.
(B) External heating should be considered.

(viii) Fail-safe engineering should be used such as:

(A) High level alarms
(B) High level pump cutoff devices
(C) Communication between tank gauger and pumping station
(D) Visual or remote system to indicate liquid levels
(E) Testing program for sensing devices

(ix) Plant effluent discharge points should be checked frequently to detect any spill control system upsets.

(x) Any oil leaks in tanks should be repaired.

(xi) Nonfixed oil storage tanks should be located within secondary containment able to hold the contents of the largest tank in an area not subject to flooding.

(3) Transfer and processing (onshore—excluding production)

(i) Buried piping should be protected from corrosion. If any is exposed, it should be regularly inspected.

(ii) Terminal connections for out-of-service pipelines should be capped and marked.

(iii) Pipe supports should be designed to minimize abrasion and corrosion.

(iv) All above-ground valves and pipelines should be regularly inspected and tested if necessary.

(v) Vehicular traffic should be warned of any danger to above-ground pipelines.

(4) Loading/unloading (onshore—excluding production)

(i) Procedures should comply with regulations of the Department of Transportation.

(ii) Containment should be provided to hold the contents of a tank truck or compartment of a rail car.
(iii) A system should be provided to prevent departure of the vehicle before proper disconnecting.
(iv) Lower drains and valves on tankers should be inspected for leakage before filling and departure.

Similar guidelines continue in Section 112.7 for (5) onshore oil production facilities; (6) onshore oil drilling and workover facilities; and (7) offshore oil drilling, production, and workover facilities. It then continues:

(8) Records of all inspections should be signed by an inspector or supervisor and made part of the SPCC plan. They should be kept for at least three years.
(9) Security (excluding oil production)
(i) Plants should be fenced with locked or guarded gates.
(ii) Valves permitting discharge of a tank's contents to the ground should be locked closed when not in use.
(iii) Pump switches should be locked "off" or made inaccessible to unauthorized people when not in use.
(iv) Load/unload connections should be capped when not in use.
(v) Lighting should be such that:
(A) Spills can be seen after dark.
(B) Vandalism will be deterred.
(10) Personnel training
(i) Training should include applicable water pollution regulations and procedures to prevent spills.
(ii) One individual should be designated accountable for spill prevention.
(iii) Spill prevention briefings should be held often enough to ensure operation of the SPCC plan.

THE SPCC PLAN AUDIT

The SPCC plan audit could well be initiated by asking the environmental coordinator for a copy of the plant's SPCC plan. If the plant has one, it should be close at hand, as its function necessitates that it be readily accessible for reference in case of a spill emergency. Also, the regulations call for it to be available for review by the EPA regional administrator. A spill could happen at any time, for instance, at night or on a weekend as well as during regular hours; so the location of the SPCC plan should be well known to several plant staff members. Thus, the auditor's first clue of the adequacy of an SPCC plan is the ease with which it is located and the plant's familiarity with it. It should be noted that the SPCC plan could be contained in a comprehensive contingency plan (required by several states). Pennsylvania, for example, requires qualifying plants to have a PPC (Preparedness, Prevention and Countermeasures) plan covering hazardous waste, best management practices, and NPDES as well as SPCC.

The first step in the oil spill prevention audit is to confirm the plant's status as an oil storage facility under 40 CFR Part 112. Many smaller plants may not have SPCC plans because they do not have the above-ground and underground oil storage capacities that trigger the requirement for a plan. To confirm this status, the auditor should review all oil storage tanks at the plant. A data inventory form, such as that illustrated in Figure 6–4, would be helpful in this regard. Each tank should be listed, together with its location, capacity, type (above-ground or underground), contents, and proximity to storm drains or surface waters. All tankage should be reviewed, including:

Fuel oil storage
Gasoline storage
Petroleum-based raw materials or products
Lubricating, cooling, and hydraulic oil drums
Waste oil storage
Hydrocarbon-based solvent drums
Large oil-cooled transformers (not utility-owned)
Oil-filled switches and circuit breakers
Replacement or waste transformer oil in drums
Heated asphalt in tanks

This review will either confirm that the plant does not need an SPCC plan or reveal that one should be prepared. If the latter is the case only because of excessive oil storage in drums, the plant may want to reduce this inventory rather than manage it as an oil storage facility. The fact that an SPCC plan is required should not be intimidating to a

ENVIRONMENTAL AUDIT
PLANT________________
DATE________________

OIL SPCC TANK NO.____ CONTAINMENT AREA____
ABOVE GROUND____ BELOW GROUND____
CONTENTS______________ GAL. OF____________ TEMP.__________
CONSTRUCTION____
LOCATION____
SPILL PROTECTION____________________________________
____
REMARKS____
____
____

OIL SPCC TANK NO.____ CONTAINMENT AREA____
ABOVE GROUND____ BELOW GROUND____
CONTENTS______________ GAL. OF____________ TEMP.__________
CONSTRUCTION____
LOCATION____
SPILL PROTECTION____________________________________
____
REMARKS____
____
____

OIL SPCC TANK NO.____ CONTAINMENT AREA____
ABOVE GROUND____ BELOW GROUND____
CONTENTS______________ GAL. OF____________ TEMP.__________
CONSTRUCTION____
LOCATION____
SPILL PROTECTION____________________________________
____
REMARKS____
____

Figure 6–4. Example of an oil storage data inventory form.

small plant because the complexity required is generally in direct proportion to the volume of storage capacity. Another viewpoint is that the SPCC plan is a regulatory tool designed to confirm the existence of responsible precautions that the plant should be taking in any case.

For the plant without an SPCC plan, the auditor must review the tankage records in the plant's engineering office and double-check this review during the plant tour. If the oil storage capacity exceeds the minimums, the proximity to navigable waters, as defined in the act, should be checked. In the absence of obvious nearby lakes or rivers, a local quarter section USC&GS map should be examined for evidence of still or flowing water of any magnitude. The contour lines of the map can be used to estimate the possibility of an oil spill's reaching these surface waters. Storm drains, run-off ditches, and natural swales should not be ignored. If surface water contamination appears possible, the audit report should so indicate, and it should contain a recommendation that an SPCC plan be prepared and put into operation.

For the plant with an SPCC plan, the auditor can provide a useful service by checking on certain items that will indicate its comprehensiveness and effectiveness. However, because larger plans were undoubtedly put together by one or more engineers, the auditor would not be in a position or have the time to conduct a complete review of such a plan. On the other hand, the auditor should be able to recognize evidence of inadequacy and therefore recommend to plant management the need for further engineering work on the plan. The difference between the SPCC plan audit and an engineering review of the plan should be pointed out to the environmental coordinator at the plant and mentioned in the audit report.

The review of the SPCC plan starts with the document itself. The following questions should be asked:

1. Is the plan readily available?
2. Is there a current plant employee named as spill coordinator, and at least one alternate? Are their current home phone numbers listed?
3. Is the phone number of the National Response Center run by the U.S. Coast Guard given (800/424-2675)? It would also be advisable to list the phone numbers of the regional EPA office, the nearest agency state office, the county or municipal board of health, and if one or more spills have occurred in the past, any neighbors who might be affected by a spill.
4. Has the plan been prepared or updated within the past three years and certified by a professional engineer registered in the same state?

5. Does the plan include an active and effective tank inspection program? There should be a description of the type of inspections done; for example, yearly visual inspections of aboveground tanks or periodic pressure tests of underground tanks. The results of these tests, initialed by the inspector, should be appended to the plan.
6. If the plan includes impervious dikes, are records included in the plan of each time accumulated precipitation was drained? Drain valves and sump pumps should be locked. They should be opened to drain accumulated rainfall only after a responsible individual has checked for oil contamination. Each opening should be recorded on a form filed with the plan and initialed.

The plan should be reviewed to determine the extent and complexity of the plant as an oil storage facility. The following information is pertinent:

1. A listing of all tankage with the type, location, construction, and content of each.
2. A listing of all loading or unloading facilities with the location, material, and frequency of use.
3. Previous reportable spill events, the quantity and direction of flow, countermeasures taken, and changes made to prevent recurrence.
4. Predictions of direction, flow rate, and quantity from potential spills.
5. Containment or diversionary structures such as dikes, berms, culverts, etc.
6. Location and content of emergency equipment such as sorbents, hay bales, and booms.
7. Description of plant security with respect to fencing, gate control, and lighting.

The auditor should judge the SPCC plan's usefulness as an emergency guide. How quickly would an inexperienced reader be directed to the proper response? The names and phone numbers of the emergency coordinators should be readily apparent. If these people could not be reached, would a supervisor be able to determine the need to report a spill? Would he learn how to locate emergency materials and understand the necessity to protect storm drains or surface waters? These questions should be asked by the auditor as he reviews the SPCC plan.

Training and Records

Personnel training is probably more important than flow diversion barriers, tank containment, or overfill protection because operator error is responsible for more spills than equipment failure. Seals on dike

Figure 6-5. Drain valve on a concrete dike is chained closed and padlocked.

drain valves, for example, are useless unless the operators know when to break them and what precautions to take. An important function of the SPCC audit is to ensure that an effective employee training program exists and has been implemented.

The training program should be part of the operator training for all operations involving oil processing, transfer, or storage. It should be prefaced by: (1) a description of the SPCC regulations, (2) a description of the plant's spill control and spill contingency plans, and (3) a statement of management policy on oil pollution. The latter should forbid intentional oil pollution and commit resources to cleaning up unintentional oil pollution. Each training program should provide familiarization with the spill control equipment at each facility and include a plan of action for its proper operation. In addition, another action plan should be provided for emergencies. This training should be repeated or reviewed at regular intervals.

Routine maintenance of spill control equipment is another area of training. This should include regular checks of all valves, pumps, and fittings for malfunction or leakage, and preventive maintenance of oil skimmers, overfill prevention devices, and other mechanical spill control equipment. Larger equipment should have maintenance records on file that are updated after each inspection. These records should be filed along with the tank inspection records in the SPCC plan.

Operator training will also involve some record keeping in connection with spill control. Impervious dike draining, for example, requires a supervisor to inspect it for oil on the surface. His OK is then recorded before accumulated water is released. The date of the release and the operator's initials are also recorded. These records are a required part of the SPCC plan.

If the auditor's tour of the plant shows the SPCC plan to be working well, little attention needs to be paid to the actual operator-training procedures. Likewise, properly filled-out drainage records as part of an up-to-date SPCC plan indicate effective training. On the other hand, if problems are found in the plant or in the records, inadequate training is a likely cause. Any investigation should start out with the supervisor of the operation in which the problem was found. The auditor should find out why the problem occurred, and what lapsed in the operator training program to allow it to happen.

Emergency Coordinator

The SPCC plan should designate one individual as the coordinator of spill prevention at the plant. Usually, this duty will be assigned to the environmental coordinator or the plant engineer. His most important function is to serve as emergency coordinator in the event of a major spill, first notifying the Coast Guard and local authorities, and then implementing a proper response. The auditor should interview the coordinator of spill prevention with respect to plant emergency preparedness, including location and maintenance of supplies and emergency response team training. The extent of these precautions should be in direct proportion to the likelihood of a major environmental impact resulting from an oil spill. The past history of oil spills at the plant should be reviewed to determine the adequacy of the emergency preparedness program.

The Plant Tour

In the plant tour, the auditor will be able to determine whether or not a plant without an SPCC plan should prepare one. For the plant with a plan, the auditor will be able to estimate its effectiveness by inspecting the tankage and other spill potential points, together with the spill control and prevention measures. He will also be able to check the effectiveness of the training program and the condition of any spill control facilities at the time of the audit. On the other hand, the auditor will not confirm the adequacy of any of the elements of a spill control program, such as a system of dikes or a tank inspection program. If they appear inadequate, the auditor can only recommend that they be reviewed by a competent engineer. It is important to reiterate that the environmental audit of a plant's SPCC plan does not substitute for an engineering review of spill control measures.

In preparation for the plant tour, the auditor should have a plot plan showing the location of all tanks, drum storage areas, fluid transport piping, load and unload points, and storm drain inlets. Each of these facilities must be carefully inspected. A topographical map would also be useful to show the presence of surface waters in the area of the plant. If the plant borders a body of water, or if the storm drains or any plant process water outfalls discharge to surface waters, the locations of all outfalls should be noted. The tour should include a walk along any plant water frontage and visits to all outfalls even if they are located off the plant site. The auditor should be alert during the tour for any unlisted tankage such as oil-filled electrical substations, drum storage areas, waste oil sumps, or small-vehicle refueling points.

Underground Tanks. The SPCC plan should list the location, contents, volume, throughput, construction, and age of each underground tank. In addition, the fill points should be described, as well as any ancillary equipment such as vent pipes, heaters, or gauges. Special procedures relating to each tank, such as safety precautions taken during filling, should be described. This information should be reviewed during the plant tour with respect to each tank. Any variance from the

Figure 6-6. Earth-covered fuel oil tanks are partially above grade and therefore are considered to be above-ground tanks.

Figure 6-7. An underground solvent tank. The only evidence is the pump and dispensing valve.

reported information that is evident by inspection should be noted on the data inventory form. Other than checking the reported information, there is very little for the auditor to observe at the location of an underground tank. Nevertheless, each underground tank location should be inspected during the plant tour to see if the tank actually is an underground tank. EPA has proposed regulations that specifically exclude tanks in underground vaults or basements and tanks only partially below grade from the definition of underground tanks. The latter include tanks with dirt piled over them. If the plant has incorrectly identified a tank, that error might change the plant's status with respect to the requirement of an SPCC plan.

If an underground tank were leaking, that would not be evident on the surface. The plant's method of testing for leakage should be reviewed during the plant tour, particularly if there are no formal records of tests. If testing is done, the method, schedule, date of the next test, and recent results should be noted. Testing at many plants may only consist of the liquid storage inventories and the annual records that would indicate a loss during storage. Unfortunately, a minor loss may not be detected by this procedure because it must allow for meter errors, spillage, and evaporation. The auditor should find out how the tank contents are gauged during inventorying and what the procedure is for reporting a shortage. If this is the only method of detecting a leak, a program of periodic testing (e.g., pressure testing) should be recommended.

Above-Ground Tanks. Each above-ground tank on the plant property must be found in the course of the plant tour and inspected. This generally means walking around each tank, looking for obvious details, and noting them on the data inventory forms. For example, is the construction riveted or welded, does it have a fixed or floating roof, is it insulated, is it heated, and is there a fume collection system? The apparent condition of each tank should also be judged, particularly if there is evidence of deterioration. Fill control devices should also be noted, such as floats, sensors, or alarms. Any evidence of past overfills would be indicative of the effectiveness of these systems. Oil-filled transformers usually have the coolant volume printed on the manufacturer tag. The volumes and contents of all other tanks should be recorded from the SPCC plan or information provided by the environmental coordinator. It is also important to know the age of the tanks and the date of the last major inspection or cleaning.

The log of the tank inspection program, which is part of the SPCC plan, should be reviewed with respect to the appearance of each above-ground tank. Most inspection programs consist of a yearly visual check for leaks or damage. In effect, the auditor should do the same thing, but he will be comparing his observation with that of a plant employee. For an above-ground tank, the inspection consists of looking for any signs of lessening of the integrity of the tank. Deformation of the tank walls, deep rust, chemical corrosion, damage, or any sign of weepage at seams should be noted and included in the audit report. The base of the tank should be examined for cracks or breaks in the curbing. The auditor should not try to assess the condition of a floating roof tank, nor should he check the accuracy or operation of any level sensing equipment, other than to confirm that it appears to be operational and is being used.

Spill Control. Several types of spill control are used for aboveground tanks. These include watertight concrete dikes, earthen dikes, flow diversion barriers (curbing), and drainage ditches. To be acceptable as part of an SPCC plan, dikes must be large enough to hold the entire contents of the largest tank plus sufficient freeboard to allow for precipitation (usually based on the five-year storm for the region). In most cases, the auditor should be able to estimate whether or not this volume requirement has been met, but if it appears to be very close, he may recommend an engineering review. In the case of concrete dikes, careful attention should be paid to the condition of the structure and the drainage system. The latter might consist of a sump or a side wall drain, equipped with a gate valve in either case. These valves should be closed and tagged at all times. Large volumes of standing water in the dike should be noted, as well as any evidence of rust or oil floating on the water. The SPCC plan should outline a procedure whereby accumulated precipitation is checked for oil before being drained off. Each draining should be noted in a log attached to the SPCC plan. There should also be a procedure for draining condensed water out of the tanks. These valves should be locked when not in use.

Earthen dikes around tanks that contain flammable hydrocarbons are often required for protection against spreading of a tank fire. These dikes are also acceptable for oil spill control if they are large enough to hold the volume of the largest tank and if their berms are sound. Rainwater usually percolates into the ground at the bottom of the dike; so no drains are required. Oil, on the other hand, will permeate the soil at a very slow rate, providing time for plant personnel to react to a spill into the dike. This reaction time must be used to transfer the spilled oil to alternate tankage. Once such a spill has occurred, the oil-soaked dirt should be removed and replaced with fresh gravel. Over the years, minor spills will gradually reduce the soil permeability to the point where rainwater will form a pond in the dike. The capacity for oil spillage may then be reduced to the point where

Figure 6–8. High grass or underbrush in an earth dike may provide a haven to burrowing animals.

the dike is no longer adequate. Unless the audit is conducted in a rainy season, the auditor will have no way to determine the rate of water percolation. He will be able to assess the general condition of the dike, however. High grass or undergrowth should be noted because it provides havens for burrowing animals. Erosion, oil stains, trash accumulation, and undergrowth are all signs that the dike requires attention.

Assessing the adequacy of curbing or drainage ditches is also beyond the scope of an audit unless a problem is very obvious. For example, if the auditor visualizes the path that a catastrophic spill would take and feels that the curbing is too low or that the drainage ditches are too narrow, he should recommend an engineering review of the diversion system. It may be possible to discuss questions such as these with an engineer responsible for the design if it was done at the plant. It is more likely that any problems found will be the result of poor maintenance (e.g., trash or debris accumulations) or construction subsequent to the date of the plan. An example of the latter would be an access road cut through a diversion curb. This should be corrected during the three-year updating of the SPCC plan.

A flow diversion system must include a containment area where spilled oil can be removed and precipitation released to the surface waters or a sewer. This could be a pond, impoundment, separator, or settling pit. The latter should be equipped with oil skimmers if minor oil spills occur frequently. The auditor should look for any obvious clues that the system might not work, as well as any examples of poor or improper maintenance of the spill control system. These should be noted in the audit report.

Loading/Unloading and Transfer. The presence of tanks at a plant means there must also be unloading stations for trucks, rail cars, or barges. The plant may also have bulk loading facilities if it is a manufacturer of oil-based liquid products. In either case, the spill liabilities are the same. The trucks, tank cars, and barges are

Figure 6-9. Poor percolation allows rainfall to accumulate within a dike, thus reducing its capacity.

themselves tanks that could develop leaks or fail while connected to the load or unload point. Furthermore, the caps, flexible hoses, pumps, and valves required to move liquids into or out of tankers constitute additional spill hazards. Because of this liability, there should be a rigorous personnel training program, backed up by a written oil-transfer procedure on file listing all safety precautions and emergency procedures. These should be reviewed by the auditor before he inspects the transfer stations.

Full diking around truck transfer stations is impossible in most cases because of the access routes of the trucks. Nor is it necessary. The probability of a full load spill due to tank failure is very low; tankers are very strong, and DOT enforces a periodic inspection program. Minor spills, however, are more likely to occur at transfer stations than at fixed tanks, because of the frequent manipulation of the loading equipment. Leakage and failure of transfer equipment must be considered as normal operational problems. Thus, flow diversion barriers and stormwater run-off protection are necessary.

Figure 6–10. The probability of a major spill at a bulk loading terminal is small, but precautions must be taken to contain minor spills.

A common example of a spill at a bulk loading station for bottom-fill tankers is one caused by the incomplete sealing of the fill hose to the truck. This allows a slow leak to occur during the entire loading cycle. Proper operator training requires either that the loading by stopped as soon as a leak is noticed, or that a bucket be used to catch the leak. Some loading racks have drip pans connected to a waste tank as part of the facility. Another frequent cause of spills is draining of the fill hose between fills. This should be done into a bucket or an underground tank. The bucket should be emptied into a wastetank after each use.

Overfilling of tankers is a source of spills, just as the overfilling of stationary tanks is. Protection against it involves metered fill volumes, sensors on top-fill nozzles, and tank-vent liquid alarms. As in the case of stationary tank overflow protection, the auditor will not be in a position to assess the effectiveness of this equipment. Proper operator training is mandatory for transfer stations, but still minor spills are unavoidable. The auditor's task is to review the capability of the facility to contain them.

Run-off. In a plant storing or handling oil, some means must be provided for protecting run-off rainwater from oil contamination. In assessing this situation, the auditor must become familiar with the stormwater run-off system. Inlets are particularly important. When they are located in the vicinity of load/unload stations or pipelines, they must be protected not only from spills but also from minor oil contamination. One way to accomplish this is to build a water seal into the inlet. This has an underflow baffle in it that retains any oil floating on the surface of the run-off while allowing the water to pass through. One drawback is that dry weather can lower the water level below the water seal so that the next rain will carry any accumulated oil out with the first flow. Another is that even an intact water seal can be overwelmed by a large oil spill and allow the bulk of the oil through. In addition, accumulated oil is difficult to clean off the surface of the water seal. Despite these objections, this type of inlet is an effective "first line of defense."

Stormwater inlets in the vicinity of oil transfer operations should have positive oil spill control for all run-off leaving the plant property, whether it joins a municipal stormwater system, flows to a POTW, or is discharged to surface waters. This control could consist of an oil/water separator, or a catch basin designed to be pumped out whenever necessary after inspection for oil on the surface. If contamination is routinely present on the water, an oil skimmer should be installed. If not, a supply of absorbent pads should be stored nearby. The auditor should examine the oil removal system for proper operation. The belts, tubes, or floats should be operational, and there should be adequate storage volume for captured oil. There should not be quantities of oil on the surface of the water during routine operation.

Security. The auditor should ensure that proper security measures have been taken to comply with the SPCC plan. These include fencing around oil storage areas (or the entire plant) and a locked or guarded entrance. Tank valves and pump switches should be locked or made inaccessible to unauthorized persons to prevent unplanned oil discharges. Adequate lighting should be provided to deter vandalism and allow early detection of spills. Electrical substations located outside the plant property are often overlooked oil storage locations. These should be kept locked and well lighted at all times for safety reasons, but they should also be reviewed for potential vandalism.

THE SPCC PLAN REPORT

The report covering the SPCC plan audit must provide information in the following areas:

1. Confirmation of the status of the plant. Does the plant have an SPCC plan? Does the plant need an SPCC plan and not have one, or does the audit confirm that a plan is not needed?
2. Quality of the SPCC plan. If the plant has an SPCC plan, does it appear to meet the minimum requirements set by EPA? Would it provide useful information in the event of a spill emergency?
3. Adequacy of procedures and equipment. If the plant is storing oil or hazardous materials, is there an effective training program? Are the spill prevention facilities properly designed and

Table 6-1. EPA Inspection Instructions.

FACILITY DESCRIPTION

(a) Make detailed in narrative style; use extra sheets if needed.

(b) Include all storage; indicate capacity and actual amounts and type of oil in each tank, including tanks not in use—above ground or buried. Indicate percent of oil in mixed storage and annual throughput where possible. If this information is included on attached drawing or lists, state this here.

(c) Describe all types and adequacy of prevention measures—dikes, catchment areas, drainage systems, separators, tank level alarm systems, drainage pumps, etc. Describe major security measures taken—locks, guards, fencing, etc.

(d) Describe maintenance at facility. Use such terms as "neat and well maintained," "messy and poorly maintained," etc. Describe any unsatisfactory maintenance such as oil pools, broken dikes, etc.

(e) Obtain a statement about past spills at this facility; observe drain controls; look for evidence of past spills.

RECEIVING WATER

(a) This should be a recognizable river, stream, lake, estuary, etc., which can be expected to contain water at least part of the year.

(b) Explicitly describe, using approx. distances in meters or kilometers (feet or miles), all of the drainage paths from facility to receiving water or storm drain in (a).

(c) Add here any statements obtained about annual rainfall, runoff, flooding, etc.

COMMENTS

Describe soil conditions as they relate to spill runoff and whether spills have a reasonable chance of reaching drainage channels, storm drains or waterways. Obtain statements from owner/operator which indicate whether the person is aware of 40 CFR 112.

SPCC PLAN REVIEW

State whether facility has an SPCC plan and whether it is adequate. Describe in detail any inadequacies in SPCC plan or its implementation. Include references to pertinent paragraphs of Spill Prevention Regulations.

SPCC AMENDMENT RECOMMENDATIONS (Amendment Inspection only)

Describe areas of past and potential oil spills and corrective actions, preventive measures and countermeasures carried out in facility. Based on your inspection, will these features of the post-spill SPCC plan adequately minimize the possibility of recurrence? Why? If not, state recommendations for SPCC plan amendments in detail—attach quantitative information, drawings, etc.

FIELD DRAWINGS (attach more sheets if needed and show north arrow or other orientation)

Show: all major features with spill potential requiring spill prevention measures; all drainage features that relate to potential spills such as catch basins, storm drains, channels, ponding areas, dikes, sumps, etc.; the appropriate distances in meters or kilometers (feet or miles) along drainage paths from spill potential areas to water course or water body in 2(a).

PHOTOGRAPHS (attach more sheets if needed)

Show inadequate SPCC features, spills, poor maintenance, proximity to waterways, and so forth. Mount photographs on page 7; attach more sheets if needed.

well maintained? Are adequate stores of emergency equipment on hand?

The report should include a comprehensive listing of all storage tanks, identifying each as to type, volume, location, contents, fill point, spill control facilities, and general condition. The tanks containing oil as defined by EPA should be listed separately in above-ground and underground groups, and these totaled to confirm the need for an SPCC plan. Storage areas of oil in drums must be included in the list and the total volume added to the volume of above-ground storage. It might be useful to identify each tank by a number and mark its location on a plot plan of the plant. For plants with substantial amounts of liquids in bulk storage, the tankage may already be listed and numbered. These lists should be used if available.

The SPCC plan should provide descriptions of any oil spills that have occurred within the past year. The audit report should go beyond this to discuss all major spills that have occurred in recent history. The extent of each spill should be mentioned, as well as the cause and the steps taken to ensure against future spills. This discussion will provide an indication of the effectiveness of the SPCC plan. If there have been several spills due to the same cause, such as tank overfilling, the spill prevention equipment or procedures may need to be upgraded. On the other hand, if a number of costly spills have occurred for different reasons, perhaps the training and response activities should be examined. Recommendations based on the auditor's perception of the adequacy of the SPCC plan should be made.

The audit report should assess the adequacy of the records required as part of the SPCC plan, including tank inspections, spill prevention equipment inspections or tests, and dike draining records. Where they are inadequate, recommendations should be made for improvement. The auditor must be familiar with the regulations, however, to guard against recommending burdensome procedures that are not warranted by either the size of the facility or the law. Table 6–1 lists the instructions from EPA Form 7500–53(9–80), entitled "SPCC Inspection Field Sheet." These instructions represent what EPA expects in a review of an SPCC plan. They provide an excellent outline for an SPCC plan audit report.

7
PCBs, Asbestos, and Superfund

Many environmental liabilities might exist at a manufacturing plant besides those covered in the previous chapters. One large area of concern is toxic and hazardous materials that are not wastes. Another involves the extensive body of federal, state, and local environmental regulations in force in addition to the major statutes reviewed thus far.

Industrial products and raw materials, often very useful and widely distributed ones, are suspected of containing harmful substances with alarming frequency. Vinyl chloride, lead compounds, chlorinated solvents, formaldehyde, and fluorocarbons are examples of these hazardous materials. The Comprehensive Environmental Response, Compensation, and Liability Act of 1980 (Superfund) was enacted to provide a broad regulatory basis that would encompass problems arising from past disposal practices and future releases for this ever-expanding list of hazardous materials. It is incumbent upon an auditor to be aware not only of all regulated substances but also of those about which questions have been raised in the press. Communicating information to plant management about possible future liabilities is as important a function of an audit as uncovering present problems.

Most hazardous materials encountered in industrial plants are related to specific manufacturing processes. They might be raw materials, solvents, by-products, catalysts, or substances otherwise connected with the manufacture of a specific product. Mercury, in the chlor-alkali industry, is an example. Mercury is used as an electrode in the electrochemical manufacture of chlorine gas. Hydrogen gas and alkali hydroxides are by-products of the reaction. An auditor of a chlor-alkali plant would have to be familiar with the specific regulations covering mercury, such as The National Emission Standard for Mercury (Part E—Section 114 of the Clean Air Act), in order to be able to evaluate the effectiveness of the compliance program at the plant.

One way to prepare for making an audit in an unfamiliar industry would be to find out all the materials that could be involved in the processes utilized in that industry. Each material should then be checked against all environmental regulations, including Section 311 of the Clean Water Act (CWA), Section 3001 of the Resource Conservation and Recovery Act (RCRA), and Section 7 of the Toxic Substances Control Act (TSCA). The regulations pertaining to any of the materials identified as hazardous in that industry should be reviewed. The auditor would then be well prepared to evaluate the compliance measures in effect at the plant for each of the hazardous materials in use.

In this environmentally enlightened age, an auditor will often find that the more hazardous the material involved in an industrial process, the more awareness the plant will have of the proper precautions, compliance measures, and legal requirements that must be met. Thus, an auditor's job will be relatively straightforward with respect to extremely hazardous materials. On the other hand, less hazardous substances in the form of coolants, lubricants, solvents, cleaners, insecticides, or boiler chemicals often pose a far greater problem to an auditor because the plant personnel may not be aware of the composition of common or proprietary materials. It is incumbent upon an auditor to check for these situations and alert plant management if necessary.

Two very widely encountered hazardous substances are PCBs and asbestos. Many plants that are more than ten years old contain these materials, but, because of their innocuous roles as transformer fluids or insulation, plant personnel may not be aware of their presence. Both materials are strictly regulated, and severe penalties and liabilities can result from their mismanagement (see later discussion in this chapter). Other common substances that should be checked during an audit include: solvents such as benzene and the chlorinated solvents; corrosives such as those found in boiler and water treatment chemicals; flammables including thinners and liquid fuels; and toxics such as insecticides, laboratory chemicals, and cleaning agents.

With regard to environmental regulations, an auditor will find that many apply to only a few industries, because of either the location or the type of industry. The Coastal Zone Management Act is an example of a location-specific regulation; it applies only in states with designated coastal zones and affects only industries located within those zones. The New Source Performance Standards promulgated under the Clean Air Act apply only to specific classes of major stationary sources (fossil-fired steam generators, catalytic cracking unit catalyst regenerators, sulfuric acid plants, nitric acid plants, and kraft pulp mills). The National Emission Standards for Hazardous Air Pollutants apply only to industries that are sources of hazardous air pollutants (asbestos, beryllium, mercury, or vinyl chloride). Petroleum refineries, glass plants, seafood plants, and organic chemical manufacturers must comply with industry-specific pretreatment regulations under the Clean Water Act. Other regulations cover specific activities that might be undertaken by industries. Examples include Section 404 of the Clean Water Act requiring permits for dredging and filling operations, and the Safe Drinking Water Act regulations covering underground injection. A detailed review of these regulations and what the auditor should look for to ascertain compliance is beyond the scope of this book. In studying the industry to be audited, an auditor should review all environmental regulations and note any that might seem to impose special requirements. The Appendix contains an outline of the major and some minor federal environmental programs that the auditor should be aware of. Equally important are the state or local environmental regulations affecting the plant being audited. These must be reviewed on a case-by-case basis.

PCBs

Polychlorinated biphenyl, PCB, refers to a family of chemicals based on the biphenyl molecule, on which from one to ten chlorine atoms are substituted. There are 209 possible members in the family, but they are almost always encountered as mixtures of isomers with specific percentages of chlorine substitution. The level of substitution is often indicated by the trade designation for the mixture, such as Arochlor 1254, which was Monsanto's trade name for a mixture of

PCBs containing 54% chlorine. Depending on this percentage, the mixture might range in viscosity from a light oil to a wax.

PCBs were developed in the 1930s for use as nonflammable cooling oils for electrical devices. They work extremely well in this capacity because they are very stable and have high heat capacity. PCB-filled electrical equipment quickly became the industry standard for all applications where fire danger was a design consideration. This included virtually all installations within buildings and railroad equipment and many outside utility installations near residential properties. PCBs also have a high dielectric constant, which enabled compact, nonflammable capacitors to be manufactured. These devices have found widespread application throughout manufacturing, power distribution, and transportation industries as motor starters and power factor controllers.

PCBs have many other uses that are based on excellent properties such as low vapor pressure and high solvency. For example, PCBs have been used as hydraulic fluids, plasticizers, sealants, and caulks. An application that has resulted in a very wide distribution of PCBs in the environment is as a dye carrier in carbonless copy paper. This product was manufactured between the years 1957 and 1971 in very large amounts. Some of it is still in use, and, as a result, PCBs are occasionally found in waste paper stocks that are recycled. One recycled product is cardboard packaging for food. The Food and Drug Administration has placed a PCB limit of 10 ppm in food packaging because of the possibility of contamination.

It has been estimated that, in the half century since their discovery, over a billion pounds of PCBs have been manufactured, and nearly all of this is still in existence because of the extreme stability of the PCB molecule. One calculation several years ago placed the amount that had degraded naturally or had been incinerated at only 4%. Since the promulgation of the EPA ban, however, increasing quantities of PCBs are being destroyed by incineration. The rest are either still in service, in landfills, or dispersed in the environment.

PCBs were discovered in the environment a little more than a decade ago when minute quantities started showing up in soil samples as well as in fish and other wildlife tissue samples. A 1974 EPA study showed the presence of PCBs in over 90% of human tissue samples collected nationwide. With such vast amounts of PCBs in use or in storage, these pieces of evidence were considered the first signs of a major contamination of the biosphere. The contamination could only get worse indefinitely unless something were done to interrupt the manufacturing and disposal cycle.

The effects of the contamination are not easy to determine at the low concentrations manifested thus far. Chlorinated pesticide residues such as DDT at somewhat higher concentrations have been shown to have a direct effect on reproductive cycles in some species of wildlife. Because of the long time constant for PCB decay, by the time similar effects are noted, it may be too late to react.

Acute symptoms from direct worker contact with PCBs are either completely absent or minimal. One symptom, chloracne, which has been noted in certain sensitive individuals, is typical for chlorinated solvents. Cohort studies of electrical workers for chronic symptoms have failed to show any consistent adverse effects of long-term exposure. These studies may be questionable, however, because of the difficulty in establishing actual exposure histories and because of the long latency periods for some diseases. There have been a few isolated incidents of PCB toxicity, but they have not been very convincing because, in every case, there has been the possible presence of highly toxic impurities in the PCB oils. Thus, the chronic toxicity of PCBs is still an open question.

Regardless of the health effects issue, the potential for massive environmental contamination by PCBs was sufficient to induce Congress through the Toxic Substances Act of 1976 to mandate the promulgation of regulations to ban the manufacture of PCBs, limit their distribution in commerce, and control their disposal. EPA rules promulgated in 1978 (43 FR 7150) and "the Final Ban Rule" in 1979 (44 FR 31514) accomplished these objectives by regulating all PCBs down to a concentration of 50 ppm. Several aspects of the regulations were challenged in the courts. As a result, EPA promulgated more stringent rules for inspection, maintenance, and disposal of PCB electrical equipment (46 FR 27614).

EPA PCB Regulations

The regulations by which EPA controls the handling and disposal of PCBs are structured around definitions based on PCB concentration ranges (Table 7-1). Three discrete ranges were established, each with definite rules for handling and disposal. The ranges are: 0–49 ppm,

Table 7-1. Examples of PCB Definitions (40 CFR Section 761).

PCB—Any chemical substance or combination of substances that contains 50 ppm, or greater, PCB.
PCB item—Any PCB article, PCB container, or equipment that contains any concentration of 50 ppm or more.
PCB article—Any manufactured item, other than PCB containers, that contains PCBs.
PCB unit—Any PCB transformer or PCB-contaminated transformer in use or stored for reuse.
PCB transformer—Any transformer containing 500 ppm, or greater, PCB.
PCB-contaminated transformer—Any transformer containing 50–499 ppm PCB.
Non-PCB transformer—Any transformer containing less than 50 ppm PCB as determined by manufacturer certification or laboratory analysis.
Large capacitor—Any capacitors, either high or low voltage, that contain three pounds or more of PCBs.
Small capacitor—Any capacitors containing less than three pounds of PCBs.
PCB container—A device (drum, barrel, etc.) used to contain PCBs or PCB articles.
Leak—Any instance in which a PCB unit has any PCBs on any portion of its external surface.
Moderate leak—Any leak that results in any quantity of PCBs running off, or about to run off, the external surface of a PCB unit.

50–499 ppm, and 500 ppm and higher. The regulations accomplish the following: ban the manufacture of PCBs, require labeling and inspection of certain PCB items in service, establish timetables for phasing out PCB articles, and set disposal criteria for each class of PCB items. The rules are straightforward, and an auditor should become familiar with them before conducting any industrial audit where PCB equipment might be present. Some states have established PCB regulations that are more strict than the EPA regulations. California, for example, has established a 7 ppm cutoff for PCB contamination. The auditor should call the state agency before the audit to ascertain any substantive differences between the EPA regulations and the state regulations affecting the plant. Below are some specific points from the federal regulations.

The regulations allow:

- PCB transformers to continue in use as long as they perform their intended function and do not leak PCBs into the environment.
- Disposal of PCB liquid and large capacitors by incineration in EPA-approved equipment.
- Storage of waste PCBs for up to one year.
- Landfilling at specially approved chemical waste landfills of soil, rags, or other debris generated from spills or contaminated with PCBs.
- Servicing of PCB transformers until June 30, 1984, excluding core removal.
- Rebuilding of PCB-contaminated transformers (with certain restrictions).
- Disposal of small capacitors at ordinary sanitary landfills.
- Reclassification of PCB transformers to PCB-contaminated transformers if, after draining and refilling, the transformer is kept in service for three months (and the PCB concentration is below 500 ppm).
- Labeling of all PCB items except PCB-contaminated transformers. (It is probably a good idea to label these anyway.)
- Continued use of carbonless carbon paper.

The regulations do not allow:

- Manufacture, processing, distribution in commerce, and use of PCBs in other than totally enclosed, nonleaking containers.
- Addition of dielectric fluid containing 500 ppm or more of PCB to any other dielectric fluid containing less than 500 ppm PCB, regardless of the resulting concentration.
- Addition of any PCB to a heat transfer system or a hydraulic system.
- Servicing of any PCB-containing electromagnets that require removal of the coil.

The regulations require:

- Visual weekly inspection for leaks of PCB units posing an exposure risk to food and feed products. Inspection logs and leak reporting are required.
- Visual inspection for leaks at least every three months of all other PCB units in use or in storage for reuse. Inspection logs and leak reporting are required.

Compliance

Any plant more than a few years old should have initiated a PCB compliance program whether there was known PCB equipment in use or not. For many plants, the result of the PCB compliance program would be confirmation of the absence of PCB equipment. For others, replacement or disposal projects might be necessary to achieve the no-PCB status. Still others might find it advantageous to manage their existing PCB equipment for the rest of its useful life. The initial PCB compliance program consists essentially of four steps:

1. Inventory all equipment for obvious PCB status.
2. Test all suspect equipment for PCB content.
3. Assess the risk of each piece of proven PCB equipment.
4. Dispose of all high-risk items and manage all low-risk items.

Equipment Inventory. The first step in achieving compliance with the PCB regulations is to inventory all oil-filled equipment. For most PCB capacitors, transformers, switches, and other electrical equipment, the label may contain sufficient information to identify the cooling fluid. For example, a trade name for a proprietary PCB fluid or an indication of nonflammability is sufficient evidence of the presence of PCBs. Table 7–2 lists the more common trade names for PCB fluids. Also, virtually all oil-filled capacitors made before 1978 can be assumed to be PCB-filled. On newer equipment, made since PCB manufacture was banned, the label often states "Non-PCB."

Figure 7–1 shows an example of a PCB data inventory form that could be used to inventory all oil-cooled electrical equipment. The inventory should be organized into categories of non-PCB equipment,

Table 7-2. Trade Names of PCB Transformer Fluids.

TRADE NAME	MANUFACTURER
Arochlor	Monsanto
Asbestol	American Corp.
Chlorextol	Allis Chalmers
Clophen	Bayer (Germany)
Diaclor	Sangamo Electric (Japan)
Dykanol	Cornell Dubilier
Elemex	McGraw Edison
Fenclor	Caffaro (Italy)
Hyvol	Aerovox
Inerteen	Westinghouse
KD	Caffaro (Italy)
Kennechlor	Mitsubishi (Japan)
No-Flamol	Wagner Electric
Phenoclor	Prodelec (France)
Pyralene	Prodelec (France)
Pyranol	General Electric
Saf-T-Kuhl	Kuhlman Electric
Santotherm	Mitsubishi (Japan)

small capacitors, large capacitors, contaminated transformers, PCB transformers, other PCB articles, and PCB items in storage. The filled-out forms will provide the basis for the plant's PCB management program, including all inspection, record-keeping, reporting, storage, or disposal requirements that must be met. Used in this manner, they must be updated regularly as required. If no PCB items or suspect PCB items are found in the inventory step, no further compliance steps are necessary. The forms and any test results should be retained by the plant as proof that a comprehensive check was made for PCBs.

Testing Suspect Equipment. Once all obvious PCB items have been identified, the next step is to test all "suspect" equipment. No capacitors will be in this group, as they can be safely assumed to be PCB capacitors unless labeled otherwise. Other oil-filled systems that are suspect should also be tested. This precautionary testing is expensive, but it is advisable because it only must be performed once to prove an item is non-PCB. This assumes that the equipment is prop-

Plant ______________________________

Item ______________ Manufacturer ______________

Rating ______________ Serial Number ______________

Equipment Owner ______________ Maintenance by ______________

Coolant ______________ Amount ______ Gal. ______ lbs ______

PCB ______________ ppm Test Date ______________

Installed ______________ Age at Installation ______________

Location ______________________________

Description of Surrounding ______________________________

Area (> 500 ppm ONLY) ______________________________

____

____

Inspections

Date	Leakage	Label	Comments	Initials

Figure 7-1. PCB item inventory.

Service

Date	Item	Service Company

Out of Service Status

Removed from Service, Date ______

Placed in Storage, Date ______

Preparation for Storage ______

Name of Storage Facility ______

Location of Storage Facility ______

Placed in Transport for Disposal ______

Transport Company ______

Location of Disposal Facility ______

Name of Disposal Facility ______

Date of Disposal ______

Note: EPA requires this record to be maintained on the premises or at a central location for a period of at least five years after the disposal of the PCB item. The record must be available for inspection by EPA compliance officers and must be current as of July 1 of every year.

Figure 7-1. (*Cont.*)

erly labeled "Non-PCB" once tested, and that no subsequent contamination takes place. Many vendors provide comprehensive services to test and inventory PCB equipment. For transformers, this service is often included with routine dielectric testing.

EPA requires that transformers about which nothing is known be assumed to be PCB transformers. Likewise, transformers that are labeled as mineral-oil-filled must be assumed to be PCB-contaminated. There must be an actual test result showing the PCB concentration to be less than 50 ppm before a transformer may be handled as a non-PCB transformer. The reason is that, in the pre–PCB-ban days, transformer service companies would use the same equipment and mixers for both PCB and non-PCB fluids, contaminating most non-PCB fluids. It is necessary to test all suspect equipment for PCBs to avoid unnecessary expenses of labeling, inspecting, and disposal. Contamination is also common in waste oil due to pre-ban practices of mixing waste transformer fluids with other waste oils. Thus, testing is also recommended for purchased waste oils, products made from

Figure 7-2. Transformers about which nothing is known must be assumed to be PCB transformers.

waste oils (e.g., dust suppression oil, cut-back asphalts) unless certified PCB-free by the suppliers, and in-plant waste oil storage where the possibility of contamination exists. A good rule is: when in doubt, test.

All test results, either positive or negative, should be filed with the PCB inventory. Sample location, sampling method, and the date should be recorded with or on the laboratory report. This information will be invaluable if there is ever a question about equipment status.

Testing should be done at laboratories that have been certified by EPA for PCB analyses. This is not only important for satisfying any EPA inspectors; it will also provide assurance that the methods used have adequate sensitivity. PCB analysis is different from most environmental pollutant analyses in that it does not seek to quantify a single compound or element such as DDT or arsenic. Rather, families of different PCB species in proportions characteristic of specific Arochlor fluids must be identified and quantified. When impurities are present or several industrial PCB fluids have been mixed, this quantification step takes great skill and precise technique.

Analysis is usually done by gas chromatography (GC). EPA has developed a number of preparation and analysis procedures for samples in various substrates such as oil, soil, and water. A typical method calls for extraction and concentration prior to GC analysis. The results consist of recorder tracings that are characteristic of the PCB fluids present. These "fingerprints" must be identified by comparing the retention times of certain components with known Arochlors run under the same conditions.

Other procedures include the following: GC detection by mass spectroscopy for positive identification of specific PCB molecular weights; chlorination to the decachloro PCB followed by quantification as a single species; and prescreening for chlorinated organic compounds. The latter method is useful for surveying large numbers of oil samples where the possibility of PCB contamination is considered unlikely. Positive results would have to be quantified by a chromatographic technique.

Risk Assessment. Many plants discover from their inventory one or more PCB transformers or capacitors in their facilities. They are then faced with the choice of disposing of the items or initiating a PCB management program. The latter choice is often the better one for a number of reasons: (1) EPA allows the continued use of totally enclosed PCB items that are not leaking (although EPA does intend to phase out PCB capacitors by 1992); (2) the management requirements for PCB equipment are not excessive; (3) the full service life of expensive electrical equipment can be obtained; and (4) more competition and better technology can be expected to lower disposal costs in the future.

A risk assessment should be performed before this decision is made. Table 7-3 gives a comprehensive format for ranking transformer risks recommended by the U.S. Navy Environmental Support Office (PCB Compliance, Assessment, and Spill Control Guide, NEESA 20.2-028A, August 1982). It considers not only the concentration of PCBs in the equipment but also the location, condition, and spill potential; and it provides four categories of risk, based on the total points assigned after completion of the assessment. For all but the lowest category, the best choice may well be disposal of the equipment and replacement with non-PCB equipment, or flushing and replacement of the PCB fluid.

Table 7-3. Transformer Risk Assessment Sheet.

POINTS ASSESSED	RISK FACTOR	TRANSFORMER TYPE
	(0)	Non-PCB filled (determined by analysis)
______	(1)	PCB contaminated liquid (determined by analysis or nameplate)
	(2)	PCB filled (determined from nameplate or by analysis)
	(2)	Contents unknown
		LABELING
	(0)	No label required (Non-PCB)
______	(1)	Properly labeled
	(2)	Requires label but not present
		QUANTITY
	(1)	Fluid level on transformer register *full*
______	(2)	3/4 full
	(3)	Less than half full
		PCB dielectric fluid in transformer:
	(1)	Less than 10 gallons
______	(2)	More than 10 but less than 100 gallons
	(15)	More than 100 but less than 500 gallons
	(20)	More than 500 but less than 1,000 gallons

Table 7-3. (*Cont.*)

POINTS ASSESSED	RISK FACTOR	TRANSFORMER TYPE
		LOCATION
	(1)	Located in isolated area
______	(2)	Located in open area occasionally visited or used by people
	(3)	Located outdoors in transformer vault
	(4)	Outdoors on pad
	(5)	Outdoors in underground vault
	(6)	Outdoors on pole
	(7)	In vault in occupied building
	(8)	In basement of occupied building
	(25)	On upper floor inside building or on roof
	If entire content of the transformer were to spill, fluid would:	
	(1)	Be contained or confined.
______	(2)	Contaminate pad and exterior of transformer only.
	(105)	Contaminate nearby soil, gravel, or other materials.
	(120)	Contaminate occupied areas.
	(150)	Contaminate water drains, ditches, sewer, etc.
	(150)	Contaminate bodies of water located nearby, and migration of fluid into waterways or groundwater would cause extensive contamination.
	(150)	Contaminate food storage, preparation, or serving area.
	Susceptibility to damage:	
	(1)	Not susceptible to damage.
______	(2)	Moderate; unit has some protection (e.g., fence or curb) runaway vehicles could cause damage.
	(3)	Unit is fenced or has lightweight guard posts, but machinery or vehicles operated close by.
	(4)	Unit is not protected at all and vehicles or machinery operated very close by. Unit is accessible to nonauthorized personnel.
	Transformer vent system:	
	(1)	Vents outside in area away from windows, air intakes, people, food, water.
______	(2)	Vents outside, near windows, air intakes, people, food, water (high probability for contamination).
	(3)	Transformer vents to inside of building where people are located.
		CONDITION
	(0)	Transformer not leaking.
______	(1)	No active leak; however, old stains visible on casing or pad.
	(100)	New small stains noted, mainly around bushings or gaskets.
	(150)	Moderate active leak requiring control by drip pan or other means.
	(175)	Large leak needs immediate repairs.
	(200)	Active spill contaminating transformer pad and surrounding area.
	(0)	Transformer pad has no drain, cracks, or open spaces around conduits or ground wire.

(*continued*)

Table 7-3. (*Cont.*)

POINTS ASSESSED	RISK FACTOR	TRANSFORMER TYPE
______	(1)	Pad has drain, no cracks.
	(2)	Pad has drain, cracks, and open spaces around conduits or ground wire.
	(3)	Metal plates present on pad where leaking PCBs would be difficult to remove.
	(4)	Transformer located in pourous concrete block or wooden building.
	(5)	Transformer located on wooden floor or pad.
	(6)	Transformer in below-ground vault with sump-pump which could become contaminated with PCBs.
	(0)	Area around transformer clean, neat, clear of trash, extraneous equipment and materials absent.
______	(1)	Fire suppression equipment readily available.
	(2)	Tools and machinery nearby where damage could occur to transformer.
	(3)	Area surrounding transformer contains trash, or is used to store tools or equipment which could damage transformer, or no fire suppression equipment available.
	(1)	Transformer and pad or vault has dike or curb to contain spill material.
______	(2)	Dike or curb deteriorated or damaged.
	(100)	No spill containment (dike or curb), transformer located over or near water or food-handling areas.
	(100)	Dike or curb insufficient to contain at least 10% material if spill occurs.
	(100)	No spill containment, transformer located in occupied building.
______	Total Points	

RISK FACTORS
Schedule

POINTS	RISK EVALUATION
300 and above	*Extreme hazard*—Transformer requires immediate major corrective action.
200–299	*Potential hazard*—Requires minor repairs.
100–199	*Poor*—Requires mainly spill containment, berm, dike, etc.
0–99	*Good*—Requires regular inspection and normal maintenance.

Management. Continued use of PCB equipment must comply with EPA requirements as listed in 40 CFR Section 761. EPA allows the indefinite use of PCB transformers (>500 ppm) to the end of their service life, but they must bear a label (Figure 7-3) and be inspected at

Figure 7-3. PCB warning label.

regular intervals. Some plants may wish to label PCB-contaminated transformers (50–500 ppm) as well, to warn service personnel to avoid spills and contamination. All records of inspections and maintenance must be retained for five years after final disposition of the equipment. The inspections are required every three months unless the transformers have secondary containment; annual inspections are then sufficient. Items that have any potential exposure to food or feed products must be inspected weekly, and those in storage areas must be inspected monthly.

An inspection of a piece of electrical equipment such as a transformer consists of a visual search for any leakage of dielectric fluid on the exterior and surrounding surfaces of the item, to the extent allowed by its location without necessitating shutting the equipment down. A small leak is any instance in which a PCB unit has any PCBs on any portion of its exterior surface. A moderate leak is one that results in any quantity of PCBs running off, or about to run off, the exterior surface of the PCB unit.

If a leak is discovered, any leaking material should be cleaned up immediately, and the leak repaired as soon as possible. The record should show the transformer location, the date of each inspection, the name of the inspector, the date of any leak, an estimate of the amount of fluid leaked, and any servicing performed. The inventory form provides for this information.

Servicing of PCB transformers is allowed up to the point of core removal. For this purpose, PCB fluids can be stored, provided that the conditions for storage are met. Servicing can result in reclassifying the equipment if the fluid is drained and refilled by non-PCB fluid. In this way, PCB transformers can be converted to PCB-contaminated or even non-PCB transformers. The test to confirm the equipment status must be conducted after no less than three months of in-service use following refilling. This gives any PCBs trapped in the core a chance to migrate into the fluid. Such migration makes it very difficult to convert a PCB transformer into a non-PCB transformer unless a permanent PCB-absorbing filter is attached to the cooling tubes.

The same labeling and inspection rules apply to PCB capacitors as to PCB transformers. One major difference is that a capacitor found to have a leak in any quantity must be removed from service and any contamination cleaned up. Continued use of large PCB capacitors is allowed by EPA until October 1, 1992. In determining the risks involved in the continued use of PCB electrical equipment, EPA regulators felt that capacitors were more likely than transformers to fail by rupturing their casings, thereby spreading PCBs around a wider area than a simple leak. This type of failure could not be planned for or anticipated by an inspection program. Therefore, EPA set a time limit on the use of large PCB capacitors.

Storage of PCB Items

Any plant with PCB electrical equipment in use is likely to have spare capacitors or replacement fluid for servicing transformers and switch gear. There also may be stored PCB equipment that has failed or has been removed from service for some other reason. All these items must be stored in accordance with EPA regulations until they are reused or disposed of. In addition, new or used PCB transformer fluid and any cleanup debris from PCB spills must also be stored in the same manner.

One option for storage is to use the facilities of a contractor. This may be an attractive alternative compared to contending with the storage regulations, but there are risks involved. The generator of controlled substances is always ultimately responsible for those materials, and this responsibility cannot be contracted away. Thus, if the storage facility is cited for violations and goes out of business, the generator might be required to bear the cleanup costs. On the other hand, if the storage is part of a total disposal contract with a qualified contractor, it might be the most efficient way of quickly ridding a plant of a leaking transformer, spill cleanup debris, or some other PCB headache. Another example where contractor storage would be useful is the case of the sale or demolition of a plant when it would not be desirable to have stored PCBs on the property. In most other cases, storage of PCBs at the plant until disposal can be arranged is the best approach.

EPA allows for temporary storage, for up to 30 days, of nonleaking PCB articles or leaking PCB items if they are packed in absorbent materials in nonleaking containers. In addition, short-term temporary storage is allowed for low concentrations (< 500 ppm) of PCB fluids and nonliquid debris in small containers such as 55-gallon drums. The only requirements are that the date of removal from service be attached to all items in temporary storage, and that the plant storing liquid PCBs have an SPCC plan that addresses the drum storage area in which the PCB items are to be stored.

The provision for temporary storage is intended to allow plant management time to arrange for disposal of small amounts of PCBs without creating a PCB storage facility. It is useful where a one-time spill has occurred, and a quantity of contaminated cleanup material has been generated and must be disposed of. It is not so useful, however, for a plant having large numbers of PCB capacitors because it would require each failed capacitor to be disposed of within 30 days of failure. The plant would find it far more economical to consolidate such materials on site for eventual disposal at one time. In addition, a plant using capacitors for motor starters or for power factor correction may have one or more capacitors in storage as spares. Fortunately for these cases, the requirements for permanent storage are not difficult to meet.

After January 1, 1983, "permanent storage" means storage for up to one year in a facility meeting the following requirements:

1. The storage facility must be located in an area that is above the 100-year flood plain.

Figure 7-4. A PCB storage facility elevated above the 100-year floodwater elevation.

2. It shall have a roof and walls that are adequate to prevent rainwater from reaching the stored items.
3. The floor shall be impervious to PCBs and have a minimum six-inch curb around it capable of containing a volume equal to the greater of either twice the internal volume of the largest stored PCB item or a quarter of the total internal volumes of all the stored items.

For the plant with a few nonleaking capacitors to store, these requirements can be easily met. For example, the capacitors could be placed in one or more plainly marked open-top drums with the tops locked on and stored in the electrical shop. The drums would serve as the secondary containment, and the shop would provide shelter; so the requirements of permanent storage would be satisfied. If there were cleanup debris or leaking items to store, they would be placed in open-top drums along with sufficient absorbent materials to prevent any PCB liquid from accumulating in the items. These drums could then be stored with the others by placing them in a steel pan meeting the volume requirements. Alternately, a curb could be installed around the storage room.

Larger storage facilities might require a separate building or fenced area to provide enough room for large transformers. Good highway access and loading areas should be available so that disposal operations are not impeded. A comprehensive spill kit should be included as part of the facility, along with a cleanup or decontamination area. Table 7–4 lists the type of equipment that should be included in a spill kit. Depending on the size of the storage facility, some or all of these items should be on hand. The instruction sheet for the spill kit should include the names and phone numbers of the plant emergency coordinator and the foreman or supervisor of the department responsible for the storage facility. It should detail specific cleanup instruction for the type of equipment or materials being stored. In addition, it should list the sources of replacements of all consumable items in the kit such as solvents, first aid supplies, respirators, gloves, and containers.

All items placed into the storage facility should be marked with the date they were first entered into storage and the PCB contents of any containers or liquid-filled equipment (and PCB warning labels, if required). They should be placed so that the label information is easily visible during inspections, and they should be raised off the floor to allow for adequate ventilation and inspection for leaks. The facility ventilation should be at least six air changes per hour. Any leaking items should be repackaged before being put into storage, and each item in storage should be inspected monthly for new leaks or other signs of deterioration. The inspection log should be maintained along with the other plant PCB records.

Spill Contingency Plan

Any facility having long-term storage of PCBs or with large volumes of PCB fluids contained in equipment in use should have a spill contingency plan on file. This should follow the general guidelines of the SPCC plan, in that it should describe: (1) the precautions that have been taken to prevent a spill, such as diking, inspections, and record

Table 7-4. Example of Equipment for PCB Spill Kit.

1	55-gallon open-head drum or 85-gallon recovery drum (may be used to hold equipment)
1	instruction sheet (should include sources of replacement supplies)
4	pairs of Neoprene gloves
2	respirators and cartridges
2	aprons (chemical-resistant)
2	pairs Neoprene boot covers
2	impermeable suits (coveralls)
1	dustpan
1	shop brush
1	square-point "D"-handle shovel
1	dozen polyethylene bags with ties
1	18" pushbroom, synthetic fibers
1	gallon liquid detergent
2	self-contained or air-supplied breathing apparatus (or identify nearest location)
80	pounds absorbent material
1	bung wrench
1	drum spigot
1	1 3/8" open-end wrench
1	drum pump (manual)
30	feet 1/2" Tygon tubing
5	blank labels and PCB labels
1	first aid kit (or identify nearest location)
2	packages absorbent paper towels or rags
1	plastic drip pan
1	polyethylene tarpaulin

keeping; (2) the emergency response actions that would be taken in the event of a spill, including prediction of possible impact, required notifications, and employee preparedness training; and (3) the cleanup activities that would be taken following a spill.

The plan should designate spill coordinators so that a trained individual will be available at all times. These coordinators should have training in emergency procedures and be familiar with the plan. Emergency phone numbers should be listed, including the National Response Center, the EPA Regional Hazardous Materials Spill Coordinator, state and/or local environmental agencies, local fire and emergency response departments, and any reliable cleanup contractors. Not all of these need be called for a spill. The coordinator decides whom to call after assessing the situation. The plan should also list any work areas near each storage area or containment that might need to be evacuated.

The contents of a spill control kit should be described. This equipment should be stored in the area of the storage facility and inspected on the same schedule as the storage area. It should contain brief instructions for handling spills as well as appropriate absorbent materials and protective clothing. Larger facilities might require medical equipment and self-contained breathing equipment.

The instructions might follow this sequence:

1. Turn off any electrical equipment involved in the spill.
2. Determine if personnel are injured and/or exposed to PCBs. If so, remove them to a safe area and provide for first aid if necessary. Removal will require the rescuer to wear protective equipment including a respirator. Provide for decontamination of all exposed personnel.
3. Arrest further spillage by repositioning leaking containers, patching any holes, or closing valves or stoppering drains.
4. Prevent the spill from spreading with absorbent materials or dike with dirt or any available materials. Cover the spill area with tarpaulins to guard against spreading by rain.
5. Estimate the amount and concentration of spilled materials. If any entered a waterway or might enter a waterway, the amount should be estimated. Note the details of the spill including time and date, equipment involved, and probable cause.
6. Report the spill if it exceeds the reportable quantity specified in the Clean Water Act (ten pounds), if it has entered or might enter the surface waters, or if it is a "moderate leak." The first report should be made to the National Response Center of the U.S. Coast Guard (800/442–8802).
7. Clean up the spilled materials and provide for proper storage until disposal can be arranged.

Disposal

A limited number of high-temperature incinerators in the United States have been approved by EPA for the disposition of high-concentration PCBs (> 500 ppm) and capacitors. They have met the requirements of high efficiency (99.9%), a two-second residency time at 1200°C, 3% excess oxygen, appropriate emission controls, and continuous monitoring of emissions. Oil that is PCB-contaminated (< 500 ppm) can be burned in approved high-efficiency industrial or utility boilers. Certain hazardous waste landfills have been approved for the disposal of stabilized contaminated oil, drained transformer bodies, and contaminated soil and other cleanup debris. Table 7–5 illustrates the various disposal options allowed by EPA for each class of PCB waste. A check with EPA's Office of Toxic Substances will yield the latest list of approved disposal facilities for each class of PCB waste. Several facilities should be contacted for price and schedule before any contracts are signed because the rapid expansion of the PCB disposal industry has brought about competitive prices. Many contractors subcontract some PCB handling steps, and it may be preferable to utilize a contractor capable of an entire removal project: storage, draining, flushing, and incineration.

A variety of processes have been developed to destroy the PCB molecules in a contaminated oil chemically without altering the properties of the oil. These processes depend on the affinity of alkali metals, principally sodium, for chlorine atoms. In practice, the PCB-contaminated fluid is mixed with a proprietary sodium reagent under specific conditions of catalysis, pressure, and temperature. An exothermic reaction occurs in which sodium chloride is formed along with a nonchlorinated organic molecule in place of each PCB molecule. A final water wash removes the excess reagent and salt so that the noncontaminated fluid can be returned for reuse.

EPA has granted permits for several of these proprietary processes. Some companies offer mobile processing facilities that can be driven to plants where large amounts of contaminated fluids justify decontamination rather than disposal. Although the basic process is expensive, the chemical destruction of PCBs has several advantages over other disposal options: there are no storage, transport, or disposal costs; there is no liability from spills or violations during storage, transport, or disposal; and the bulk of the fluid is returned to the owner. This fluid can be disposed of as a non-PCB fluid, or because transformer fluids are relatively expensive, it can be reused.

Table 7-5. Disposal Options

ITEM	INCINERATE	EPA-APPROVED LANDFILL	HIGH-EFFICIENCY BOILER	MUNICIPAL LANDFILL	SALVAGE
PCB transformers (≥ 500 ppm PCB)	Yes	[1]Yes	No	No	No
PCB-contaminated transformers (> 50 < 500 ppm PCB)	Not required—		No	[1]Yes	[1]Yes
Large PCB capacitors (≥ 3 pounds PCB)	Yes	No	No	No	No
Small capacitors (< 3 pounds PCB)	Yes	Yes	No	No	No
PCB hydraulic devices	Not required—		No	[1]Yes	[1]Yes
Other PCB articles	Yes	Yes	No	No	No
PCB containers (≥ 500 ppm PCB)	[1]Yes	[1]Yes	No	No	No
PCB-contaminated containers (≥ 50 < 500 ppm PCB)	Not required—		No	[1]Yes	No
Properly decontaminated PCB containers	Not required—		No	[1]Yes	[1]Yes
PCB liquid (≥ 500 ppm PCB)	Yes	No	No	No	No
PCB-contaminated liquid (≥ 50 < 500 ppm PCB)	Yes	Yes	Yes	No	No
Non-PCB liquids (< 50 ppm PCB)	[2]Dispose of as a waste oil; only restriction is that it cannot be used as a dust control, sealant, or coating.				
Solid PCB wastes: dredge spoils, sewage treatment sludges	Yes	Yes	No	No	No
Materials contaminated from PCB spills: soil, sand, gravel, rags, wood, etc.	Yes	Yes	No	No	No

1. Requires proper draining and flushing.
2. Certain states may have stringent requirements; i.e., California requires EPA-approved landfill, incineration, or burning in a boiler for all liquids containing > 7 ppm PCB.

Symbols used: < less than, > greater than, = equal to, ≥ greater than or equal to.

Retrofilling transformers, switches, circuit breakers, or other PCB-contaminated electrical equipment is permitted by EPA as a method of reducing the PCB concentration in the equipment. It is useful when the location of the equipment poses an unacceptable liability and the expense of replacement would be very high. An example would be a large PCB-contaminated transformer in a location where a spill could contaminate surface waters or food or feed products.

The retrofilling procedure involves draining the equipment of all fluid and flushing it three times with an appropriate solvent. The original fluid and the flushing solution must all be disposed of properly. The equipment can then be refilled with an appropriate non-PCB fluid. This could be a paraffinic or polyolefinic dielectric fluid, or, if fire resistance is important, a silicone fluid. Fluid replacement may require downrating a transformer's capacity because the high dielectric strength of the original PCB fluids cannot be duplicated in non-PCB fluids.

A transformer must be operated for a minimum of three months after refilling before the fluid can be tested to determine PCB contamination. This gives PCBs in the windings a chance to migrate into the fluid. If the transformer was contaminated with PCBs, refilling may reduce the concentration to below 50 ppm. An Askeral transformer, however, generally will still contain 4 or 5% PCB after refilling. To complete the decontamination, a filter can be attached to the transformer to scavenge PCB molecules as the fluid circulates. As long as two years may be required to reduce the PCB contamination to below 50 ppm. Each step of the refilling procedure should be recorded on the inventory form, including the final test result that enables the equipment to be reclassified as non-PCB. Until that is possible, inspections must be continued.

THE PCB AUDIT

The PCB audit is initiated by determining the status of the plant with respect to EPA's PCB regulations under TSCA Part 761. If any of the following apply, the plant is regulated:

1. The plant has PCB articles in use containing over 50 ppm PCB.
2. The plant has PCB items in storage.
3. The plant had PCB articles in use or PCB items in storage at any time within the past five years.
4. The plant produces PCBs greater than 50 ppm in waste streams.

Figure 7-5. PCB capacitors are easily overlooked (two in this photograph).

If the status is positive for PCBs, the plant should have documentation on file such as annual documents, lab reports, inventories, service records, manifests, and inspection logs. The audit consists of three steps: reviewing this paperwork; checking or at least spot-checking the equipment and facilities; and finally, in the course of the plant tour, looking for oversights. The last step is necessary whether the initial determination is positive for PCBs or not. It is very possible that some electrical devices might have been overlooked. This is especially likely at older plants.

Documentation

Annual documents are required for plants having the following minimum PCB inventories: 50 or more capacitors in use or storage; one or more PCB transformers; or 45 kilograms (99.4 pounds) or more PCBs in PCB containers. The annual documents should be available for each year since 1978 in which the plant met the PCB minimums, and should be completed by July 1 following the calendar year covered by the document. If the plant ceases using or storing PCBs or PCB items above the minimum quantities, the annual documents must be retained for at least five years.

The information required on the annual document includes the total number of PCB transformers and capacitors in use and in storage along with the dates any of the items were placed in storage or removed for disposal. The total weight of PCBs and PCB items in storage at the end of each year and all PCBs reported the previous year must be accounted for. Figure 7-6 shows a report format that would be suitable as an annual document.

The paperwork review should start with the annual documents, as they comprise a history of the plant's PCB management since 1978. The reports should be available for each year during which PCBs above the minimum quantities were on the plant property, and the quantities reported should be consistent from year to year. That is, the latest report should account for the same quantity of PCBs as the first report, less the quantities disposed of in the intervening years. If this checks out, the auditor can use the latest report to indicate the present status of the plant. It will show how many PCB items are in service, whether the plant has a storage area, and any disposal activity during the past year. Not shown would be any PCB-contaminated transformers. The absence of an annual document is not the end of the PCB audit because plants having only contaminated transformers and fewer than 50 capacitors are not required to prepare annual documents.

The annual document is not a substitute for inventory forms (Figure 7-1) for each PCB item; rather, it should be prepared each year from the data on the inventory forms. The inventory forms provide a record of each inspection, servicing, and status change for all PCB items at a plant. Thus, they are an important source of information for the auditor. They indicate how well the inspection program

PLANT ______ PCB INVENTORY – YEAR ENDING 31 December ______ Sheet ____ of ____

A. GENERAL				B. IN SERVICE			C. REMOVED FROM SERVICE				D. STORAGE						E. DISPOSAL			
ID No.	Location	Testing ppm	Testing date	Container D C T	Quantity (kg)	Condition	Container D C T	Quantity (kg)	Date Removed	Sent to	Container D C T	Quantity (kg)	Date Received	From	Date Transferred	Sent to	Container D C T	Quantity (kg)	Date to Hauler	Hauler/ Disposal Site

F. SUMMARY	B. IN SERVICE	C. REMOVED FROM SERVICE	D. STORAGE	E. DISPOSAL
Number of PCB:				
Drums	___	___	___	___
Capacitors	___	___	___	___
Transformers	___	___	___	___
Weight of PCBs in:				
Drums	___ kg	___ kg	___ kg	___ kg
Capacitors	___ kg	___ kg	___ kg	___ kg
Transforms	___ kg	___ kg	___ kg	___ kg
Subtotal	D ___ C ___ T ___ ___ kg	D ___ C ___ T ___ ___ kg	D ___ C ___ T ___ ___ kg	D ___ C ___ T ___ ___ kg
TOTAL	D ___ C ___ T ___ ___ kg	D ___ C ___ T ___ ___ kg	D ___ C ___ T ___ ___ kg	D ___ C ___ T ___ ___ kg

Figure 7–6. Example of an annual document.

meets the requirements. They should also show how the PCB status of each item was determined. It is recommended that inventory forms be retained on non-PCB items that were suspect and therefore analyzed; the analysis report should be attached. Similarly, the analysis reports on PCB-contaminated transformers should be attached to their respective inventory forms.

The document review will indicate to the auditor the adequacy of the plant's records and inspections. It will show whether any items were retained in storage longer than the year permitted by regulation. In addition, the auditor should note the areas in the plant that should be inspected during the plant tour. Large numbers of capacitors need not be individually inspected, although several should be checked for labeling and signs of leakage. Large PCB transformers should be checked and any storage area carefully inspected. Last, the document review should provide the auditor with a list of recent incidents, such as transformer servicing resulting in a status change, reported spills, and items removed from storage for disposal. Documentation for each of these should be on file. Where it appears to be lacking, the responsible individuals should be interviewed. For example, the plant electrician should have a service record on any transformer work, and the auditor should be able to track any PCB fluid removed and flushing solutions used. Spill reports should be on file showing quantities spilled, cleanup activities, and precautions taken to avoid repeats. Manifests should have been returned, proving proper disposal of all PCB items removed from storage.

Plant PCB Tour

The major PCB items noted during the document review should be examined. Examples include the following types of equipment:

- PCB capacitors
- PCB transformers
- PCB-contaminated transformers
- Transformers that have been converted to non-PCB
- Railroad transformers
- PCB hydraulic systems, electromagnets, switches, circuit breakers, or heat transfer systems

- PCB-contaminated hydraulic systems, electromagnets, switches, circuit breakers, or heat transfer systems
- PCB articles removed from service
- PCB containers in storage for disposal or reuse

For transformers, this examination includes comparing the inventory information with the auditor's observations. Is the transformer the size and make reported? Does the manufacturer's tag confirm the PCB status? Do any spill control facilities appear adequate? Next, the auditor should inspect the transformer in the same manner that the plant would during a routine inspection. The auditor could initial the inspection log if the plant so desires. The presence, content, location, and condition of the PCB warning label should be checked. An examination for leakage includes noting visible oil accumulations on the surface of the transformer as well as evidence of seepage near gaskets and oil stains on the surface below the transformer. If these are present, the auditor should recommend testing of the spilled material and a cleanup. The adequacy of any security precautions should be evaluated, and the transformer's location with respect to occupied areas, food and feed activities, and waterways or drainage should be noted. Last, the condition of spill prevention facilities should be checked.

Any locations in which spills occurred should be examined from the standpoints of (1) adequacy of the cleanup, and (2) precautions taken against further spills. Spills onto soil are cleaned up by removing the contaminated soil and backfilling with clean fill. Any evidence of oil should be sampled and tested for PCB contamination unless test reports are on file showing the contamination to be less than 50 ppm. Precautions against further spills include concrete diking, removal of the PCB equipment, or flushing and refilling.

All PCB items including switch gear, electromagnets, hydraulic systems, and large high-voltage capacitors should be inspected in a manner similar to the transformer examination. Small capacitors should be randomly checked. Any waste oil processing areas should be examined for the possibility of PCB contamination in addition to the inspection required by the SPCC audit.

If the plant is on record as having a storage area for PCBs, it should be carefully examined. The area should provide adequate protection against rainfall. Continuous curbing of at least six inches should surround the stored materials, and it should provide spill containment exceeding twice the volume of the largest article or container or 25% of all articles and containers (whichever is greater). There should be no floor drains within the curbing, or if there are, they should be valved and any openings recorded. The storage area should be above the 100-year floodwater elevation, and it should be adequately marked.

The items in storage should bear dates showing when they were removed from service or, in the case of spill residues, entered into storage. These dates should correspond to the inventory information. If the storage area contains large numbers of items, they should be arranged by date of entry to facilitate management and disposal. They should also be arranged so that they can be easily inspected for leaks. The containers should meet DOT as well as OSHA specifications. Any leaking containers should be placed in leak-tight containers and surrounded by sorbent materials.

Some items are not required to be stored in storage areas meeting the above standards. Large capacitors and PCB-contaminated transformers are allowed to be stored on pallets next to a PCB storage area. Temporary storage, up to 30 days, is allowed for nonleaking articles and equipment, leaking articles and equipment placed in nonleaking containers with sorbent materials, containers of nonliquid PCBs such as cleanup residues, and containers of PCB liquids between 50 and 500 ppm, provided they are included in a plant SPCC plan.

Equipment used in the storage area should be checked for possible contamination to outside areas. For example, forklifts should be cleaned if they become contaminated during transfers into or out of storage. The auditor should review the procedures used in the management of the storage area. Some decontamination procedure should be followed, and the proper supplies should be on hand. Table 7-4 provides an example list. Employees involved in the management of the storage area should be interviewed about their training and experiences.

Some larger plants may have facilities for draining and flushing PCB equipment. This operation requires special attention to the PCB regulations and is beyond the scope of a routine PCB audit. Likewise, facilities for disposing of PCBs by combustion, either in dedicated incinerators or large, high-efficiency boilers, cannot be reviewed in the above manner. Specific handling procedures, records, and testing regulations apply to these operations.

Plant Non-PCB Tour

Many plants will have no records of PCB equipment on file, and will not have PCB management programs. Nevertheless, a check should

Figure 7-7. Twenty-four PCB capacitors at a substation.

be made during the plant tour for suspect items. All oil-filled transformers should be checked for manufacturer data unless the plant has done testing proving the absence of PCBs. Non-PCB labels are very useful to confirm this status. Capacitors often escape notice, but they too must be checked for manufacturer data. Many capacitors installed recently bear manufacturer labels stating "Non-PCB." If PCB capacitors are found where none was expected, the auditor should also check the electrical storeroom for spare capacitors.

Waste oil handling should also be reviewed for PCB contamination. If the plant purchases waste oil for dust control or product dilution, there should be a purchasing specification requiring the supplier to test for PCBs. Large inventories of waste oil should have been tested, and provisions made to prevent future contamination. Former practices of transformer draining contributed to extensive waste oil contamination.

PCB Audit Report

If the plant is regulated, the audit report should summarize the number of pieces of regulated equipment it has in use and in storage, and provide approximations of the volumes of each class of PCB fluids (50–500 ppm and > 500 ppm) in use and in storage. The data inventory forms should be attached to the report to provide the data supporting the summaries. Any changes that occurred over the past year in the PCB inventories should be noted, as well as any changes planned for the near future. The status of the compliance program should also be evaluated. Are annual documents on file for each July 1 since 1978 or for five years following cessation of PCB activities? Did the plant tour provide evidence that the equipment labeling is proper, and that there are no obvious leaks on the surfaces of any equipment? Is there documentation that equipment in use and in storage is being inspected at the proper intervals?

If there is a storage area, the report should include a description of it and an evaluation of its adequacy, giving consideration to the following: inspection procedure being used, the spill prevention measures, the physical details of the facility such as curbing and ventilation, security measures including warning signs, emergency protective gear and cleanup supplies, adequacy of labeling and dating of items in storage, and any testing results.

Recent PCB activities should be described and evaluated according to the nature of the activities; for example, retrofilling of transformers, transfer of equipment to storage, and disposal of items. A review should be made of the manifests generated for disposed PCBs. The qualifications and documentation supplied by the contractor, the procedures utilized, and the final disposition of all wastes should be covered. The costs involved could also be included if they provide inducement for recommended activities. PCB spills should be described with details such as the cause of the spill, the cleanup activities, any agency response, and steps taken to avoid recurrences.

Last, the report could provide recommendations for PCB management where the auditor feels that the liability of present plant practices is unacceptable, or that more economical procedures might be available. The age of PCB equipment, as well as its condition and location, enter into considerations of best management practices. Future plans for the plant are also important. For example, if the plant is to be closed or sold, it might be advisable to remove all PCBs first.

ASBESTOS

Introduction

The term "asbestos" covers a group of minerals including actinolite, amosite, anthophyllite, chrysotile, crocidolite, and tremolite that are related to each other as fibrous inorganic hydrated mineral silicates. These minerals, primarily amosite, chrysotile, and crocidolite, have been valued as a natural resource with hundreds of applications in manufacturing, construction, defense industries, and consumer products. Their fibrous forms allow them to be made into cloth, felt, gaskets, and rope, or used for reinforcement in cements, asphalt, and plastic. They are nonflammable, withstand high temperatures, have low heat conductivity, resist chemical attack, and have a high tensile strength; so products made from them have such desirable properties as flame resistance, good insulation, and high strength. Asbestos is widely distributed around the world, and is inexpensive to refine.

The good reputation of asbestos has come under attack over the past two decades as more has been learned about the medical consequences of exposure to it. Aspirated fibers tend to be retained by the lungs and can bring on a variety of diseases, some of them not evident for 20 years or more after initial exposure. Foremost among these diseases is asbestosis, a respiratory disease affecting primarily asbestos workers such as insulators, miners, and factory workers involved in the manufacture of asbestos products. It involves a condition of scarring and thickening of the lungs that results in breathing difficulties. Another, more insidious disease is mesothelioma, a form of cancer affecting the pleural lining of the lungs. This rare but often fatal disease has been primarily associated with people who have been exposed to asbestos fibers. It may not have a dose–response relationship (i.e., the disease could develop after a single exposure to asbestos dust). There is some evidence, however, that mesothelioma is also related to smoking, and that both elements must be present for the disease to develop.

Asbestos Regulations

A consequence of the increased awareness of the dangers of asbestos has been numerous regulations by various governmental agencies controlling and restricting the use of asbestos. The Occupational Safety and Health Administration (OSHA), for example, has set eight-hour and peak exposure limits for asbestos fibers occurring in work areas. In addition, OSHA requires monitoring, employee notification and training, warning signs, change rooms, and numerous other specific actions or facilities for any employees involved in asbestos handling (29 CFR Section 1910). The auditor should be generally aware of OSHA's requirements because many companies may not consider that the presence of asbestos in common industrial forms such as insulation on old equipment brings them under these regulations. As a result, these companies may have their maintenance staff handling asbestos without taking proper (and required) precautions. On the other hand, the auditor should not attempt to judge the adequacy of any OSHA compliance program other than to warn of the possible need for one and recommend the services of a certified industrial hygienist.

The primary body of regulations covering the environmental impact of asbestos in industry comes from Section 112 of the Clean Air Act: the National Emission Standards for Hazardous Air Pollutants

Figure 7–8. Asbestos is commonly found as insulation on old industrial equipment.

(NESHAPS). These technology-based standards have been promulgated for beryllium, mercury, and vinyl chloride as well as asbestos. Standards have been proposed for benzene and radionuclides and are anticipated for inorganic arsenic. The standards apply to both new and existing sources and can be enforced both by the states, under an approved state plan, and directly by EPA. The National Emission Standard for Asbestos is documented in 40 CFR §61.20.

The emission standard for asbestos requires simply that there be no visible emissions to the outside air from any operation or building. "Visible emissions" are defined as any emissions that are visually detectable without the aid of instruments and contain particulate asbestos material. This standard applies primarily to asbestos milling operations and to manufacturers who use asbestos in their products.

Compliance can be achieved either by totally enclosing asbestos operations or by controlling their emissions. For the latter, EPA is quite specific. In §61.23, a fabric filter collection device (baghouse) is required which is operated at a pressure drop of no more than four inches of water and uses a fabric at least one-sixteenth inch thick, weighing 14 ounces per yard or more and with a permeability of not more than 30 CFM per square foot of woven fabric (35 for felted fabrics) as determined by ASTM method D737–69. Special authorization may be requested to use a scrubber operating at at least 40 inches of water or another device, provided it can be shown to be as effective as the baghouse described. Whatever control device is used, however, the regulations require that it be properly installed, operated, and maintained. It may be bypassed during an upset or emergency condition, but only for as long as it takes to shut down the operation that generates the asbestos emissions.

The manufacturing operations using asbestos that are regulated by EPA include the following: the manufacture of cloth, cord, wicks, tubing, tape, twine, rope, thread, yarn, roving, lap, or other textile materials; the manufacture of cement products (e.g., pipe, mill board, or shingles); the manufacture of fireproofing and insulating materials; the manufacture of friction products; the manufacture of paper, millboard, and felt; the manufacture of floor tile; the manufacture of paints, coatings, caulks, adhesives, and sealants; the manufacture of plastics and rubber materials; the manufacture of chlorine; the manufacture of shotgun shells; and the manufacture of asphalt concrete. Many of these industries have substituted other materials for asbestos or discontinued operations altogether because of the hazards involved with asbestos. Others such as the manufacturers of asbestos/cement products, vinyl/asbestos floor tile, and friction products have not been able to find substitutes with the unique properties of asbestos and therefore have had to achieve environmentally and occupationally safe operations by the application of good engineering practices and comprehensive monitoring programs.

EPA also regulates the disposal of asbestos-containing wastes under NESHAPS (rather than RCRA). These regulations are contained in §61.22(j). They require that asbestos-containing wastes either be wetted and packaged into leak-tight containers before disposal or processed into a nonfriable form. "Friable asbestos material" is defined as any material that contains more than 1% asbestos by weight and can be crumbled, pulverized, or reduced to powder when dry, by hand pressure. Both the waste containers and the nonfriable pellets must be disposed of at waste disposal sites that meet certain requirements.

Visible emissions from disposal sites for asbestos-containing wastes are prohibited. In addition, warning signs must be displayed, and access by the general public must be deterred by fencing. To prevent visible emissions, an active disposal site can be covered at least once each 24 hours with six or more inches of compacted non-asbestos-containing material or treated with a resinous or petroleum-based dust suppression agent (not waste crankcase oil). For an inactive disposal site, the non-asbestos-containing cap should be at least two feet thick.

It should be noted that approved asbestos disposal sites do not have to meet RCRA requirements for hazardous waste disposal. A liner is not required, nor is groundwater monitoring, a closure plan, or regular inspections, because of studies that have shown that asbestos does not migrate into groundwaters once it has been landfilled. Nevertheless, disposal of asbestos may eventually be included under RCRA, and some states such as California now define asbestos waste as hazardous under their state programs.

NESHAPS has a reporting requirement, promulgated in 1975, for all companies that have sources of hazardous air pollutants as defined by §61.10. Within 90 days of the effective date of the standard, these companies were required to report to EPA such information as name and address, source location, a brief description of the operation utilizing the hazardous pollutant, and the average weight per month of the hazardous materials being processed over the previous year. For asbestos sources, a description was to be included of the control device for each operation with details, such as, for a baghouse, pressure drop, fabric type, fabric weight, and permeability. It was also required that operations that generate asbestos-containing wastes be described, along with the methods of waste handling, the type of disposal site used, its location and owner, and the methods by which it achieves compliance with the standard.

Asbestos manufacturers, importers, and processors were also required under Section 8(a) of TSCA to file an extensive report on employee exposure, quantities of asbestos utilized, waste disposal, and pollution control equipment (EPA Form 7710–36 or –37). This one-time requirement, promulgated July 30, 1982, was designed to provide EPA with information about the current state of the asbestos industry in the United States, to support its ongoing asbestos risk investigation. The form was entitled "Reporting Commercial and Industrial Uses of Asbestos." Submission was required within 60 and 90 days of promulgation for secondary and primary processors, respectively. A copy of this form would be a useful starting point in any audit of an asbestos processor.

The foregoing several paragraphs are applicable only to industries specifically involved in processing asbestos or utilizing it as a raw material in their manufacturing operations. A far greater number of plants are potentially affected by these regulations because they contain asbestos either sprayed on girders, walls, and ceilings of their buildings as fireproofing or on pipes and boilers as insulation.

From 1946 until it was banned by EPA in 1973, asbestos was utilized as a fireproofing material, applied by spraying it on structural steel during building construction. When applied to ceilings and walls, the same material also provided effective soundproofing. The popularity of this practice has resulted in a legacy of thousands of apartment buildings, schools, and factories containing substantial amounts of asbestos.

Sprayed asbestos is a problem in two situations. One is building demolition. This is generally handled by demolition contractors, so that plant operators need not be concerned with complying with the applicable regulations (§ 61.22(d)). The ultimate responsibility would rest with the plant, however, if an unscrupulous or inept contractor were chosen; so it is advisable to review exactly how compliance will be achieved as part of the bidding process. In addition, the plant should request a copy of the notification that the contractor is required to make to EPA under § 61.22(d)(2).

Sprayed insulation is also a concern when it becomes loose and threatens possible contamination of a work area. This is a big problem in public schools and no less a concern in lunchrooms or offices of industrial facilities. Suspect areas should be tested unless it is known that the insulation is asbestos, because sprayed nonasbestos materials were also used for soundproofing and insulation (e.g., gypsum, vermiculite, rockwool, fiberglass, and attapulgate). Once found, deteriorating asbestos insulation should be either stripped off and replaced with nonasbestos insulation or permanently sealed by any of a number of commercial processes. These operations are best handled by contractors experienced in this work.

The use of asbestos for high-temperature insulation in industrial applications goes back to the turn of the century. Virtually every component of an industrial steam system that is more than ten years old, for example, is likely to be covered with asbestos. Generally, it is used as reinforcement in molded insulation. It may also be found as dense packing, woven cloth, or paper. All these insulating forms are likely to release fibers in the course of handling or removal. Thus, workers in contact with it must be in compliance with OSHA as well as EPA regulations.

EPA provides an exemption to its notification requirement for

Figure 7-9. The use of experienced contractors for asbestos removal ensures that the proper safety precautions will be taken.

small asbestos insulation removal projects. The cutoffs are 260 feet of pipe insulation and 160 square feet of insulation on ducts, boilers, tanks, kilns, or even structural steel. Not exempted, however, is the requirement for proper disposal. The wastes must be thoroughly wet and sealed into airtight containers bearing a warning label. A special arrangement with the local industrial hauler will be necessary to meet landfilling requirements.

The OSHA requirements for the protection of workers exposed to asbestos fibers are very stringent. There is no exemption for small jobs, and proper protection and work practices are always required. When the potential liabilities of working with asbestos are taken into consideration, the use of a contractor who is experienced in this work may become more attractive. Some large industries such as refineries have crews working every week of the year in asbestos stripping. They must provide personnel monitoring, change rooms, and medical surveillance for these workers.

THE ASBESTOS AUDIT

Asbestos Processors

EPA defines a primary asbestos processor as a person (plant) who processes bulk asbestos for commercial purposes. A secondary processor processes asbestos mixtures. A plant, for example, that mixes raw asbestos with resins to form brake shoe pads is a primary processor, whereas a plant that attaches the pads to brake shoes is a secondary processor. Either plant should be thoroughly familiar with audits, surveys, and questionnaires by government and corporate officials. Thus, the environmental auditor has only to follow the trail left by others and ensure that other required elements of an environmental compliance program are being followed. In addition, he must check over the entire facility just as he would a nonasbestos manufacturer for evidence of exposed or deteriorating asbestos insulation or soundproofing.

A copy of "Reporting Commercial and Industrial Uses of Asbestos" (EPA Form 7710–36 or –37) is a good place to start an audit of a primary or secondary asbestos processor. A copy should be requested in advance because there was no requirement that it be kept at the plant or even that it be kept. Thus, it may be buried in a file at corporate headquarters and take some time to find. It will be useful, as it lists all emission control equipment and waste disposal procedures. This information should be reviewed with the environmental coordinator as the first step at the plant.

Any company using asbestos in its process should have a vigorous industrial hygiene program in force. It is not the job of the environmental auditor to provide a definitive review of employee safety and health programs. On the other hand, obvious problems should be pointed out when they are noticed during the plant tour. For example, accumulations of dust in work areas where asbestos is handled suggest the possibility that insufficient cleaning is being done. The use of any brooms, brushes, or air hoses for cleaning is improper—vacuums are required unless the waste is wet down first. Fiber-unloading, transfer, warehousing, and bag-opening areas should all be kept scrupulously clean. Torn bags should be immediately taped closed and any spilled fiber removed.

The data collection phase of the audit should result in documentation of the same information required by EPA under 40 CFR §61.24. Obviously, the original report would also be useful to the auditor, but it was most likely prepared many years ago and may be difficult to locate. Also, the information may be substantially out of date. Thus, if it is available, it will have to be carefully updated. The air pollution source data inventory form would be useful for recording asbestos emission control equipment, adding where necessary the special requirements imposed by 40 CFR §61.23. Likewise, data inventory forms for waste disposal and water effluent point sources can be used to log these impact points.

In the plant tour, the special requirements of NESHAPS and the CWA for asbestos sources should be checked for each emission point, waste-handling area, and water effluent source. Where baghouses are used to control emissions, the pressure drop should not exceed four inches. If a scrubber is used, the pressure drop minimum should be 40 inches. Good management would call for a daily or shift log of these readings, which could be checked for variances. The environmental coordinator should be able to find out what fabrics are used for filtration for comparison with the regulations. At waste disposal sites, there should be warning signs and barriers. Wastes should be covered at re-

Figure 7-10. The plant tour should include the scrap yard.

quired intervals. Wastes produced during manufacturing should be wet and sealed into leak-tight containers. A warning label meeting EPA or OSHA specifications must be attached to each waste container. Emission sources and waste-handling areas must comply with the requirement of no visible emissions. Water effluent sources should meet the individual requirements of the NPDES permit. At a minimum, total suspended solids (TSS), acidity (pH), and chemical oxygen demand (COD) would be required. The records of these tests should be available for review.

Non-Asbestos Processors

For plants that are not processors of asbestos, the auditor should check for asbestos in the form of insulation, packing, soundproofing, or fire protection. The plant steam system is the first place to look for asbestos insulation. It might be a part of the lagging on the boilers or the insulation on the distribution system. Where it is found or suspected, the condition should be noted. If it is flaking off, a recommendation should be made for stabilization or replacement. If it is in good condition, its presence should be noted in the audit report so that the plant will take the proper precautions during maintenance procedures. If the auditor is not sure about the identity of an insulation, he should recommend sampling and analysis by the plant.

Between the years of 1946 and 1973, asbestos was often applied to building surfaces by spraying, for noise control and fire protection. Any areas suspected of having this treatment should be checked for deterioration. Other materials such as gypsum, vermiculite, rockwool, attapulgate, and fiberglass are also used for the same purpose; so a recommendation should be made for testing if the content is not known. Employee cafeterias and auditoriums are good candidates for acoustical treatment. Flaking asbestos should be sealed or removed. Sound asbestos should be noted for future reference.

NESHAPS includes specific requirements for asbestos demolition under 40 CFR §61.22(d). The auditor should not be concerned with them because demolition and construction cannot be considered to be routine plant operations. If demolition involving asbestos materials is intended, the auditor might suggest using an experienced contractor instead of plant personnel unless they are specifically trained in the OSHA procedures. The plant tour should include the scrap area or "bone yard" because debris from previous asbestos demolition operations may have been disposed of there.

Asbestos Audit Report

The audit report will be substantially more extensive in the case of a primary or secondary asbestos processor than for a plant having asbestos as part of its process equipment or buildings. In the former case, the report should follow the outline provided by 40 CFR §61.24, with commentary concerning the compliance of each emission control device or waste-handling area. Recommendations should first list all situations where compliance is questionable. Second, recommendations should be made in areas of good management practices. Examples include the routine logging of control device pressure drops and the use of preventive maintenance.

For plants that are not processors of asbestos, the audit report should confirm the presence or absence of asbestos on the premises. If asbestos is present, its extent and condition should be reported. Recommendations could be made for its proper handling. If asbestos is only suspected, a recommendation should be made to sample the areas in question and test for asbestos content.

SUPERFUND

Introduction

On December 11, 1980, the United States Congress enacted the Comprehensive Environmental Response, Compensation and Liability Act, commonly known as Superfund. In some respects, the act represents the first major piece of environmental legislation that attempts to address the effects of any pollutant release into the environment by any pathway. Unlike the Clean Air and Clean Water acts, Superfund is not restricted to regulating certain industrial processes or pollutants. One of the hallmarks of Superfund is its incorporation, by reference, of many pollutant lists from other environmental statutes. The broad authorities that Superfund invests in the EPA can potentially affect every industrial plant in the nation. For this reason, it is imperative to address compliance with the act during an environmental audit.

Legislative Background

Unlike many other environmental acts, Superfund does not currently rely on an exhaustive body of regulations to be effective. The law itself details the major requirements that industrial plants must comply with. In order to inform potentially affected plants of these provisions, EPA published summaries of the act in several *Federal Register* notices (see FR 4/15/81, FR 7/16/82, and FR 5/25/83). It is these three publications that provide the guidance and interpretation necessary to achieve compliance.

Spill Notification. The major concerns associated with Superfund center around two different notification requirements. The first provision, which became effective upon enactment, requires persons in charge of plants or vessels to notify the National Response Center when the release of a hazardous substance occurs in amounts equal to or greater than its reportable quantity. The act established authority for the federal government to respond to these releases under a revised National Contingency Plan. The act also imposes liability for cleanup and damages upon the responsible party. Notification under Superfund acts as a trigger for informing the federal government of a release so that it may evaluate the need for response. Notification does not necessarily mean the government will respond in all cases, nor does it release the responsible party from liability for cleanup or damages. The term "hazardous substance" is defined in the act, and basically includes all pollutants regulated under other environmental statutes. The initial list of 696 substances included:

- Hazardous substances designated under Section 311 of the Clean Water Act.
- Hazardous wastes under Section 3001 of the Resource Conservation and Recovery Act.
- Toxic pollutants under Section 307(a) of the Clean Water Act.
- Hazardous air pollutants under Section 112 of the Clean Air Act.
- Imminently hazardous chemicals under Section 7 of the Toxic Substances Control Act.

In addition, EPA has been given the authority under Superfund to designate hazardous substances beyond this initial list.

The reportable quantity for a release of hazardous substances was originally set in the act at one pound. For materials with existing reportable quantities, the act did not supersede these levels. For hazardous substances listed under Section 311 of the Clean Water Act, the reportable quantity varies from 1 to 5000 pounds.

Superfund specifically exempts four classes of releases from the statutory reporting requirement. Although they have been the subject of much interpretation, it is important for plant personnel to be familiar with these exemptions in order to reduce unnecessary spill reporting. In summary, these exemptions include:

1. Releases already reported under the emergency provisions of the Resource Conservation and Recovery Act.

2. Certain continuous releases, provided they are stable in quantity and rate, and notification has been given under Section 103(f) of Superfund. EPA is currently developing a special reporting scheme for continuous releases that may result in an additional notification requirement.
3. The application, storage, and handling of a pesticide product registered under the Federal Insecticide, Fungicide, and Rodenticide Act (FIFRA) consistent with manufacturer label instructions.
4. Federally permitted releases as defined in Section 101 of the act. These include discharges in compliance with the following programs:
    - National Pollutant Discharge Elimination System (NPDES) permits.
    - Dredge and Fill permits (Section 404 of the Clean Water Act).
    - Final permits under the Resource Conservation and Recovery Act.
    - Permits under the Marine Protection Research and Sanctuaries Act (ocean dumping).
    - Underground Injection permits under the Clean Water Act.
    - Permitted emissions under the Clean Air Act.
    - Injections related to crude oil or natural gas development.
    - Discharges to a publicly owned treatment works under an approved pretreatment program.
    - Releases of nuclear materials under the Atomic Energy Act.

One important aspect of compliance with Superfund's ongoing notification requirement is determining when a reportable release has occurred. Congress defined this term to include virtually all ways that a hazardous substance may enter the environment:

> ''release'' means any spilling, leaking, pumping, pouring, emitting, emptying, discharging, injecting, escaping, leaching, dumping or disposing into the environment. (Section 101(22))

The key term in the definition is the phrase ''into the environment.'' Although environment is broadly defined in Superfund, some releases may not result in substances entering the environment. For example, EPA does not require reporting of a spill onto a concrete floor inside a manufacturing plant. Some plants interpret this provision to exclude spills of nonvolatile substances in containment areas specifically designed for this purpose.

Past Disposal Notification. The second major notification requirement under Superfund entails reporting prior disposal activities and sites. When Superfund was enacted, Congress was specifically concerned with potential environmental and health effects associated with facilities that treated, stored, or disposed of hazardous waste. Recognizing that detailed information was lacking on such sites, Congress provided in Section 103(c) that:

> Within one hundred and eighty days after the enactment of this Act, any person who owns or operates or who at the time of disposal owned or operated, or who accepted hazardous substances for transport and selected a facility at which hazardous substances (as defined in section 101(4)(C) of this title) are or have been stored, treated, or disposed of shall, unless such facility has a permit issued under, or has been accorded interim status under, subtitle C of the Solid Waste Disposal Act, notify the Administrator of the Environmental Protection Agency of the existence of such facility, specifying the amount and type of any hazardous substance to be found there, and any known, suspected, or likely releases of such substances from such facility.

The deadline for filing this notification was June 9, 1981. On April 15, 1981, EPA published guidance and a proposed notification form in the *Federal Register*. A sample of this form appears as Figure 7–11.

For notification of hazardous waste sites, several exclusions existed either in the act itself or in EPA interpretations. In summary, the following were excluded:

- Wastes not considered hazardous under RCRA. Examples include household trash, fly ash, slag, drilling fluids, and certain mining wastes.
- Petroleum, including crude oil, any fractions and natural gas not specifically listed in RCRA. "Listed" and "characteristic"

EPA Notification of Hazardous Waste Site

United States Environmental Protection Agency
Washington DC 20460

This initial notification information is required by Section 103(c) of the Comprehensive Environmental Response, Compensation, and Liability Act of 1980 and must be mailed by June 9, 1981.

Please type or print in ink. If you need additional space, use separate sheets of paper. Indicate the letter of the item which applies.

Person Required to Notify:

Enter the name and address of the person or organization required to notify.

Name ______

Street ______

City ______ State ______ Zip Code ______

Site Location:

Enter the common name (if known) and actual location of the site.

Name of Site ______

Street ______

City ______ County ______ State ______ Zip Code ______

Person to Contact:

Enter the name, title (if applicable), and business telephone number of the person to contact regarding information submitted on this form.

Name (Last, First and Title) ______

Phone ______

Dates of Waste Handling:

Enter the years that you estimate waste treatment, storage, or disposal began and ended at the site.

From (Year) ______ To (Year) ______

Waste Type: Choose the option you prefer to complete

Option I: Select general waste types and source categories. If you do not know the general waste types or sources, you are encouraged to describe the site in Item I—Description of Site.

General Type of Waste:
Place an X in the appropriate boxes. The categories listed overlap. Check each applicable category.

1. ☐ Organics
2. ☐ Inorganics
3. ☐ Solvents
4. ☐ Pesticides
5. ☐ Heavy metals
6. ☐ Acids
7. ☐ Bases
8. ☐ PCBs
9. ☐ Mixed Municipal Waste
10. ☐ Unknown
11. ☐ Other (Specify)

______
______
______

Source of Waste:
Place an X in the appropriate boxes.

1. ☐ Mining
2. ☐ Construction
3. ☐ Textiles
4. ☐ Fertilizer
5. ☐ Paper/Printing
6. ☐ Leather Tanning
7. ☐ Iron/Steel Foundry
8. ☐ Chemical, General
9. ☐ Plating/Polishing
10. ☐ Military/Ammunition
11. ☐ Electrical Conductors
12. ☐ Transformers
13. ☐ Utility Companies
14. ☐ Sanitary/Refuse
15. ☐ Photofinish
16. ☐ Lab/Hospital
17. ☐ Unknown
18. ☐ Other (Specify)

______
______
______

Option 2: This option is available to persons familiar with the Resource Conservation and Recovery Act (RCRA) Section 3001 regulations (40 CFR Part 261).

Specific Type of Waste:
EPA has assigned a four-digit number to each hazardous waste listed in the regulations under Section 3001 of RCRA. Enter the appropriate four-digit number in the boxes provided. A copy of the list of hazardous wastes and codes can be obtained by contacting the EPA Region serving the State in which the site is located.

Form Approved
OMB No. 2000-0138

EPA Form 8900-1

Figure 7-11. Notification of hazardous waste site.

Notification of Hazardous Waste Site Side Two

F Waste Quantity:

Place an X in the appropriate boxes to indicate the facility types found at the site.

In the "total facility waste amount" space give the estimated combined quantity (volume) of hazardous wastes at the site using cubic feet or gallons.

In the "total facility area" space, give the estimated area size which the facilities occupy using square feet or acres.

Facility Type

1. ☐ Piles
2. ☐ Land Treatment
3. ☐ Landfill
4. ☐ Tanks
5. ☐ Impoundment
6. ☐ Underground Injection
7. ☐ Drums, Above Ground
8. ☐ Drums, Below Ground
9. ☐ Other (Specify) __________

Total Facility Waste Amount

cubic feet __________

gallons __________

Total Facility Area

square feet __________

acres __________

G Known, Suspected or Likely Releases to the Environment:

Place an X in the appropriate boxes to indicate any known, suspected, or likely releases of wastes to the environment.

☐ Known ☐ Suspected ☐ Likely ☐ None

Note: Items H and I are optional. Completing these items will assist EPA and State and local governments in locating and assessing hazardous waste sites. Although completing the items is not required, you are encouraged to do so.

H Sketch Map of Site Location: (Optional)

Sketch a map showing streets, highways, routes or other prominent landmarks near the site. Place an X on the map to indicate the site location. Draw an arrow showing the direction north. You may substitute a publishing map showing the site location.

I Description of Site: (Optional)

Describe the history and present conditions of the site. Give directions to the site and describe any nearby wells, springs, lakes, or housing. Include such information as how waste was disposed and where the waste came from. Provide any other information or comments which may help describe the site conditions.

J Signature and Title:

The person or authorized representative (such as plant managers, superintendents, trustees or attorneys) of persons required to notify must sign the form and provide a mailing address (if different than address in item A). For other persons providing notification, the signature is optional. Check the boxes which best describe the relationship to the site of the person required to notify. If you are not required to notify check "Other".

Name __________

Street __________

City ______ State ______ Zip Code ______

Signature __________ Date ______

☐ Owner, Present
☐ Owner, Past
☐ Transporter
☐ Operator, Present
☐ Operator, Past
☐ Other

Figure 7-11. (*Continued*)

Form **6627**
(May 1981)
Department of the Treasury
Internal Revenue Service

Environmental Taxes

▶ See instructions on back
▶ Attach to Form 720

OMB No. 1545-0245
Expires April 1, 1983

Name	Employer identification number as shown on Form 720	
	Date quarter ended	S.I.C. Number

Part I Tax on Petroleum

		(a) Barrels	(b) Rate	(c) Tax
1 Crude oil received at a U.S. refinery	bbls.			
2 Crude oil taxed prior to receipt at refinery	bbls.			
3 Taxable crude oil (Subtract line 2 from line 1) ▶		bbls.	$ .0079 bbl.	$
4 Petroleum products entered into the U.S. ▶		bbls.	$ .0079 bbl.	$
5 Crude oil used in or exported from the U.S. before the tax was imposed		bbls.	$ .0079 bbl.	$
6 Total petroleum tax. Enter here and on Form 720 on the line for IRS No. 53 ▶				$

Part II Tax on the Sale or Use of Certain Chemicals

Chemical	(a) Tons	(b) Rate	(c) Amount	Chemical	(a) Tons	(b) Rate	(c) Amount
1 Acetylene		$4.87		22 Hydrochloric acid		$0.29	
2 Ammonia		2.64		23 Hydrogen fluoride		4.23	
3 Antimony		4.45		24 Lead oxide		4.14	
4 Antimony trioxide		3.75		25 Mercury		4.45	
5 Arsenic		4.45		26 Methane		3.44	
6 Arsenic trioxide		3.41		27 Naphthalene		4.87	
7 Barium sulfide		2.30		28 Nickel		4.45	
8 Benzene		4.87		29 Nitric acid		0.24	
9 Bromine		4.45		30 Phosphorus		4.45	
10 Butane		4.87		31 Potassium dichromate		1.69	
11 Butylene		4.87		32 Potassium hydroxide		0.22	
12 Butadiene		4.87		33 Propylene		4.87	
13 Cadmium		4.45		34 Sodium dichromate		1.87	
14 Chlorine		2.70		35 Sodium hydroxide		0.28	
15 Chromite		1.52		36 Stannic chloride		2.12	
16 Chromium		4.45		37 Stannous chloride		2.85	
17 Cobalt		4.45		38 Sulfuric acid		0.26	
18 Cupric oxide		3.59		39 Toluene		4.87	
19 Cupric sulfate		1.87		40 Xylene		4.87	
20 Cuprous oxide		3.97		41 Zinc chloride		2.22	
21 Ethylene		4.87		42 Zinc sulfate		1.90	

43 Total Chemical Tax. Enter here and on Form 720 on the line for IRS No. 54 ▶ $

For Paperwork Reduction Act Notice see back of form.   Form 6627 (5-81)

Figure 7-12. Environmental taxes.

hazardous wastes from the petroleum industry were subject to this requirement."

- Polychlorinated biphenyls (PCBs). The EPA did encourage "voluntary" notification by facilities that formerly stored, treated, or disposed of PCBs.
- Active facilities that had interim status or a final RCRA permit. This exclusion extended only to the actual permitted portion of the property. It did not exclude former facilities that did not qualify for interim status.
- Facilities that may have held hazardous wastes due only to short-term transportation stoppages.

Environmental Taxes. The final major provision of the act and the reason it came to be known as Superfund was the establishment of a \$1.6 billion trust fund administered by the EPA. This trust is earmarked to fund response and remedial activities at former hazardous waste disposal sites in which responsible parties are either unable or unwilling to finance cleanup. The fund was created by taxes on oil and chemicals (87%) and general federal appropriations (13%). Although the fund was scheduled to expire after five years, proposals exist to extend it and begin levying taxes against the amount of hazardous waste disposed of. This tax provision of the act specifically affects plants in the petroleum and chemical industries and may eventually affect all plants that dispose of hazardous wastes. The audit should assure that management is aware of this responsibility to pay certain taxes and identify the department responsible for compliance. A copy of the IRS tax form that was used to calculate these taxes appears as Figure 7-12.

Good Management Practices

Good management practices under the Comprehensive Environmental Response, Compensation and Liability Act of 1980 include more than recognition of the requirement to report spills. Well-managed plants show evidence of attention to the following areas:

Superfund Inventory. Efforts are made to prepare a comprehensive inventory of all "hazardous substances" the plant purchases and produces. This list is kept current through the involvement of the plant purchasing department and includes each substance's reportable quantity. This task is sometimes complicated by suppliers' reluctance to divulge product compositions.

Reporting "Chain of Command." Some industrial plants vest all reporting responsibility in a single department. This clear accountability encourages compliance and assures good decision making. Personnel responsible for notification have access to legal counsel so that "gray" areas or interpretations can be reviewed in a timely fashion. Some plants have complemented this effort by preparing a spill report checklist that serves as a guide for the information needed to report a spill. Plants that operate on a 24-hour basis issue appropriate guidance to off-shift supervisors and guards so that precious time is not lost in responding to a spill.

Employee Awareness. All employees are made aware of the company's responsibility to clean up and report spills. This can be accomplished by holding short briefing sessions, posting appropriate bulletin board notices, or preparing guidance materials. The goal is to encourage the reporting of all spills to appropriate plant authorities.

Proper Storage. The storage, use, processing, and disposition of hazardous substances are evaluated to minimize the chances for catastrophic spills and reduce potential cleanup costs. Spill containment structures are in evidence, as are appropriate loading, unloading, and user procedures.

Past Disposal Notification. The plant shows evidence of a conscious effort to identify past hazardous waste management practices. These efforts can include interviews with former employees and transporters and file searches for old disposal contracts and purchase orders. Some plants have reviewed old aerial photographs and also examined property they may have leased to or from others.

Environmental Taxes. Plants in the chemical and petroleum industry have sufficient documentation to prove the preparation of an accurate environmental tax return. Typically, responsibility for preparation is vested in the tax department to assure compliance.

THE SUPERFUND AUDIT

Pre-audit Preparations

Preparations for a Superfund audit consist of securing a basic understanding the act's reporting requirements as well as the plant's process and layout. If access to plant files is available prior to the audit, any spill reports or notification of hazardous waste site reports should be closely reviewed. In addition, the auditor should seek information regarding all property subject to plant control, whether leased or owned. Examples include date of purchase and sale, other companies involved, the use of the property, and whether any disposal activities ever occurred on-site. If possible, the auditor may want to forewarn the plant's environmental coordinator and purchasing agent that a list of raw materials, chemicals, and products will be prepared during the audit. This list may already have been prepared during the solid / hazardous waste audit of the plant. This courtesy will give plant personnel the opportunity to begin preparations prior to the actual visit.

Superfund Inventory

The first step in the Superfund audit is the preparation of a comprehensive inventory of all hazardous substances found on-site. At many plants, this inventory may have already been prepared. If so, the auditor should merely confirm that the list is accurate and current. At plants where this inventory has not been prepared, the auditor should begin preparations, perhaps using the list of hazardous wastes prepared during the waste audit as a starting point. In either event, the plant purchasing agent should be interviewed to assure completeness. This step is important because new chemicals, additives, or cleaning agents are frequently brought on-site without the knowledge of the environmental coordinator.

If this seems to be a frequent occurrence that could materially affect the plant, the auditor may wish to recommend the institution of a formal reporting mechanism for new purchases. In some plants, the environmental and safety departments are required to "sign off" on new chemical purchases. This mechanism assures that each department remains current and aware of the plant's material inventory. The Superfund inventory of hazardous substances should be recorded using a format similar to that of Figure 7-13.

As an additional check on the inventory's completeness, the auditor may interview the plant's safety coordinator. Often the safety department is also responsible for the proper management of certain toxic materials found at the plant. In some cases, this department maintains an inventory of these materials, their location, use, and potential

Hazardous Substance	RQ	Amount on Site		Storage Method	Storage Area	Receiving Area	Shipping Area	NOTES
		Min	Max					

Figure 7-13. Superfund inventory.

employee exposure routes. Time permitting, the final interview to prepare the inventory is conducted with the plant's warehouse manager. This individual is aware of material flow throughout the plant and receiving and storage methods, as well as their shipping containers. In addition, he may be aware of any inventory of off-specification or obsolete chemicals on-site.

It is useful for the auditor also to include each hazardous substance's reportable quantity on the inventory. These figures appear in the proposed rules published by the EPA in the May 25, 1983 *Federal Register*. During the several interviews with plant personnel, the auditor should also secure some information regarding the amount of each hazardous substance typically found on-site. In some cases it may be necessary to express this estimate as a minimum/maximum figure.

Plant Tour

The next logical step in the Superfund audit is the listing and inspection of each area in the plant where hazardous substances are stored or otherwise processed. This step is conducted by touring the plant. For each substance on the inventory, the containers used and their condition and proximity to potential spill escape routes should be noted. Areas where storage or use occurs near sewers, drains, or bodies of water should be specifically reviewed for spill prevention. These areas, as well as shipping and receiving areas, should exhibit spill containment provisions. In the absence of engineered approaches, evidence of loading/unloading procedures should be present. The largest motivation for recommending spill prevention measures is the plant's responsibility to clean up all spills and its liability for damages. Figure 7–13 contains space for recording the results of the plant tour.

Spill Reports

The next step in the audit is a review of the plant's spill history using any reports on prior incidents as a start. If such documentation is unavailable, the environmental coordinator should be asked to estimate the number and extent of reportable releases experienced in the last year or so. It is beneficial for the auditor specifically to examine and tour the site of any "major" spills and review the effectiveness of any corrective measures taken to prevent future occurrences. A lack of corrective actions deserves mention in the audit report. Plants that experience more than a few minor spills should be encouraged to implement an internal spill report system. At a minimum, the spill report serves as a convenient checklist of concerns for the environmental coordinator to consider prior to official agency notification. Figure 7–14 is a sample spill report form that summarizes

PLANT:_____________________________TIME AND DATE OF INCIDENT:________

____

EXACT SPILL LOCATIONS:____

MATERIAL SPILLED:____

QUANTITY SPILLED:___________RQ OF SPILLED MATERIAL:___________________

HOW WAS QUANTITY SPILLED ESTIMATED?__________________________________

____

SPILL DISCOVERED BY:________________________WHEN?_____________________

DID SPILLED MATERIAL REACH ANY BODY OF WATER, STORM SEWER OR SANITARY SEWER?____ DESCRIBE:____

____

TOTAL SIZE OF AREA AFFECTED BY SPILL:__________________________________

DESCRIBE AREA:____

WAS THERE ANY PERSONAL INJURY:________DESCRIBE:________________________

____

WAS THERE ANY DAMAGE TO PERSONAL PROPERTY?___________DESCRIBE:______

____

WAS THERE ANY DAMAGE TO EQUIPMENT?___________DESCRIBE:_______________

____

DID YOU REPORT ANY DAMAGE TO THE INSURANCE DEPARTMENT?______________

DID YOU REPORT ANY INJURY TO THE SAFETY DEPARTMENT?_________________

DESCRIBE CONTAINMENT MEASURES USED (INCLUDE TIMES AND DATES MEASURES WERE INSTITUTED. NOTE IF MEASURES ARE STILL UNDERWAY).__

____

____

____

DESCRIBE CLEAN-UP WORK PERFORMED. (INCLUDE ANY USE OF OUTSIDE CONTRACTORS OR PERSONNEL)____

____

____

Figure 7-14. Superfund spill report

SUPERFUND SPILL REPORT (continued)

DESCRIPTION OF CLEAN-UP WASTES GENERATED____________________

____

____

____

QUANTITY OF WASTES:____________CONTAINERIZATION:____________

DISPOSAL SITE:________________________

MANIFEST NUMBERS, DATES________________________________

LIST ALL AGENCIES NOTIFIED.

AGENCY	PERSON NOTIFIED	TELEPHONE	DATE	TIME	NOTIFIED BY

DID ANY AGENCY OFFICIALS VISIT THE SCENE?____________________

LIST AND DESCRIBE:____________________________________

____

____________________ ________________
Signature Date

the information normally required by the National Response Center when a release is reported.

Past Disposal Activities

The last step in the Superfund audit is a nominal review of the plant's prior disposal activities. The review begins by examining any "Notification of Hazardous Waste Site" forms (Figure 7-11) the plant may have filed to meet the June 9, 1981 deadline in the act. If any notifications were filed, the auditor should review the documentation used by the plant to prepare these submissions. This body of information often contains "guesstimates" and assumptions made by the company to meet the statutory deadline. Additional information may now be available regarding the site, increasing or decreasing its seriousness. The auditor should specifically tour any notified areas and note any obvious environmental impairments. If the plant's exposure to liability appears significant, the auditor may consider recommending additional study.

In order to help gauge the completeness of any site notifications, the auditor should determine if any outside information sources were used by the plant to prepare the forms. An example might be transportation firms used for prior waste disposal. In some cases, these transporters were also required to file notifications, which may contain information regarding the plant and sites it may have used. Some large firms have gone so far as to retain outside consultants to conduct thorough investigations into past disposal practices. These are sometimes justified as a means to reduce the company's uncertainty regarding potential remedial action costs.

Even if the plant has not filed a notification form under Superfund, the auditor should tour each plant facility looking for signs of past disposal activities. Evidence may exist in the form of large built-up areas with little plant growth, areas of obvious fill, or shallow depressions and ponds. Existing areas should be reviewed with the environmental coordinator to assure their inclusion in the notification.

It should be noted that the government has instituted an inspection program whereby EPA employees or contract personnel tour registered sites and file written reports on their findings. These reports are used to update government files on the site and may be used to help rank their seriousness. EPA has generated a general checklist for use during these inspections that includes information regarding:

- Site and owner identification
- Generator and transporter information
- Activities conducted on-site

- Wastes handled and methods used
- Sampling and analysis data
- Potential exposure routes
- Descriptions of other potential hazards

By reviewing such information during the audit, the auditor serves to better prepare plant representatives for future agency inspections.

Bibliography

American Institute of Chemical Engineers. "Environmental Auditing Presentation," September 1, 1982.

Arthur D. Little, Inc. *Environmental Audit Reporting: A Study of Current Practices,* 1982.

Arthur D. Little, Inc. "Auditing—A New Entry on the Environmental Balance Sheet," *Public Policy Notes,* Vol. II, September 1981.

Baumer, Ronald A. "Making Environmental Audits," *Chemical Engineering,* Vol. 89, No. 22, November 1, 1982, pp. 101–104.

Cahill, L. B. "Creating an Environmental Audit Program," National Conference on Environmental Auditing, The Energy Bureau, Inc., Arlington, Virginia, October 1982.

Cahill, L. B. and Bailey, S. W. "Developing and Implementing Compliance Assessment Programs," Engineering Foundation Conference on Accountability in Hazardous Waste Management, Rindge, New Hampshire, August 1981.

Cahill, L. B. and Bailey, S. W. "A Perspective on Environmental Audits," *Proceedings of the ASCE National Conference on Environmental Engineering,* July 1982.

Cahill, L. B. and Burns, H. L. "Compliance Strategies: An Analytical Framework You Can Put to Work," Booz, Allen and Hamilton, Inc., Boardroom Briefing on Regulatory Risk Management, Washington, D.C., July 1981.

Cahill, L. B. et al. *Environmental Audits,* Second Edition, Government Institutes, Inc., Rockville, Maryland, 1983.

Chemical Manufacturers Association. "Environmental Auditing Seminar," September 27–28, 1983.

Chester, Frank W. "A Quality Assurance Management Plan," *Journal of the Air Pollution Control Association,* Vol. 29, No. 7, July 1979, pp. 701–703.

"Corporate Environmental Auditing Called Essential Tool in Ensuring Compliance with Standards," *Journal of the Air Pollution Control Association.* Vol. 32, No. 5, May 1982, p. 540.

Cutler, Robert W. "Environmental Auditing: The Keystone to a Management Compliance Control and Risk Assessment Program," *Environmental Analyst,* April 1982, pp. 12–16.

Duvel, William A. "Environmental 'Termite' Inspections Pay Off in Corporate Real Estate Transactions". *Hazardous Materials and Waste Management,* January/February, 1984, pp. 36–40.

Edison Electric Institute. "EEI Position Paper on Voluntary Environmental Audits," 1982.

"Environmental Audit Programs Win CMA, Government Backing," *Chemecology,* November 1983, p. 4.

"Environmental Audits Catch Industry's Eye," *Industry Week,* April 5, 1982, pp. 29–31.

"Environmental Audits Cut Compliance Risks," *Chemical Week,* Vol. 126, No. 22, May 28, 1980, pp. 72–73.

"The Exploding Market for Environmental Audits," *Business Week,* June 6, 1983, pp. 92–94.

Frick, William G. *Conducting An Environmental Audit,* VanNess, Feldman, Sutcliffe, Curtis and Levenberg, Washington, D.C., October 1981.

Goldman, Harvey. "A Businessman's Approach to Environmental Compliance," *Proceedings of the 1983 Hazmat Conference,* pp. 89-92.

Guido, Joseph. "A Practical Look at Environmental Audits," *Journal of the Air Pollution Control Association,* Vol. 32, No. 5, August 1982, p. 568.

Harrison, Lee. "Big Business Pollution Problems Spawn A New Breed of Auditors," *New York Times,* Business Section, May 17, 1981, pp. 8–9.

Harrison, Lee. *Environmental Auditing Handbook,* McGraw-Hill, 1984.

Henz, Donald J. "Safeguarding Confidential Business Information Part I: Environmental Audits and Litigation," *Pollution Engineering,* January 1984, pp. 30–33.

Henz, Donald J. "Safeguarding Confidential Business Information Part II: Freedom of Information," *Pollution Engineering,* March 1984, pp. 44–47.

Kane, Raymond W. "Designing a Good Corporate Program for Environmental Management and Compliance," *The Environmental Forum,* Vol. 1, No. 6, October 1982, pp. 18–27.

Kennedy, Bingham. "The Need for Environmental Audits," *Pollution Engineering,* July 1982, pp. 28–30.

Lawson, J. T. and Cane, N. G. "Hazardous Waste and the Real Estate Transaction," *Environmental Research & Technology, Inc. Newsletter,* pp. 1–5.

Milvy, Paul. "Environmental Impairment Liability Insurance and Risk Assessments," *The Environmental Forum,* Vol. 1, No. 6, October 1982, pp. 30–37.

"Multi-Media Compliance Audit Inspection Procedures," USEPA, National Enforcement Investigation Center, July 1983.

Murphy, M. J. and Stern, C. D. "An Internal Environmental Audit Can Help Firms Navigate the Stormy Seas of Regulation," *Risk Management,* November 1982, pp. 20–28.

Nakles, D. V. and Schenck, P. "Environmental Audits for Industry," *Environmental Research and Technology Inc. Newsletter,* March 1982, pp. 1–6.

Palmisano, John. " The Evolution of Environmental Auditing: Implications for Firms and for Regulators," USEPA, Presentation at the Air Pollution Control Association Annual Meeting, Atlanta, Georgia, June 1983.

Penna, Richard A. "Environmental Auditing: The Policy and the Prospects," *The Environmental Forum,* Vol. 2, No. 1, May 1983, pp. 16–20.

"Self-Auditing Program Monitors Compliance," *Hazardous Waste and Pollution Management Bulletin,* Vol. 1, February 10, 1983, pp. 1–2.

Singh, Jaswant. "Environmental Auditing: What it is, What it does, How to do it," *Plant Engineering,* February 23, 1984. pp. 43–44.

Sittenfield, Marcus. "A Hazardous Waste Audit Could Save Your Firm Money and Keep You Out of Regulatory Hot Water," *Professional Engineer,* Spring 1983, pp. 20–23.

Splendore, John L. "The How and Why of Environmental Audits," *Industrial Wastes,* March/April, 1983, pp. 14–15.

Truitt, T. H. et al. *Environmental Audit Handbook: Basic Principles of Environmental Compliance Auditing,* Wald, Harkrader & Ross, Washington, D. C., March 1981.

U.S. Environmental Protection Agency. *NEIC Policies and Procedures Manual,* National Enforcement Investigations Center, October 1979.

U.S. Environmental Protection Agency. *NPDES Compliance Evaluation Inspection Manual, MCD-75,* January 1981.

U.S Environmental Protection Agency. *Performance Audit Inspections of Wastewater Sources,* National Enforcement Investigations Center, August 1979.

U.S. Environmental Protection Agency. *Resource Conservation and Recovery Act Inspection Manual,* Government Institutes, Inc., Rockville, Maryland, 1982.

U.S. Environmental Protection Agency. *Toxic Substances Control Act Inspection Manual,* Vols. 1 and 2, Government Institutes, Inc., Rockville, Maryland, 1982.

Vanderver, Timothy A. "Environmental Auditing" in *Environmental Law Handbook.* Seventh Edition by J. G. Arbuckle et al., Government Institutes, Inc., Rockville, Maryland, 1983.

Appendix Other Federal Environmental Programs

CWA, Section 404—Dredge or Fill Permit Program. Provides permitting program for major projects, administered by the Department of the Army. Some categories of activities having minimal impact on the environment may be permitted under state or Corps of Engineers authorization. Environmental Impact Statement may be required. EPA has issued guidelines for acceptable projects and has the authority to veto any activity having unacceptable adverse effects.

Coastal Zone Management Act of 1972. Defines a coastal zone as an area along the ocean and gulf shores of the United States extending three miles out to sea. For the Great Lakes, the coastal zone extends to the border with Canada. The act encourages the states with territory within the coastal zone to develop Coastal Zone Management Plans. Where these have been enacted, permits or approval may be required for industrial development within the coastal zone.

Endangered Species Act of 1973. Provides for the protection of endangered species of wildlife, fish, and plants.

Deepwater Port Act of 1974. Establishes procedures for the location, construction, and operation of deepwater ports off the coast of the United States for the purposes of regulating commerce, promoting efficiency in transportation, and protecting the environment.

Federal Insecticide, Fungicide, and Rodenticide Act. Defines pesticides as substances intended to prevent, destroy, repel, or mitigate pests. All pesticides must be registered every five years for either general or restricted use. They must be labeled, specifying ingredients, uses, warnings, registration number, and any special use restrictions. Tolerance levels for certain pesticides are specified for agricultural commodities. Recommendations are made for transportation and disposal of pesticides.

Marine Protection, Research and Sanctuaries Act. Regulates the dumping of materials into the ocean and the transportation for dumping of materials into the ocean.

Noise Control Act of 1972. Gives to EPA the responsibility for administering all federal anti-noise programs. Regulations are directed toward controlling aircraft noise, but the act also covers products distributed in commerce, interstate railroads, and interstate motor carriers.

Rivers and Harbors Act of 1899. Provides for the protection, preservation, and safety of the navigable waters of the United States.

Safe Drinking Water Act of 1974. Provides primary and secondary standards for public drinking water systems. Also requires the states to establish underground injection control programs to prevent endangerment of any underground source of drinking water. Five classes of wells are defined: Class I—hazardous and municipal waste injection wells below but within a quarter mile of an underground source of drinking water; Class II—oil and gas injection wells; Class III—wells related to mineral or energy extraction; Class IV—hazardous and radioactive waste injection into or above an underground source of drinking water; and Class V—all other injection wells. Class I and IV wells are regulated by RCRA; new Class IV wells are prohibited, and existing wells will be phased out. Standards for construction and operation of Class I through III wells are established, and a survey is provided to study regulatory mechanisms for Class V wells.

TSCA, Section 7—Imminent Hazard. Authorizes EPA to bring action in U.S. District Court to seize a chemical substance or mixture having an imminent and unreasonable risk of serious or widespread injury to health or to the environment, or to require the recall, replacement, or repurchase of the substance.

TSCA, Section 8—Reporting and Recordkeeping. Authorizes EPA to collect and make available information on toxic chemicals used in commerce. Under 8(a), EPA surveyed industry for production and exposure data on 2300 existing chemicals. 8(c) requires records of significant adverse effects on human health or the environment from chemical substances, and retention of records of alleged adverse reactions for at least five years. Where data on a chemical substance or mixture support a conclusion of substantial risk of injury to health or to the environment, 8(e) requires a manufacturer, processor, or distributor to notify EPA immediately.

INDEX

INDEX